Crime Scene Investigation
Procedural Guide

Crime Scene Investigation
Procedural Guide

Michael S. Maloney, MFS
Special Agent NCIS, Senior Instructor FLETC (Retired)
Independence, Missouri, USA

Donald G. Housman, MFS
Forensic Consultant Division, Chief, NCIS (Retired)
Nashville, Indiana, USA

Edited by Ross M. Gardner
Bevel, Gardner & Associates
Atlanta, Georgia, USA

CRC Press
Taylor & Francis Group
Boca Raton   London   New York

CRC Press is an imprint of the
Taylor & Francis Group, an **informa** business

CRC Press
Taylor & Francis Group
6000 Broken Sound Parkway NW, Suite 300
Boca Raton, FL 33487-2742

© 2014 by Taylor & Francis Group, LLC
CRC Press is an imprint of Taylor & Francis Group, an Informa business

No claim to original U.S. Government works

Printed on acid-free paper
Version Date: 20140325

International Standard Book Number-13: 978-1-4665-5754-3 (Paperback)

Visit the Taylor & Francis Web site at
http://www.taylorandfrancis.com

and the CRC Press Web site at
http://www.crcpress.com

Contents

22   Child Sexual Assault or Abuse   153

23   Child Physical Abuse   165

Section IV

EVIDENCE PROCESSING AND DOCUMENTATION

* Available for download from www.crcpress.com/product/isbn/9781466557543.

Foreword

When one considers the application of forensics to the solution of crime, no single role is as critical as that of the crime scene investigator. Often thought of as secondary, if one considers the criminal justice process the crime scene investigator's importance cannot be overstated. Why? The answer is simple; it is the crime scene investigator who starts and ultimately defines the overall process. Forensic scientists, investigators, and the court rely on the information and data the crime scene investigator is tasked to collect.

If the crime scene investigator fails to collect items or collects them in a manner that makes them unusable to the forensic scientist, science itself cannot undo that failure. If specific context in the scene is not captured then later in the investigation when the detectives are trying to resolve some claim, they may not have the information necessary to resolve the issue. If forensic scientists are unable to offer conclusions and detectives are unable to resolve issues, the court (jurors, judges, and lawyers) is left with highly subjective ways to try and decide guilt or innocence. The CSI role is clearly the weakest link in the chain. Without proper crime scene investigation, the criminal justice system can and will fail.

Unfortunately, the role of the crime scene investigator is a daunting one. Crime scene investigators (CSI) come to scenes with little or no context, and their efforts are judged months or years later in the light of a much clearer context. As the investigation develops, witnesses, victims, and even suspects have provided perspective, the probative investigative issues are clearer, and those making that judgment *expect* and *rely* on the CSI's efforts to resolve all issues.

The role of the CSI is no easy task. It is the CSI who must decide what is or is not evidence and how to collect it in the very limited contextual light. To do this well, crime scene investigation demands an understanding of every type of forensic evidence: what to collect, how to collect it, and how to properly store it so it has value to the forensic scientist. In addition to collecting all of the necessary evidence, the CSI is expected to capture the full context of the scene (e.g., notes, photographs, and sketches) under conditions that are rarely conducive to such effort. The CSI is very much a "Jack of all Trades" and has only one opportunity to get it right.

It is only through properly training and outfitting the crime scene investigator that this is accomplished. Yet formal training may have been years before and when presented with a complex case or one which the CSI has not dealt with routinely, it is easy to forget a critical aspect of the scene examination. The *Crime Scene Investigation Procedural Guide* is designed to assist properly trained crime scene investigators in their efforts. It offers effective strategies for routine tasks associated with crime scene investigation (e.g., initial response, crime scene management, photography and sketching), strategies for specific criminal events (e.g., larcenies, burglaries, and assaults) as well as strategies for less common situations (e.g., aquatic recoveries and post-blast). Additionally, it provides the CSI with guidance on how to deal with nearly every type of physical evidence that might be encountered. This book is not intended to go on a bookshelf, but rather to be with the CSI as a ready reference at the scene.

The authors come to you with literally years of extensive on-scene experience dealing with both simple and highly complex scenes. They have been "down in the trenches" and now share through this guide the extensive knowledge they gained working scenes over their careers. They also have extensive experience managing crime scenes and criminal investigations, thus they understand the role of the CSI in its entirety. Novice or highly experienced, this book is an indispensable part of any working CSI's toolbox.

Ross M. Gardner

Preface

This book is meant to be used at the scene, as a practical field guide when responding to the scene of a crime. Some information in the various chapters of the guide may seem repetitious; this is meant to facilitate its field use by minimizing the need to flip back and forth while processing the scene. The guide is separated into the following sections for ease of use, with primary processing accomplished through Section I.

Section I, "Crime Scene Investigation," includes initial response, crime scene organization and management, crime scene tasks, and responsibilities, as well as search methods.

Section II, "Crimes against Property," covers a protocol for processing as well as the various types of evidence that might be present.

Section III, "Crimes against Persons," details a protocol for their processing as well as the various types of evidence that might be present.

Section IV, "Evidence Processing and Documentation," is used to supplement crime scene investigation by providing detailed steps to refresh the crime scene investigator's (CSI) memory on friction ridge, trace, impression, biological, bloodstain, and shooting scene evidence processing and documentation.

The appendices* contain a variety of reproducible, easy-to-use worksheets to help organize documentation and notes while at the scene.

---

* Appendices B through O are available for download from www.crcpress.com/product/isbn/9781466557543.

Acknowledgments

The foundation for this guidebook was established in 1996 while we were involved in coauthoring a government publication, *The Field Guide for Crime Scene Processing*, for the Naval Criminal Investigative Service. It is our hope that following the concept of that publication, a comprehensive procedural guide for the crime scene investigator (CSI) specifically formatted for field use will be useful. Though the concept for this guidebook is borrowed from that publication, the information and procedures have largely been rewritten, updated, and expounded upon. We thank Special Agents Bill Herzig, Tom Brady, and Fred Ewell, and all other NCIS special agents who served or are serving in the Forensic Science Division and scattered about the globe; Ted McDonald, Chris Stewart, and Dan Chancellor, senior instructors at the Federal Law Enforcement Training Center, for their incredible technical expertise in all aspects of crime scene processing; Dana Sutton and Michael Hullihan, instructors at FLETC for their expertise; and our editor, Ross Gardner, for his expertise and help throughout the years as well as allowing us to link this procedural guide to his very successful *Practical Crime Scene Processing* text.

A special thank you to Doug Peavey and the Lynn Peavey Company for providing the crime scene equipment and supplies used in the photographs and illustrations.

A special acknowledgment to Maxine and Patti and our children, who supported us throughout our careers of midnight, holiday, birthday, anniversary, and vacation callouts.

About the Authors

Michael Maloney is a private consultant and trainer after retiring from a career in Federal law enforcement. He holds a master of forensic science degree from GWU, fellowship in forensic medicine, twenty years experience as a special agent with the Naval Criminal Investigative Service (NCIS), senior instructor-Federal Law Enforcement Training Center for Death Investigations and Sex Crimes and is the author of *Death Scene Investigation: Procedural Guide* and *Crime Scene Investigation: Procedural Guide* from CRC Press. He is a contributing author to *Practical Crime Scene Processing and Investigation* published by CRC Press.

Don Housman is a private consultant, educator, and trainer. He retired from a career with the Naval Criminal Investigative Service (NCIS) where he was chief of the Forensic Consultant Division. He holds a master of forensic sciences degree from GWU, a fellowship in forensic medicine, and has twenty-three years' experience as a special agent with NCIS and the FBI. He has co-authored four forensic related books for the Department of Defense and is the co-author of *Crime Scene Investigation: Procedural Guide* from CRC Press.

Ross Gardner is a private consultant, educator and trainer. He retired as a command sergeant major and special agent with the US Army Criminal Investigation Command and subsequently served four years as the Chief of Police for Lake City, Georgia. He is a graduate of the scenes of crime officers course, New Scotland Yard and holds a master's degree in computer and information systems management from Webster University. He is the author of *Practical Crime Scene Processing and Investigation* and co-author of *Bloodstain Pattern Analysis, with an Introduction to Crime Scene Reconstruction* and *Practical Crime Scene Analysis and Reconstruction*.

Crime Scene Investigation

I

Initial Response

1

Notification

The first receipt of information of a crime, or possible crime, by the crime scene investigator (CSI) formally begins the crime scene documentation process. Though covered more thoroughly later, crime scenes are documented through notes, photography, and sketching. Notification, however, begins the note-taking phase. Record the following information:

- Method of notification.
- Person making notification.
- Time of notification.
- Location and nature of the crime scene (e.g., outdoor, indoor, residential, commercial).
- Who is present at the crime scene (e.g., law enforcement, victim, witnesses, fire department)?
- What is the reported crime?
- Has the scene been initially identified and secured? (What agency is currently in charge?)
- If this is an assault or sexual assault, is the victim still at the scene? If not, where is he or she?
- Are there any safety hazards or unique considerations with the scene (e.g., electrocution, poisonous gases, unstable terrain, civil insurrection)?
- Are suspects and witnesses still in the area?
- Who else or what other agencies have been notified and are responding?

Scene Coordination

It is important to determine who has investigative jurisdiction over the physical location of the crime scene, the type of offense committed, as well as any interdepartmental responses.

- Determine investigative jurisdiction and what agency will have lead investigative responsibility.

- If tasked with an out-of-jurisdiction response, coordinate with the requesting agency.
- If an interdepartmental response between patrol, the crime scene unit, or investigative units is anticipated, coordinate with the on-scene patrol supervisor and whoever will be the lead investigator assigned to the case.
- If the victim has been transported to a medical facility, remember that the victim may *be* the primary crime scene. Ensure someone is responding to the victim's location.
- If the initial scope and description of the crime scene indicate the need for interagency assistance, begin coordination with the appropriate agencies or departments. For example, a scene with an unstable building or requiring lighting, or an underwater crime scene, may demand assistance from the fire department, rescue squad, or other specialized investigative unit.

Arrival at the Scene

Initial arrival at the scene may be chaotic, depending on the scope and nature of the crime. The presence of first responders, law enforcement, fire or rescue, emergency medical services, and multiple jurisdictions' agencies has an impact on scene order. During these initial moments, scene safety, determining who has primary responsibility, the scene parameters, and protecting physical evidence are of primary concern.

Immediate Actions

- Note arrival time.
- Determine if there are any injured who require medical assistance; provide or arrange to have aid provided as appropriate.
- Determine if there are specific scene hazards that must be addressed. These would include continuing tactical operations, a toxic environment, or imminent structural collapse.

Emergency Medical Services (EMS)

- If emergency medical services (EMS) is on scene, immediately photograph any injured they are tending to in order to document spatial relationships within the crime scene.
- If EMS is present, take the steps necessary to expeditiously document and collect perishable items of evidence that may be disturbed through their lifesaving efforts.

- If the victim or suspect has already been transported from the scene, ensure a CSI response to that location to collect and document evidence and injuries.

Law Enforcement First Responders

- Determine who has entered the crime scene and all actions they took, to include any items they may have touched or disturbed.
- It is not unusual or unexpected for first responders to touch items within the scene or move objects. Lights may have been turned on, a weapon made safe, doors opened or closed.
- Ensure such changes are noted.

Legal Concerns

Determine if the police have a legal right to be present conducting the crime scene investigation. A crime scene investigation is basically the **search** for evidence and properly documenting, preserving, and collecting this evidence. The key word is *search*; the CSI must ensure that a person's Fourth Amendment rights against unreasonable search and seizure are protected. It is incumbent upon the crime scene investigator to ensure that he or she has legal authority to be present conducting the scene investigation.

The key legal premise to determine is who has a **reasonable expectation of privacy** in the area where the crime scene investigation is being conducted. This may not necessarily be the titleholder of a piece of property. Lawfully rented property requires the authority of the lawful renter, not necessarily the property owner. A roommate may allow a search, but that authority extends to his or her personal area and any shared area (such as the kitchen and living room); such consent would not extend to his or her roommate's bedroom. Either the individual that has a reasonable expectation of privacy in the area to be searched grants approval, or a judge with appropriate jurisdiction may grant permission to search through a search warrant.

- Consult with appropriate legal counsel if there is any question as to the CSI's authority to be present conducting a crime scene investigation.
- **Public lands and property** hold no expectation of privacy for the individual who chooses to be present on the public land. Individuals do not have a reasonable expectation of privacy in public parks, public wooded areas, streets, etc. A warrant is generally not required in these areas; seek legal counsel to determine if there is a specific need in your jurisdiction.

- **Exigent circumstances** apply to the initial uncertainty surrounding an emergency response. They include searching for victims, ensuring no threat to safety remains at the scene (e.g., searching for suspects). Exigent circumstances do not allow for the routine law enforcement function of processing a crime scene. That said, during the execution of the duties called for under exigent circumstances, the law enforcement officer does not have to ignore evidence of a crime that is in plain view. If exigent circumstances required an initial law enforcement presence, that authority expires when:
  - The search for additional victims is complete
  - The search for an immediate threat from a perpetrator is complete
  - All emergency aid to the injured is complete, and they are removed from the scene
  - When a threat to public safety (gas leaks, structural collapse, etc.) has been mitigated
- A **permissive search** is perhaps the easiest method to obtain authority to conduct the crime scene investigation. A permissive search is easily granted when the victim is also the one that has a reasonable expectation of privacy for the property or area in question. Most departments maintain a standard form for the individual to grant a permissive search.
- A **search warrant** is obtained by providing probable cause to a judge that there is evidence of a crime on the property, the nature of that evidence, and generally where it is. The judge will then decide if a warrant will be issued. This is by far the legally safest method of conducting a search. Anytime the search involves an area where a potential suspect exercises a reasonable expectation of privacy, a warrant should be considered.

Identifying the Scope of the Scene

Primary Scene

- Determine if the scene has been adequately identified and its perimeter secured. If not, enlarge the perimeter as necessary (Figure 1.1).
- Determine the likely areas a perpetrator would have entered or exited the scene and any subsequent paths of travel. If noted, ensure they are secured.

Identifying Ancillary Scenes

- Determine if the initial information would indicate the possibility of ancillary, or secondary, crime scenes.

Figure 1.1 Inner (working) perimeter.

- Surveillance location, where the perpetrator observed the location while planning or waiting for the opportune time to commit the crime.
- Consider dump sites where the perpetrator may have discarded items after the crime (such as purses or wallets after removing valuables, or weapons, tools, or clothing used to commit the crime).
- Surveillance location, where the perpetrator observed the victim, the victim's habits, or selected a victim or planned the attack. This may also include the area where the perpetrator lay in wait for the victim.
- Surveillance location, where the perpetrator made contact with the victim and gained control.
- Consider methods of transportation or conveyance for moving the victim either before or after the crime.

Each of these is an ancillary, or secondary, crime scene. All secondary scenes must be secured in the same manner as the primary scene.

Administrative Scene Controls

- Identify a point of entry and exit for those working the scene, and establish an entry control point and a controller (preferably someone from law enforcement) using a crime scene entry log (Appendix B).
- Determine what level of personal protective equipment (PPE) is required for the scene and establish PPE guidelines for entry (Appendix A).
- Once a scene's perimeter is established, designate an area outside of the perimeter for CSIs to work in (e.g., sketching, on-scene

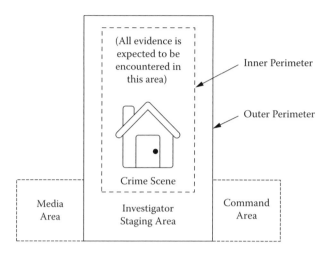

Figure 1.2 Extended perimeter including administrative areas.

evidence processing, changing PPE, trash collection, and for breaks) (Figure 1.2).

- CSIs or other law enforcement personnel should never take food, drinks, or tobacco products into a crime scene area.

Major Scene Considerations

On major scenes where departmental, governmental, and media interests are expected, the following should be established as soon as possible:

Media area:
- Designate a media area for news personnel to have indirect access to the scene.
- This area prevents direct access but provides a visual site of interest that allows them to capture video of an area of interest (e.g., CSIs moving in and out of the scene with equipment or the front entrance of the structure). At the same time, it should be positioned in such a way as to prevent the media from filming the critical investigative area (Figure 1.2).
- This location should also be far enough removed from the command briefing area as to preclude any chance of the media capturing, recording, or hearing any part of command briefs.
- A failure to designate a media area may result in the media having 360-degree access to the crime scene perimeter.
- The media will be either in a designated area or where they want to be; the choice rests on how quickly the CSI designates an area

that provides the media what they need while containing the flow of case-sensitive information.

Command briefings:

- Designate an area for command briefings.
- This area should be outside of the crime scene perimeter and allow easy access for crime scene supervisors to hold briefings.
- The location should also be sufficiently isolated to limit law enforcement command personnel from becoming involved in routine crime scene investigation decisions and direction. This will help avoid any appearance of unusual influence over the processing procedure (Figure 1.2).

Crime Scene Management

2

Processing of a crime scene requires certain roles to be filled and tasks to be accomplished no matter what the size and complexity of the scene or response. The management of these tasks as well as the overall approach to the crime scene will generally fall to the lead crime scene investigator. The primary tasks and roles are described below. It is important to note if one CSI or a team processes the crime scene, each of the roles must at some level be fulfilled.

Arrival and Initial Organization

The lead CSI should refer to Chapter 1, "Initial Response," for detailed guidance. The lead CSI must:

- Exercise overall control of the crime scene
- Ensure appropriate legal authority exists to examine the scene
- Establish a crime scene entry control point and designate access routes into and through the crime scene
- Be responsible for the initial walk-through and formulation of the crime scene strategy
- Make assignments to other CSIs, as available, to accomplish crime scene observations, photography, sketching, search, processing, and evidence collection
- Ensure required equipment and support are available
- Ensure safety and comfort (in as far as possible) of CSIs

Investigative Plan/Scene Strategy

At the conclusion of the walk-through an investigative strategy for processing the scene should be developed. This is an opportunity to **slow down** and determine investigative priorities, tasking, and assignments. The videotape from the walk-through (or pictures) may be helpful during this process. Once a strategy is developed, it should remain sufficiently flexible to allow for unforeseen developments.

Scene Considerations

- Consider tasks at hand and manpower available and make appropriate assignments.
- Consider any unique equipment requirements, such as auxiliary lighting, side scanning sonar, or safety equipment.
- Consider the need for support through specialists, such as explosive ordnance disposal, underwater evidence unit, computer forensics, fire cause and origin, or search and recovery teams.
- Consider unique weather or terrain requirements. The area may be on a steep grade or unstable ground that would require rope work, in a tidal area, or along a busy roadway that requires traffic control.

Investigative Direction

A critical function of crime scene analysis is placing the evidence within the context of the scene to assist the lead detective in determining investigative direction and developing investigative leads.

- Frequent communication between the lead CSI and lead detective is critical to ensure that information developed during scene processing may be integrated into the investigative and interview strategies.
- Information from the lead detective can often be used at the scene to focus or refine searches and processing strategies.
- Under each investigative chapter of this guide is a section titled "Establishing Context"; this serves as a guide in determining investigative direction from the indicators present at the scene.

Scene Processing

Order of Processing

Ensure that the order of processing is meticulously maintained by all crime scene investigators.

- **Observe** without disturbing anything.
- **Record/document** through notes, photography, and sketches.
- **Process and preserve** physical evidence, ensuring that all known evidence is sampled and collected in as pristine and appropriate condition as is possible (e.g., friction ridge prints are properly protected, biological and trace evidence is sampled and collected).

- **Collect** and properly package the evidence and enter it into the evidence custody system.

Available Personnel

The following tasks are routinely completed during the investigation of a crime scene. A team approach may be conducted when a coordinated and trained crime investigation team responds to the scene. In many instances one or two CSIs will be the only available assets. If this is the case, they are responsible for filling each of the following roles:

- **Scene observation** (refer to Chapter 3, "Crime Scene Notes and Observations")
- **Videography** (refer to Chapter 4, "Crime Scene Videography and Photography")
- **Photography** (refer to Chapter 4, "Crime Scene Videography and Photography")
- **Sketching** (refer to Chapter 5, "Crime Scene Sketching")
- **Searching** (refer to Chapter 6, "Crime Scene Search Procedures")
- **Processing/collection**—recovery of evidence (refer to Section IV, "Evidence Processing and Documentation")

Scene Documentation

- Ensure documentation of the scene through appropriate notes, photography, and sketches.
- Ensure all items of evidence are properly collected, preserved, and entered into the evidence custody system.

Command Function

- Brief organizational command structure as appropriate.
- Establish command post if necessary.
- Establish media control point if necessary.

Scene Completion and Post Scene Activities

- Determine the appropriate time to release the scene and ensure the scene is secured and turned over to an appropriate responsible person.
- Consider if the scene should be held until after interviews or medical examinations.

- Have a fresh set of eyes go through the scene to determine if anything has been missed, collect any gear that may have been left at the scene, and act as a confidence check of the processing methodology and procedures used.
- Ensure all evidence is screened for forensic value and sent to the appropriate forensic laboratory for analysis.
- Ensure all crime scene reports are completed.

Crime Scene Notes and Observation

3

Scene Observer Duties

The scene observer records all objective data at the crime scene. Each CSI is still responsible for his or her own observations and notes as they relate to his or her specific assignments. General crime scene notes worksheets are provided in Appendix C. The CSI assigned observation duties is:

- Responsible for overall scene documentation
- Responsible for recording overall observations

Notes

- Written notes are the best method for recording observations.
  - Number each page.
  - Initial and date each page.
  - Include case reference on each page.
  - Complete in pen.
  - Strike through mistakes with a single line and initial.
  - Generally record in chronological order.
  - Do not contain extraneous data; limit to facts, observations, and logical leads developed from observations.
- An audio recording may be appropriate when time does not allow for written notes in situations such as a hostile area, imminent danger, heavy bloodborne pathogen contamination, etc.
  - Lead-in narration on the recording should include time, date, location, and case number/name (if available).
  - Recordings must be transcribed at some point.

Observations (Scene Indicators) for Indoor Scenes

Structure Type/Location

Document static nonchanging characteristics of the involved scene, including:

- Exact address or location of structure
- Type of structure (e.g., apartment, house, townhouse, commercial building)
- Number of stories (e.g., single story, two stories)
- Construction (e.g., brick, wood, masonry)
- Entry and exit points (e.g., all doors, windows)

General Appearance

Document specific scene conditions.

- Evidence of criminal activity
- Forced entry or lack thereof
- Evidence of struggle
- Evidence of ransacking
- Evidence suggesting missing items
- Evidence of personal injury, such as blood on floor or other surfaces

Possible Related Video Coverage

- Is there video coverage of avenues of approach to the area?
- Is there on-scene video coverage of the scene itself (e.g., security, nanny cams)?

Entry/Exit

- Are doors open or closed?
- Are doors locked or unlocked?
- What types of locks are on doors?
- Are the doors bolted from inside?
- Is there any evidence of forced entry?
- Who has keys or a passkey and are all keys accounted for?

Windows

- Are the windows open or closed?
- Are the windows locked or unlocked?
- What types of locks are on the windows?
- Are there screens on the windows? Are the screens in place?
- Is there any evidence of forced entry?
- What window covering (e.g., curtains, blinds, and shades) are in place and what are their positions?

- Continuity aspects of windows and screens (e.g., the presence or absence of cobwebs or dirt on the sill)

Kitchen and Dining Room

- Is there food preparation indicating recent eating before, during, or after the crime?
- Are there indications of cleanup after a meal?
- Does food preparation indicate multiple parties present at the scene?
- Is the oven on, and if so, what is the status of the food within (raw, undercooked, overcooked, burnt)?
- Are there dated or spoiled foodstuffs in the pantry or refrigerator?

Environmental Controls

- What is the temperature in the room?
- What is the thermostat setting? If there is a program mode how far into the cycle is it?
- Is thermostat on a timer and what are the settings?

Laundry and Utility Areas

- Are appliances running or warm (to include washer/dryer)?
- Is there clothing in the washer or dryer, wet or damp?
- If suspect's clothes were believed to be laundered, consider the lint trap as evidence.

Lighting (in Each Room as well as Outside Lights)

- Are the lights on or off?
- Are the lights working?

Telephones and Cellular Phones

- Is there any record of incoming and outgoing calls? Attempt to determine those calls.
- Are there any answering machine messages?
- Is there an off-site answering service? What does it take to ascertain those messages?
- Can mapping of cellular towers indicate location of where a call was made?
- Are there text messages? Ensure charger is included with the mobile phone.

Mail

- What is the date on any outgoing mail?
- Are there any time-dated receipts?
- What is the date of mail outside the home or in the box?
- What is the date of mail brought in or opened?

Contents of Wastebaskets and Ashtrays

- Check and document the contents of wastebaskets and trashcans if appropriate.
- Check ashtrays. If there are indications of multiple parties being present, consider collecting cigarette butts for DNA analysis.

Bath and Toilet Areas

- Are there damp or bloodstained towels or washcloths?
- Is there evidence of recent bathing or washing activity (e.g., wet tubs, towels)?
- If victim is a single female living alone, is the toilet seat raised?
- Is there evidence of suspect cleanup?
- What drugs or medicines are in medicine cabinets?
- What are the dates on prescription medication and number of tablets missing?

Calendars and Planners

- What are the entries on any calendars for the time period before and contemporaneous to the crime?
- What are the diary or day planner entries for the time period before and contemporaneous to the crime?

Computers and Internet

- When was the victim last on the computer?
- Is there computer activity after the suspected time of the crime?
- Is there email, chat, or telephone activity contemporaneous to the time of the crime?

Observations for Outdoor Scenes

Environmental Conditions

- What is the temperature?

- What is the humidity?
- Is there ongoing precipitation or evidence of recent precipitation?
- What are the past temperatures, precipitation, and humidity covering the time since the crime?
- Is it daylight, nighttime, or evening?
- What time was sunrise or sunset (if applicable)?
- What are the moon phase and cloud cover?
- What is the ambient lighting? Consider streetlights, porch lights, and even city sky glow.

Immediate Area of Crime Scene

- Is there evidence of a struggle?
- Are there footwear impressions, scuff marks, or tire marks?
- Is there any video coverage of the area? Consider ATMs, surrounding store video, and traffic surveillance systems.
- Is there evidence discarded in nearby trash receptacles?

Extended Area of Crime Scene

- What are the likely paths of travel to and from the scene?
- Is there evidence discarded in trash receptacles, ditches, underpasses, etc.?
- Is there any video coverage of avenues of approach to the area?
- Are there nearby convenience stores or gas stations that might have video coverage and trash receptacles that could be searched for evidence?

Observations for Motor Vehicle Scenes

Exterior

- Are there signs of damage, particularly signs of recent damage, to include indications of collision, bullet holes, etc.?
- If the vehicle was suspected of being involved in a personal injury, do the mirrors, bumpers, grill, or undercarriage have possible human hairs, fibers, blood, etc., present?
- Are there areas likely handled/touched by suspects that need to be protected for possible latent fingerprint detection/touch DNA recovery?
- Record VIN, plate number, and any other identifying feature of the vehicle, to include the make, model, color, and distinguishing features.

- For pickups, record contents of the bed.
- Observe tires, rims, and wheel well areas for possible mud, dirt, etc., that would indicate the presence of materials that might be needed for subsequent alibi comparisons.
- Is there a need for later towing and raising the vehicle to search for evidence of the crime deposited on the undercarriage?

Interior

- Is blood or other evidence of personal injury present?
- Are tools present that might have been used in the crime?
- Are items present (mail, written messages, other objects with names on them) that would indicate the identity of passengers/drivers of the vehicle?
- Are items missing from any separate, but related, scene present in the vehicle?
- Are there items in the trunk that are related to the crime or that help identify persons?

Crime Scene Videography and Photography

4

Videography

Setup

- If date and time stamp are to be recorded, ensure they are correct.
- Synchronize all team members' watches with video recorder's time stamp. This may seem unnecessary, but consider how opposing counsel might represent a critical item of evidence that based on the camera's time stamp does not appear in a crime scene photo or video 5 minutes before its recorded collected time.
- When possible, disable the recording of audio.
- Record the image of a head slate (identifier card with photographer, date, case title or number, and organization). (See Appendix D, "Photographic Identifier Slate.")

Technique

- Remember to pause for at least 3 seconds before changing camera direction, angle, or before and after zooming.
- Remove all personnel from the area being recorded and remove all CSI equipment that might appear in the recording.
- Do not walk or move with the camera recording unless demonstrating a path of travel.

Recording

- Record the address of the scene (mailbox, street sign, address on front of house, etc.).
- Record the scene during initial walk-through or shortly thereafter.
- Record the general location of the incident.
- Record any bystanders or onlookers near the scene.
- Record both general and specific conditions at the scene.
- Record items of evidence and their spatial relationship to the scene and other items of evidence.

- Consider recording the scene again prior to leaving it. This can help to defend the agency in any action the owner of the property may bring against it later.

Photography

Setup

- Begin and maintain a photo log. This is often easier when an assistant aids the photographer by filling out the log. (See Appendix E, "Photography Log.")
- The detail required in the photographic log will differ based upon your camera and capture method. At a minimum, exposure/image number and description of the view are necessary.
- Capture digital images in raw format (e.g., NEF format) as well as JPEG.
- If shooting digital with metadata, as long as ISO, f-stop, aperture setting, and flash are recorded as a part of the metadata, they do not need to be recorded on the log.
- The use of any external flash, lighting, or filters that are not recorded on the metadata should be noted in the photography log.
- Ensure date and time stamps on exposures or their recordings in metadata are correct.
- If using digital media, ensure that the card or memory stick is new or has been appropriately reformatted. Do not start taking photographs on a partially filled data source.
- If using film, do not start photos on a roll that has already been partially exposed. Use a fresh roll.

Technique

- The first photograph should be of the head slate (identifier card with photographer, date, case title or number, and organization). (A template is provided as Appendix D.)
- If practical, use the highest-resolution image available on your camera.
- Raw images allow for the highest resolution as well as digital documentation that they have not been compressed or altered.
- Raw images should be transferred to an evidence quality CD or agency server at the soonest possible opportunity, prior to viewing or image enhancement.
- Working copies may be made from the raw images and stored as .jpeg or other more portable files. These copies may be enhanced digitally as necessary.

- When working with a program that allows digital enhancement and correction, ensure that each step of alteration to the original image is recorded.
- If working with film instead of digital, it may be necessary to "bracket" your exposures. In other words, expose the same photograph at ±1 f-stop to ensure proper exposure. In arson cases consider bracketing using several f-stops.

General Photography Guidelines

- Keep crime scene processing equipment and investigators out of photographs.
- The evidence should be photographed without scale first, and then with scale (Figure 4.1).
- When slower shutter speeds are used, consider a tripod to ensure sharpness.
- In examination quality photographs fill the frame with the evidence and take the photograph with the film/CCD plane at parallel to from the portion of the evidence that is of most interest (Figure 4.2).
- If using film, ensure it is appropriate for the lighting. As an example, the surgical lights during autopsy are generally tungsten and will not render true color if daylight film is used. A tungsten type film is recommended.

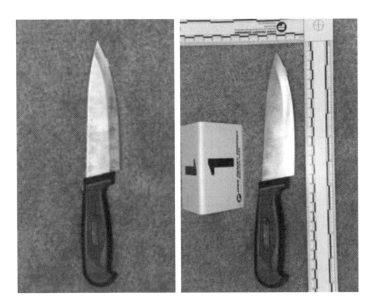

Figure 4.1 Evidence photographed without and with scale.

Figure 4.2 Examination quality photograph of developed print on knife blade.

- Ensure with digital exposures that the white balance is correct for the lighting. This may involve setting the camera for automatic white balance or, in the situation described above, choosing tungsten lighting.

Use of Flash

- Flash should be used on most indoor and many outdoor exposures. The flash will correct for white balance as well as filling in the shadows.
- If using a digital camera, whenever possible set the camera to flash mode; however, some digital cameras may not allow such a setting.
- Shadows often accentuate detail and highlight impressions. Use a detachable electronic flash unit to manipulate or eliminate shadows.
- Front lighting eliminates unwanted shadows and highlights evidentiary details. In some situations, too much light will wash out detail or eliminate accentuating shadows.
- An off-camera flash capability is critical for crime scene photography. This allows for both oblique lighting and fill flash.
- The flash may be angled across the surface being photographed to provide low-level oblique lighting that enhances surface texture. This is an important technique when photographing footwear or fingerprint impressions, toolmarks, and bite marks, as well as trace evidence.
- An off-camera flash capability also allows for specifically aiming the flash to fill in shadows naturally created by the scene (Figure 4.3).
- An off-camera flash may also be used to "paint" the background of photographs taken of luminol or other darkened conditions.
- An off-camera flash is also used in the technique called painting with light, which illuminates large areas in the dark.

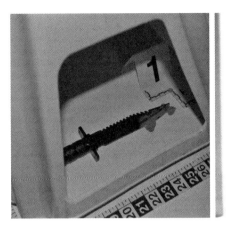

Figure 4.3 Use of fill flash to remove shadows within the scene.

Use of Filters

- A polarizing filter allows for visibility of objects under shallow water or through windows, diminishing the glare from the water or glass (Figure 4.4).
- A neutral density (ND) 30 filter or series of ND filters may be useful in photographing green laser (or alternate light source (ALS)) in daylight conditions.
- A variety of colored filters may be useful in photographing friction ridge detail from colored surfaces. When photographing in black and white color filters may be used to "drop out" the background color, making the print more readily visible.

Figure 4.4 Photograph with and without polarizing filter.

- For print photography on multi- or brightly colored surfaces color filters closely matching the background will cause that background to drop out, making the print more readily visible.

Scene Photography

- Photograph areas around the scene, including possible points of entry and exit. Remember to include exterior shots of the structure if working inside.
- Consider aerial photography to show spatial relationship within the scene. Aerial photography is accomplished from an aircraft, aerial ladder, or an elevated vantage point.
- If strong, natural back lighting conditions exist, use a flash aimed in a direction that would eliminate shadows, or take the photograph from a different angle.
- Avoid taking a photograph that includes the CSI or CSI equipment in it, either directly or as a reflection from any surface. Also avoid taking a photograph where the CSI's shadow is visible.

Overlapping Method/Panographic

- Take a series of photos in a circular, clockwise direction to get 360 degrees of coverage, or take photographs from overlapping vantage points (e.g., shooting from the four corners of the room).
- Overlap each photo with items or areas appearing in the preceding photo to permit matching or comparison.
- Be sure to include floors and ceilings in your photographs.

Progressive Method

- Pinpoint a specific item in a scene and show its relationship to other items in the scene.
- Take a series of overall, evidence-establishing (also known as mid-range or relationship photographs), and close-up photographs (without and with scale) from the same angle and from the same perspective (walk toward the evidence).
- Micro- or macro-photographs may be needed to show greater detail on close-ups.

Photographing Items of Evidence

- Photograph all evidence before moving it.

- Photograph the item as it is found, with an evidence-establishing shot (placing it in context with its surrounding) and close-up shot.
- Repeat the evidence-establishing and close-up shots after placing an evidence placard and scale (if not a part of the placard) by the item.
- Take an examination quality photograph if required.
- Coordinate with the sketcher, on-scene evidence custodian, and evidence collection team before moving the item.
- At the time of collection capture all aspects of the item (e.g., photograph the side of a pistol or body that was not visible as it lay in the scene).

Photographic Perspectives

- **Overall**—Shows a general area as found and helps establish the relationship between the area/scene and its surroundings (Figure 4.5).
- **Evidence establishing (mid-range/relationship)**—Establishes relationship between items of evidence and some known landmark in the scene (Figure 4.6). This photo effectively establishes where in the scene a specific item is.
- **Close-up**—Shows the item of evidence in detail (fill the frame with the item), taken both without and with scale (Figure 4.7).

Figure 4.5 Overall photograph.

Figure 4.6 Evidence establishing photograph.

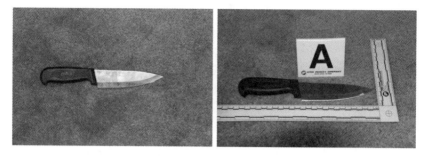

Figure 4.7 Close-up photograph.

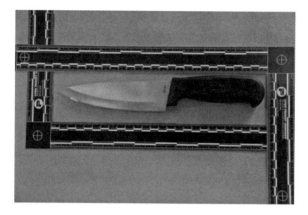

Figure 4.8 Examination quality photograph.

- **Examination quality**—Used to document evidence that will later undergo examination, such as latent prints, bite marks, toolmarks, etc. (Figure 4.8).
- Work closely with the sketcher; photographs and sketches must augment each other in accurately depicting the crime scene.

Crime Scene Sketching

5

The crime scene sketch documents spatial relationships between items of evidence and the scene. A series of sketches may be required when documenting a crime scene. An overall sketch shows the location where the crime occurred; an area sketch shows the relationship of the room or area within a structure to the floor plan, or the location of specific evidence categories such as bloodstain patterns.

- Rough sketch: The original sketch that is drafted at the scene is the rough sketch. It may be drafted onto graph paper and is generally done in pencil with a straight edge and other simple drawing tools or perhaps a template (Figure 5.1).
- Finished sketch (final diagram): From the rough sketch a finished sketch will be prepared. It will be the sketch attached to the crime scene report and quite likely will be used in court. It needs to be a professional-looking product. The finished sketch may be simply prepared by using templates, ink pen, and straight edges or through use of computer software or advanced CAD programs. Sketches may also be prepared from laser and photographic mapping systems (Figure 5.2).

General Components of a Sketch

- A north arrow is placed on the sketch showing orientation. In certain instances (a ship or boat on the water, an airplane in flight) a north arrow would serve no purpose. In these instances the sketch should be oriented to a logical feature of the craft, such as the bow of a boat or ship and the flight deck/nose of an aircraft.
- The sketch should be marked "not to scale" unless an actual scale is used. The latter is not recommended, unless agency protocol requires it. If used, the scale must be very accurate, or the CSI risks having the opposing counsel make an issue at trial of any minor error.
- A title block indicating the case title, location, dates, and who prepared the sketch should be included.

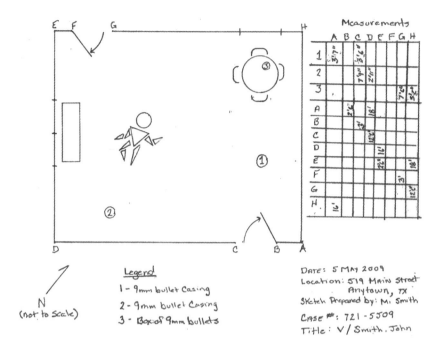

Figure 5.1 Example of rough sketch.

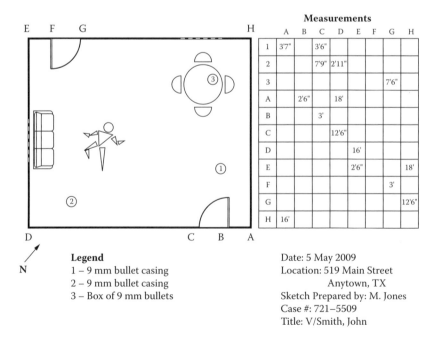

Figure 5.2 Example of finished sketch.

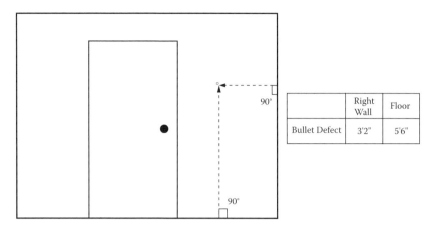

Figure 5.3 Example of bullet defect location sketch.

- Measurements: Overall measurements of the room or space should be provided. Important room features, such as doors, windows, and furnishings, should also be measured in relation to room corners, walls, and each other. Of course, individual items of evidence need to be measured from two fixed reference points to place them in their location within the scene. Measurements need to be made in a straight line. If used, tape measures need to be held taut, and the plane used to measure distances should be the same plane as the items being measured. For example, if measuring the distance from the corner of the room to an item on the floor, the tape measure or other device should be held parallel to the level of the floor, not at an indiscriminate angle that would add to the actual distance involved.

Depictions

- An area sketch depicts the general location or area of the crime scene. It would include surrounding homes and properties, street names, and any other pertinent area features the CSI considers important.
- A scene sketch includes all areas where evidence is located.
- A detailed sketch shows the spatial relationship of specific items of evidence and their immediate surroundings.
- Additional sketches may be prepared that show specific evidentiary findings, such as all bloodstain patterns or bullet defects and trajectories (Figure 5.3).

Types of Sketches

- Bird's-eye view (aka overview or plan view) provides the perspective of looking down onto the area being sketched (Figure 5.4).

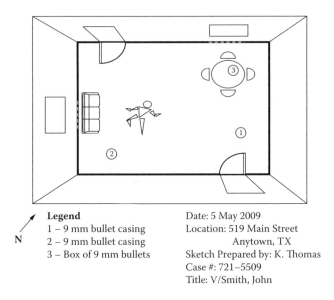

Legend   Date: 5 May 2009
1 – 9 mm bullet casing   Location: 519 Main Street
N   2 – 9 mm bullet casing   Anytown, TX
3 – Box of 9 mm bullets   Sketch Prepared by: K. Thomas
                                        Case #: 721–5509
                                        Title: V/Smith, John

Figure 5.4 Example of bird's eye view sketch.

- Exploded view (aka cross-projection) is a way of including walls and ceilings in relation to the floors by laying down adjacent surfaces onto a two-dimensional format (Figure 5.5).
- Elevation usually shows a side view, such as the perspective of a vertical wall looking from the side.

Scene Measurements

- Measurements are taken to identify general scene dimensions and specific locations of evidence where the crime occurred. A standard tape measure or an electronic/laser tape measure may be used.
- Evidence measurements are generally made to the nearest 1/4 in. If a greater degree of precision is required to document a specific spatial relationship, a smaller unit of measure on the scale may be used. For instance, in showing extreme details, the use of the metric system (in centimeters or millimeters) may be more applicable, as used in close-up or examination quality photography.
- In documenting close-up photographs of bloodstain patterns and bullet defects, the most precise unit of measure available should be photographically depicted. These measurements are generally represented using a metric scale with millimeter demarcations (Figure 5.6).
- Measurements to the evidence may be taken to center mass of the evidence if spatial orientation does not matter. An example would be

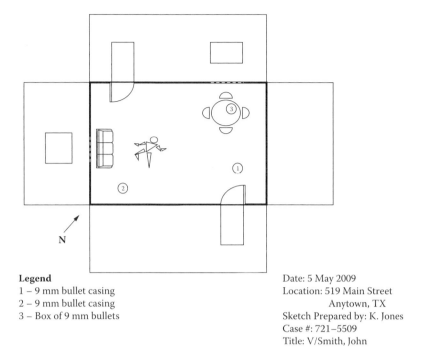

Legend

1 – 9 mm bullet casing
2 – 9 mm bullet casing
3 – Box of 9 mm bullets

Date: 5 May 2009
Location: 519 Main Street
　　　　　Anytown, TX
Sketch Prepared by: K. Jones
Case #: 721–5509
Title: V/Smith, John

Figure 5.5 Example of exploded view or cross projection sketch.

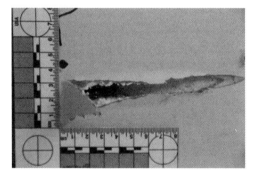

Figure 5.6 Bullet defect with ABFO (metric) scale.

measuring to the center of a strand of hair on the carpet or an ejected bullet case (Figure 5.7).

- At least two separate sets of measurements to two different points on the evidence may be taken if spatial orientation is important. An example would be measuring to both the handle and tip of the blade of a knife, or to the front sight, rear sight, and tip of the trigger on a handgun.
- Permanent features of the area, such as walls, door openings, or room corners, are the primary reference points. Additional reference

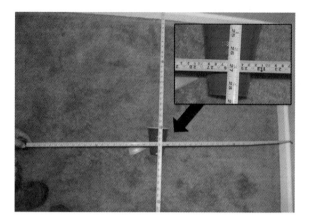

Figure 5.7 Measuring an object to center mass when axial orientation is not significant.(demonstrative only, photographs normally not taken with measuring tapes in place).

points can be established on such features (e.g., reference point 1 is located on the west wall 2 ft north of the southwest corner of the room). Reference points are usually designated by an uppercase *R* followed by a number (R1, R2, R3).

- If there are very few items of evidence, the measurements may be depicted on the primary sketch with straight lines and the measurement represented beside them.
- Representing all measurements on the primary sketch very quickly becomes confusing and difficult to decipher. A table may be prepared (on the sketch or a supplemental page) that shows the distances between the fixed points, the fixed points and furnishings, and the fixed points and items of evidence (Figure 5.8). An alternative is to create an additional sketch that depicts only the evidence measurements.

Methods of Measuring

- **Triangulation:** Commonly used to fix furnishing and items of evidence on any surface. Measurements are taken from two fixed points to the item of evidence. The distance between the two fixed points must be known. It is critical that the fixed points be just that; they cannot be moveable. Examples are corners of rooms and the edges of door or window openings (Figure 5.9).
- **Rectangular coordinates:** Commonly used to document the location of any item of evidence and is effective when fixing evidence on a vertical surface such as a wall. This method is used for documenting the location of bloodstain patterns and bullet defects. Measurements

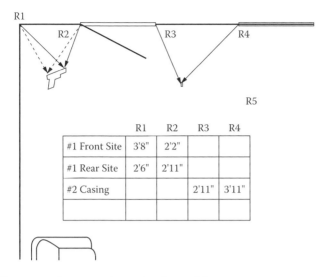

	R1	R2	R3	R4
#1 Front Site	3'8"	2'2"		
#1 Rear Site	2'6"	2'11"		
#2 Casing			2'11"	3'11"

Figure 5.8 Triangulation and use of a data table.

are taken at 90 degrees to the floor and the nearest intersecting wall or feature (such as a door frame) (Figures 5.10 and 5.11).

- When items lie adjacent to or flush to a surface, a single measurement from a known point effectively fixes its position when using either triangulation or rectangular coordinates. An example would be a spent bullet casing located 6 ft 2 in. from the south corner along the wall running south to north.

Figure 5.9 Triangulation of item of evidence (demonstrative only, photographs normally not taken with measuring tapes in place).

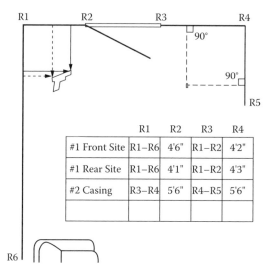

Figure 5.10 Rectangular coordinates method of documenting evidence.

- **Baseline:** The interior baseline is commonly used in large areas where limited reference points exist (e.g., a warehouse). A single baseline is established down the center of the room, and measurements are taken at 90 degrees from the baseline and represented as plus or minus, depending on which side of the line the measurement is made from. Baseline is particularly effective when the floor consists of tiles or something similar with known measurements, for instance, when 12 in. tiles are on the floor. The distance out from one

Figure 5.11 Rectangular coordinates method of documentation. (demonstrative only, photographs normally not taken with measuring tapes in place).

wall can be easily measured, and the distance from a designated line (created by the tiles) can be determined.

- **Baseline method with an outdoor scene:** Baseline is a form of modified rectangular coordinates. It involves running a long tape measure between two fixed points (telephone poles, trees, or other landmarks) after fixing the two points with a global positioning system (GPS). Measurements are then taken at 90 degrees from the baseline and represented as plus or minus, depending on which side of the tape the measurement is from (Figure 5.12). The baseline's fixed points (beginning and end) can be further fixed if required by driving a metal stake or short piece of concrete reinforcing bar (rebar) into the ground at the respective point. This will allow for subsequent location of the fixed points if needed by using a metal detector. This technique is effective if the baseline is located in an area with limited or changing features (e.g., a wooded area). Baseline is also effective if an existing linear permanent feature such as the edge of a road or a sidewalk is present, so long as the feature is straight. The use of

Figure 5.12 Baseline method of documenting evidence.

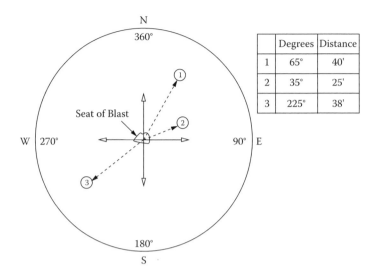

	Degrees	Distance
1	65°	40'
2	35°	25'
3	225°	38'

Figure 5.13 Polar coordinates method of documenting evidence. All measurements taken from seat of blast or pre-established location near the center of the scene.

curved feature (e.g., a roadway with a gradual turn) should not be used as the baseline.

- **Polar coordinates:** In this method a fixed reference point is established and a compass heading (azimuth) is noted as well as the distance along that azimuth to the evidence. The azimuth is most accurately taken with the use of surveyor's transit, although a lensatic compass may also be used. An example would be that an item of evidence lies 137 degrees and 62 ft 8 in. from the reference point (Figure 5.13). This technique is often used for outdoor scenes that have an obvious center of attention, such as the seat of an explosion.

Evidence Identification

- Items of physical evidence that will be removed from the scene are usually represented by numbers (1, 2, 3).
- Pattern evidence, such as two-dimensional footwear impressions or bloodstain patterns, or items of evidence that cannot be taken from the scene, such as a bullet defect in asphalt or concrete, are designated by uppercase letters (A, B, C). If the pattern is collected or sampled as physical evidence, it is codesignated with a number for the evidence custody form.
- The use of either numbers or letters for the evidence is acceptable; however, use the alternative for the patterned evidence.

- A legend (on the sketch or a supplemental page) should be prepared to identify each of the numbers and letters, or other symbols used, with a description of the item of evidence they represent.

Crime Scene Search Procedures

6

Some evidence may be readily apparent to the CSI, such as toolmarks on a jimmied door, or an obvious knife or gun lying in the scene. Other evidence will not be so easily detected. At some point, or during multiple points in the processing, detailed searches for evidence must be made. This includes searching for the instrumentalities of the crime, items removed from or introduced into the scene, items displaced in the scene, and evidence of the presence of individuals within the scene.

General Search Guidelines

- The most time-consuming search is generally the most thorough.
- Items that may have evidentiary value should be noted and marked.
- When the search is completed, evidence identification placards may be placed. By first noting all items of evidence, a logical and methodical assignment of evidence numbers is more likely to occur (Figure 6.1).
- Negative evidence, items expected in the scene that are not present, should also be noted.
- Obviously displaced or moved items should be noted.
- Whichever search pattern is chosen, it must be methodical.
- The search pattern utilized is generally based on the nature of the scene (e.g., a confined space such as an office, room, or vehicle, compared to a field, wooded area, or body of water).
- The space may be an unconfined space, such as a field, wooded area, or body of water.
- The most logical search method chosen should be adapted to the unique aspects of the search area.

Confined Area Searches

Confined area searches are searches that occur within obvious boundaries, such as a search of a car, an office, a room, or a house.

Figure 6.1 Use of expedient evidence markers prior to number placards.

Point-to-Point Search

- Point-to-point searches are used when there is obvious perishable/fragile evidence noted in the scene.
- Direct movement to the perishable evidence is accomplished by searching and clearing a pathway to the item.
- The pathway cleared should avoid the perpetrator's suspected path of travel. This is used in crime scenes to move directly to an item of evidence where a delay would compromise the investigation (Figure 6.2).

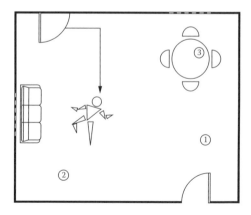

Figure 6.2 Establish pathway that avoids perpetrator's suspected travel.

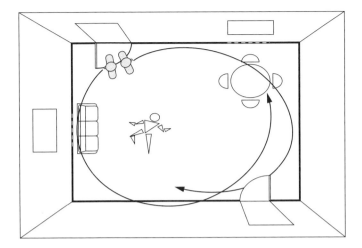

Figure 6.3 Circle search method.

Circle or Spiral Search

- The circle/spiral method is effective in defined spaces (e.g., rooms) (Figure 6.3).
- Start at a common point, such as a door or entryway or the center of the scene.
- Using a consistent swath search path, the CSI moves in a clockwise or counterclockwise path, in either an expanding or shrinking spiral.
- An alternative is for two CSIs to search the same area, one clockwise, one counterclockwise.
- When they meet, they continue past each other, researching the area previously searched by their partner.
- All areas in the search swath must be evaluated (e.g., high and low, on top of and underneath tables) (Figure 6.4).

Sector Search (Zone Search or Quadrant)

- Sector search is effective in confined spaces such as an office, room, or vehicle (Figure 6.5).
- For a room, divide it into imaginary quadrants.
- In a motor vehicle, the area may be sectored as front passenger compartment, rear passenger compartment, trunk, and engine compartment.

Open-Area Searches

An open-area search differs from a confined-area search, as there are fewer obvious boundaries that would contain the area of evidence. These areas

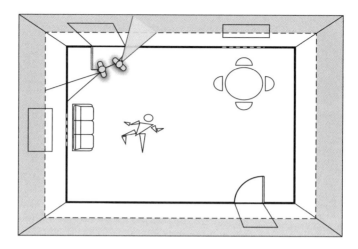

Figure 6.4 High/low search method.

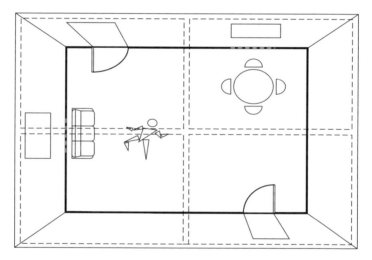

Figure 6.5 Sector (zoned) search method.

would be open fields, wooded areas, yards, or other spaces without clear boundaries. These techniques may also be used in areas with ambiguous boundaries, such as a warehouse or other large space that is better suited to these search techniques.

Strip or Line Search

- The area is divided into distinct search swaths that lie parallel to one other.
- The CSI moves down each swath strip, and then returns down the adjacent swath (Figure 6.6).

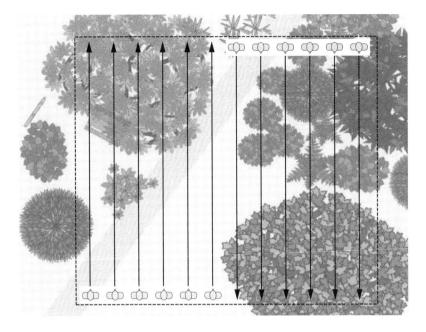

Figure 6.6 Strip or line search method.

Grid Search

- The grid search is an alternative form of the strip search.
- It is a strip search that doubles back over itself at right angles to the first search.
- It is very effective and thorough in large areas and outdoor searches.
- As with any search method, it may be repeated with an increased degree of scrutiny on each pass (Figure 6.7).

Circle or Spiral Search

- In relatively small open spaces a circle or spiral search is also effective for outdoor scenes.
- This pattern is of limited value for large outdoor areas, as it is more difficult to ensure complete coverage and it is easy to overlook areas.
- May be effective in underwater searches or when moving out from an area of known evidence in an unconfined space (Figure 6.8).

Specific Search Guidelines

- Likely point(s) of entry into a structure should be examined for latent prints, toolmarks, impressions, and trace evidence.

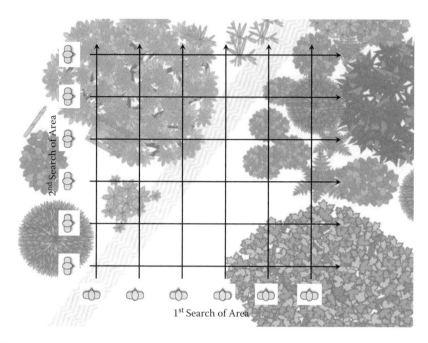

Figure 6.7 Grid search method.

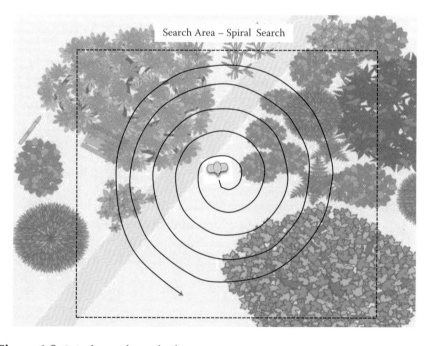

Figure 6.8 Spiral search method.

- Likely paths of travel of the perpetrator should be examined for footwear impression evidence and trace evidence.
- Any items identified as having been handled or touched by the perpetrator should be examined for latent prints and preserved for touch DNA.
- Areas where struggle or contact between the suspect and victim took place should be examined for trace and biological evidence, as well as any footwear impressions.
- Areas where the perpetrator may have cleaned up should be examined for latent prints, impression, biological, and trace evidence.
- The likely point of exit from the scene should also be processed for latent prints, impressions, biological, and trace evidence.

Vehicle Searches

Exterior

- The exterior should be examined first.
- Pay particular attention to the grille area and hood.
- Look for broken or damaged areas, imprints in dust or road grime on the automobile's finish, hairs and fibers, missing parts, and other irregularities, such as patterns from clothing.
- Examine the exterior for fingerprints around the top of the car, the areas around the door handles, and the window glass. Collect latent prints immediately to avoid destruction.
- Examine the undercarriage for fibers, hair, blood, and human tissue.
- When appropriate, collect samples of dirt, grease, and road grime from the underside of the vehicle. Look for soil in wheel wells and running boards. These samples may be valuable as samples to compare against evidence recovered from the victim.
- When obtaining paint samples from a car, take them from around the damaged area all the way to the bare metal to ensure that each layer of paint is sampled.

Interior

- Divide the interior of the automobile into specific areas and record the search and collection efforts in each of these specific areas.
- Consider the relevance of fibers and dirt from the floor of the various interior areas. If it is deemed important, collect all possible trace evidence on these or other surfaces.

- Examine with a magnifying glass and seize observable materials before any attempt to collect residues using a vacuum. If a vacuum is used, do so in a manner that keeps the materials from each floor area of the vehicle separate from one another.
- Search for items (e.g., drugs, weapons) that may be hidden in the interior.
- Have two investigators search the same areas to reduce the chance of overlooking items.
- Do not reach into places you cannot see; use mirrors and lights instead.

Trunk

- Follow the same procedures as for searching the interior.

Engine Compartment

- The engine compartment generally produces less physical evidence than any other part of a vehicle.
- Concentrate on concealed tools, weapons, drugs, etc.
- Include the area around the inside of the grille, the area around the radiator, and any containers attached to the wheel wells inside the engine compartment.

Computer Searches

- A computer or electronic information system may contain valuable information as to the crime; this may include notes or sites visited.
- In addition, the computer activity, including Internet, chats, phone calls, and emails, may indicate activities that occurred contemporaneously with the crime.

Seizure

- Seizure should be completed only for stand-alone systems; networked systems must be seized by a forensic computer specialist.
- Immediately photograph the screen, if on.
- Do not shut down the machine through standard system shutdown procedures.
- Do not touch any keys.
- Immediately isolate the system from any outside connections.

- Disconnect from any network provider by removing connection from the wall outlet.
- Disconnect any wireless LAN hub connection by unplugging power to the hub from the wall outlet.
- Unplug the power cord to the machine from the wall outlet or surge protector.
- If the machine is connected to a battery backup system, it must be disconnected from that source.
- Photograph all connections from the ports of the machine.
- Photograph all peripheral devices.
- Seize the CPU and all devices that may be used to store digital media.
- **Always** follow agency protocol/policy, if one exists, on the seizure and recovery of computer-related data.

Analysis

- On-scene evaluations should be done by those trained as forensic computer specialists or contracted experts.
- Failure to follow acceptable digital collection and analysis protocols when attempting to retrieve or review the contents of a computer system at the crime scene may unintentionally destroy evidence or render it inadmissible in court.
- Consult a forensic computer specialist if it is necessary to evaluate the contents of a computer system on scene.

Aquatic Recovery of Evidence

7

General

This chapter focuses on search techniques when evidence is in the water. In most instances this submerged evidence will have been intentionally discarded in a pond, lake, river, or saltwater environment. Under no circumstances should the CSI attempt a water recovery without proper training and experience. A properly trained and equipped underwater evidence recovery team (such skills are often resident within a local dive search and rescue team) is required for both the safety of the members of the recovery operation and to maximize the opportunity for a successful recovery that is also appropriately documented.

The CSI, however, must be versed in the techniques employed, as he or she should be a vital part of the effort, whether or not he or she acts as part of the actual dive team. In many cases aquatic recoveries will yield valuable evidence that must be uniquely handled upon recovery. The CSI, if familiar with the technology available, may be able to narrow the team's search focus and aid in the overall recovery effort.

An underwater evidence recovery team or an underwater archeology team is vital in any effort to facilitate locating, documenting, and recovering submerged items.

Visually Locating Evidence

Surface Searches

- Visual location of evidence from the surface is often very difficult, unless the evidence is located in relatively clear, shallow water and very close to shore.
- For surface searches from boats or shore, wearing polarized sunglasses may allow for better visualization just below the surface, significantly reducing the glare caused by the water (Figure 7.1).

Figure 7.1 Visual search with and without polarizing filter/lens. Photograph on the left, without polarizing filter, shows surface reflection that obscures evidence detail. The photograph on the right, with polarizing filter allows for visualization of the scale and bottom detail without surface reflection.

Aerial Searches

- Aerial search is most effective when seeking large items of evidence (e.g., a motor vehicle) in relatively shallow water or when a significant area of relatively shallow water must be searched, such as a tidal marsh area.
- The use of helicopters or other platforms that allow the observer to get well above the surface of the water and look down is very effective and should be employed as soon as practical.
- If the evidence is suspected to be close to a boat ramp or dock with sufficient access, a fire department snorkel truck may be helpful for searching the area around the dock.
- During aerial searches wearing, polarized sunglasses may allow for better visualization just below the surface.

Visual Searches (Completely Submerged)

- Underwater search for the evidence may be conducted by an underwater evidence recovery team. This skill set may reside within a local or state search and recovery team.

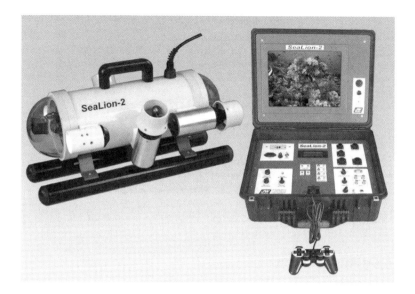

Figure 7.2 Submersible guided video platform. (Photograph courtesy of Jack Fisher, JW Fishers Underwater Search Equipment.)

Note: Underwater evidence recovery is a specialty that requires training, certification, proper equipment, and familiarity with the specific aquatic environment. This should not be attempted by sports divers.

- Underwater searches are far more effective if a search area is narrowed down through the use of technological search, such as a magnetometer or sonar.
- Underwater visual searches may also be conducted by video using a remotely operated vehicle (Figure 7.2). These remotely operated vehicles are controlled by cable and are quite portable. These devices may be available from local harbor, ship inspection, or marine construction facilities.

Modeling

- Many navigable waterways and other waters supported by the Army Corps of Engineers, Coast Guard, or state agencies have been mapped in detail. These agencies may have a detailed computer simulation or model of the waterway. If large items of evidence have been submerged for a significant period of time, using these models may allow an adept operator to simulate the conditions from the time of the submersion to determine the effects of flooding or currents on their current possible position.

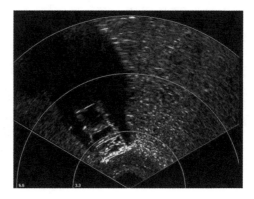

Figure 7.3 Scanning sonar. (Photograph and image courtesy of Jack Fisher, JW Fishers Underwater Search Equipment.)

Technological Search

There are various technologies that may aid the CSI and underwater recovery team. Although often difficult to locate as a resource, such technologies greatly enhance the search efforts. These include:

- **Scanning sonar:** Scanning sonar is submerged from a boat in shallow water, mounted on a tripod on the bottom, or mounted to a remotely operated vehicle. It may be used in smaller bodies of water, such as ponds where side-scanning sonar could not be effectively towed. It provides a 360-degree view of the bottom regardless of water visibility (Figure 7.3).
- **Side-scanning sonar:** Side-scanning sonar is submerged and towed behind a boat. It sends sonar waves out and analyzes their return to show details of the lake, river, or ocean bottom. Side-scanning sonar is useful in locating submerged evidence that rests on the bottom. Its disadvantage would be in locating evidence along a very rocky or irregular bottom surface, or if the evidence items have been covered by silt or debris (Figure 7.4).
- **Magnetometer:** The magnetometer detects the magnetic field of buried ferrous objects. This technique is effective for ferrous items of evidence (those containing iron).

Recovery of Evidence

- Ensure that the name of the individual who discovered the evidence, as well as all those involved in the recovery, is recorded.

Tow Fish

Figure 7.4 Side scanning sonar. (Photograph and image courtesy of Jack Fisher, JW Fishers Underwater Search Equipment.)

- Document in detail the position, condition, and location (to include depth) of the evidence.
- If visibility allows, have the item of evidence photographed in place by the recovery team. Carefully document the location of the recovery. Consider GPS marking from a marker buoy raised over the object.
- Metallic items of evidence may rapidly oxidize (rust) once they are removed from the water and exposed to open air. When practical, collect them in a watertight container that contains the same water from which they were recovered. There is no need to do this at depth; this may be accomplished (if safe) in shallow water or by the recovery platform over a catch net should an item slip or a round be ejected from a weapon while rendering it safe.
- If smaller items of evidence are in a submerged vehicle, there is usually no rush to recover them. Plan, prepare, and set up for the recovery of the evidence and the vehicle. Extended submersion, in and of itself, does not eliminate the potential for other valuable forensic evidence to be recovered.
- If there is other obvious evidence associated with a submerged vehicle or container, ensure that prior to recovery it is fully documented photographically to the extent that visibility allows.
- The process of lifting a submerged vehicle from the bottom will cause many items to shift. To the extent possible, fully document

photographically the interior condition prior to any movement of the submerged vehicle or container.

- Using underwater metal detectors, magnetometers, and visual search techniques, search the area beneath and adjacent to any submerged vehicle or container.

Releasing the Scene and Postscene Activities

8

The release of the crime scene should only be done after careful consideration. Once released, it will be more difficult to return and later seize additional items from the scene. Consider holding significant scenes until the completion of interviews, medical examinations/autopsies, and a thorough postscene assessment is completed.

Postscene Assessment

- Determines if the scene should be held until after interviews or medical examinations.
- Determine the appropriate time to release the scene and ensure the scene is secured and turned over to an appropriate responsible authority/person.

General Guidelines

- Have a fresh set of eyes go through the scene to determine if anything has been missed. Ensure no gear has been left at the scene. This final review acts as a confidence check in the processing methodology and procedures used.
- Ensure all evidence is screened for forensic value and sent to the appropriate forensic laboratory for analysis.
- Ensure all crime scene reports are completed.
- Conduct a team meeting and review all aspects of the search. Ensure no areas have been overlooked.
- Outline the plan for the next 24 hours. Identify critical issues:
  - Records checks
  - Key interviews
  - Searches
  - Evidence to the lab
  - Expert assistance (forensic consultant, computer specialist, etc.)
  - Future manpower requirements

- Clearly assign responsibility for:
  - Up-channel notifications (e.g., chain of command briefings)
  - Overall control of the case and report
  - Specific report inserts
- Arrange for continued crime scene security, if necessary.

Documentation

- Ensure documentation is complete and free of errors and inconsistencies.
- Ensure all evidence custody documents are filled out properly.

Releasing the Scene

- Prior to releasing the scene, have someone who has not worked the scene but is familiar with the investigation walk through the area with fresh eyes to note and process any additional items discovered.
- Once the scene is released, reentry generally requires another search authorization. Consult the appropriate legal authority before reentering a scene that has been released.
- Ensure that the scene is released in a secure condition. If the scene is a residence or business, make certain that it is physically secured or that a responsible person has been given control. This is usually the owner or resident of the space that has been searched, or a person designated by him or her.
- Ensure that homeowners, etc., are aware of any chemical agents used to process the scene or biological contaminates left at the scene, and the proper way to clean or handle them.
- Ensure that the final condition of the scene has been recorded by still photography, videography, or both. This is particularly important if there is concern that the owner/resident may later claim extensive damage or loss resulting from the search.
- Remember to leave a copy of any search warrant and a copy of all items seized and any other legal documents required by agency policy or state law.

Crimes against Property

Burglary and Housebreaking   9

This chapter deals with discovering and documenting physical evidence involved in acts of burglary and housebreaking. Their common elements include the unlawful entry into a building or dwelling with the intent to commit a felony therein.

Initial Actions

Specific guidance for steps in securing the scene, photography, and initial crime scene procedures is covered in Section I, "Crime Scene Investigation." Section I is applicable to all crime scenes and should be reviewed to ensure no steps are missed.

Establish Perimeter

- Without entering the structure, determine likely points of entry and exit.
- Establish a generous perimeter that includes likely paths of travel to and from the crime scene.

Legal Concerns

- Determine the legal authority to be present and conduct a crime scene examination. Remember that at some point any exigent circumstances for responding to the scene (e.g., caring for victims) will be over.
- Ensure a continued authority to remain on scene and collect evidence (e.g., search warrant, consent, no reasonable expectation of privacy).
- See Chapter 1, "Initial Response," for a detailed explanation of search and processing legal concerns.

Establishing Context

- Receive a briefing or speak with the owner or resident to determine when the structure was last known to be secured, who had legitimate access, who discovered the incident, where he or she moved, what he or she handled, and what he or she noted missing or altered.

- Determine when the location was last known to be secure. This establishes a context by which to evaluate evidence. Context examples include:
  - If the location was secure last night and there are weathered cigarette butts in the area, they may be of less significance than fresh ones associated with the scene.
  - Conversely, weathered cigarette butts or beer cans at a summer cabin broken into sometime over the winter may be very significant.
- Determine who has entered the crime scene and who had legitimate access prior to the crime.
  - Arrange to take elimination prints.
  - Photograph the tread pattern of their footwear.
  - Collect footwear if they fall under suspicion.
- Conduct a scene walk-through, avoiding paths of travel likely used by the perpetrators.
  - Note any perishable evidence and document/collect or safeguard it.
  - Note any obvious items missing or disturbed.
- Determine area of primary activity used to commit the crime.
- Determin the area of primary activity required to commit the crime.
  - If the back door is forced open and every indication is that entry and exit were made from that door, the front foyer will likely decrease in priority for processing.
  - Rooms that have clearly not been disturbed or entered may decrease in priority of processing.
  - Areas that have obviously been disturbed and furnishings that have been moved and drawers gone through will increase these areas' priority of processing.

Crime Scene Processing Guidelines

- Working from the outside to the inside, search for possible two- and three-dimensional footwear impressions along the perpetrator's likely path of travel.
- Examine points of entry and exit (and other appropriate areas) for perishable evidence, such as clothing fibers, hair, blood, or transfer evidence, to include touch DNA.
- Identify means used to gain entry and process/collect appropriate evidence, such as toolmarks (Chapter 26) and latent prints (Chapter 25).

- Examine windows and adjacent areas for clothing fibers, blood, and other trace evidence. Examine and process window frames, doors, and doorknobs for fingerprints; consider recovery of touch DNA.
- Have the victim assist in identifying areas of activity, missing items, disturbed items, or items introduced to the scene by the perpetrator.

Caution: The victim's tendency will be to touch items no matter how often you warn him or her. Consider asking the victim to place his or her hands in his or her pockets.

- Examine and process for latent prints all surfaces that might have been touched by suspects (open drawers, cabinet doors, and out-of-place objects). Consider touch DNA. Collect or process out-of-place items.
- If latent prints are recovered, obtain elimination prints from all those who logically had access to the item or area.
- Examine garbage containers for beer or soda cans, refrigerators for food items that may be missing, or food items that have been moved, touched, or partially eaten, leaving prints, bite marks, or DNA.

Stolen Property List

- Obtain detailed descriptions, including existing photos of stolen items.
- Identify unusual marks or means of identification.
- Obtain approximate values, including copies of receipts if available.
- Obtain serial numbers for entry into NCIC and pawn shop searches.

Commonly Encountered Evidence

The following evidence is commonly found at breaking and entering scenes:

- Blood
- Fingerprints
- DNA
- Cigarette butts
- Soil
- Tool impressions or discarded tools
- Hairs and fibers
- Tire tracks
- Footwear impressions

- Paint
- Glass
- Fabrics

Larceny

10

This chapter deals with discovering physical evidence involved in the act of larceny. The crime of larceny involves the unlawful taking of an item of value with the intent to permanently deprive. A larceny crime may differ from housebreaking and burglary in that unlawful entry of a structure is not always a factor.

Initial Actions

Specific guidance for steps in securing the scene, photography, and initial crime scene procedures is covered in Section I, "Crime Scene Investigation." Section I is applicable to all crime scenes and should be reviewed to ensure no steps are missed.

Establish Perimeter

- Establish the specific location from which the items were taken.
- Establish a generous perimeter that includes likely paths of travel to and from the crime scene.

Legal Concerns

- Determine the legal authority to be present and conduct a crime scene examination. At some point the exigent circumstances for responding to the scene (e.g., caring for victims) will be over.
- Ensure a continued authority to remain on scene and collect evidence (e.g., search warrant, consent, no reasonable expectation of privacy).
- See Chapter 1, "Initial Response," for a detailed explanation of search and processing legal concerns.

Establishing Context

- Receive a briefing or speak with the individual responsible for controlling access to the item or area from which it was taken to determine when the item was last known to be present, who had legitimate access, is surveillance video available of the area, who discovered the incident, where he or she moved in the scene, what he or she handled, and what he or she noted missing or altered.

- Determine when the item was last known to be secure. This establishes a context by which to evaluate evidence. Context examples include:
  - Could the item have been missing for several days or weeks and its absence was just not detected?
  - Was the container for the item still present, giving the impression the item was still there?
  - Is this an area that is seldom checked and the item's immediate absence would not be noted?
- Determine who has entered the crime scene and who had legitimate access prior to the crime.
  - Arrange to take elimination prints.
  - Photograph the tread pattern of their footwear.
  - Collect footwear if they fall under suspicion.

- Determine if this is an area with open access to the public or visitors, or if access is generally limited to employees.
- Conduct a scene walk-through, avoiding paths of travel likely used by the perpetrators.
  - Note any perishable evidence and document/collect or safeguard it.
  - Note any obvious items missing or disturbed.
- Determine the area of primary activity required to commit the crime.
  - Limit the scene through logical consideration of the progression of the crime to determine specifically where the individual had to be to steal the item and what he or she would have had to touch.
  - This specific area and item identification can greatly reduce the suspect pool. It may also assist in determining those individuals with specific contact with the scene to commit the crime from those who had casual contact with the scene. This is referred to as the zone of isolation; for example:
  - Consider a computer or electronic system stolen by an employee with access to the warehouse area, with the box and packaging returned to the shelf in order to delay detection of the crime. Though many employees would have access to the area and exterior box, the suspect would be isolated from this pool by fingerprints or touch DNA on the interior packaging that would have to be handled to remove the component from its packaging.

Crime Scene Processing Guidelines

- Working from the outside of the zone of isolation to the inside, search for possible two-dimensional and three-dimensional footwear impressions along the perpetrator's likely path of travel.
- Examine objects handled for perishable evidence, such as clothing fibers, hair, blood, or transfer evidence, to include touch DNA.
- Identify means used to access the stolen item, such as a ladder or lock mechanism, and process/collect appropriate evidence for latent prints, touch DNA, and toolmarks (Chapters 25 and 27).
- Examine any threshold to the zone of isolation that might contain traces of the perpetrator's passage, such as two-dimensional impression evidence, clothing fibers, blood, touch DNA, and trace evidence.
- Determine what the perpetrator would have had to touch or manipulate to facilitate the crime. Process these areas.
- Have the victim assist in identifying any changes within the isolation zone that contain disturbed items or items introduced to the scene by the perpetrator. *Caution*: The victim's tendency will be to touch items no matter how often you warn him or her. Consider asking the victim to place his or her hands in his or her pockets.
- Examine and process for latent prints all surfaces that might have been touched by suspects (open drawers, cabinet doors, and out-of-place objects). Consider touch DNA. Collect or process out-of-place items.
- If latent prints are recovered, obtain elimination prints from all those who logically had access to the item or area.
- If the item was packaged, examine trash containers and other logical areas for discarded packaging. These items should be documented and processed for latent prints, touch DNA, or other trace evidence.

Stolen Property List

- Obtain detailed descriptions, including existing photos of stolen items.
- Identify unusual marks or means of identification.
- Obtain approximate values, including copies of receipts if available.
- Obtain serial numbers for entry into NCIC and pawn shop searches.

Commonly Encountered Evidence

- Friction ridge evidence:
  - Patent prints
  - Latent prints

- Biological evidence:
  - Touch DNA
- Impression evidence:
  - Toolmarks
  - Footwear impressions

Larceny of a Motor Vehicle

11

This chapter deals with discovering physical evidence involved in the theft of a motor vehicle. Though the most common vehicles encountered are an automobile, motorcycle, boat, ATV, or farm equipment, any other motorized self-propelled vehicle may also be processed using these guidelines. Larceny of a motor vehicle runs a wide range of motivations and professional expertise in its execution. From the amateur that engages in a "joy ride" to professional car theft rings, entry to the vehicle, ignition override of the vehicle, and removal of the vehicle from its location all require a certain level of force and interaction that leave physical evidence both at the scene and in the vehicle. Processing of both the scene and the recovered vehicle will be covered in this chapter.

Initial Actions

Specific guidance for steps in securing the scene, photography, and initial crime scene procedures is covered in Section I, "Crime Scene Investigation." Section I is applicable to all crime scenes and should be reviewed to ensure no steps are missed.

Establish Perimeter

- Establish the specific location from which the vehicle was taken.
- Establish a generous perimeter that includes likely paths of travel to and from the crime scene.
- Include any area where a lookout or spotter may have been positioned. These areas may contain valuable trace evidence, such as cigarette butts, candy wrappings, or footwear impressions.

Legal Concerns

- Determine the legal authority to be present and conduct a crime scene examination. At some point the exigent circumstances for responding to the scene (e.g., caring for victims) will be over.
- What is the continued authority to remain on scene and collect evidence (e.g., search warrant, consent to search, no reasonable expectation of privacy)?

- See Chapter 1, "Initial Response," for a detailed explanation of search and processing legal concerns.

Establishing Context

- Receive a briefing or speak with the individual responsible for having secured the vehicle last.
  - Determine when the vehicle was last known to be present.
  - Determine who had legitimate access and keys. Determine if there is surveillance video available of the area.
  - Determine who discovered the vehicle missing. Determine what, if anything, he or she moved or handled and what he or she noted missing or altered.
- Determine when the item was last known to be secure. This establishes a context by which to evaluate evidence. Context examples include:
  - Could the vehicle have been missing for several days or weeks and its absence was just now detected?
  - Was the garage or parking area for the vehicle still secure, giving the impression the vehicle was still present?
  - Is this an area that is seldom checked and the vehicle's immediate absence would not be noted?
- Determine who has entered the area of the theft and who had legitimate access to the scene and vehicle prior to the crime.
  - Arrange to take elimination prints.
  - Photograph the tread pattern of their footwear.
  - Collect footwear if they fall under suspicion.
- Determine if this is an area with open access to the public or visitors, or if access is generally limited, such as in a garage or secure parking facility.
- Conduct a scene walk-through, avoiding paths of travel likely used by the perpetrators.
  - Note any perishable evidence and document/collect or safeguard it.
  - Note any obvious items missing or disturbed.
- Determine the area of primary activity required to commit the crime.
  - Limit the scene through logical progression to determine specifically where the individual had to be to facilitate the theft and what he or she would have had to touch.
  - This specific area is used to assist in determining who had specific contact with the scene to commit the crime, compared to those with casual contact with the scene. This is referred to as the zone of isolation; for example:
  - Consider a vehicle in a commercial parking lot. Glass fragments may indicate entrance to the vehicle was made through the driver's

side window. Another vehicle closely parked on that side might have incidental handprints from the perpetrator maneuvering in the tight space. Though many people would have access to the parking area, few would have been between the two cars. The suspect may be isolated from this pool by fingerprints or touch DNA.

Crime Scene Processing Guidelines

- Working from the outside of the zone of isolation to the inside, search for possible two-dimensional and three-dimensional footwear impressions along the perpetrator's likely path of travel.
- Examine objects handled for perishable evidence, such as clothing fibers, hair, blood, or transfer evidence, to include touch DNA.
- Identify means used to access the stolen vehicle, such as a hammer, brick, or spark plug ceramic (ninja rocks), and process/collect appropriate evidence for latent prints, touch DNA, and toolmarks (Chapter 26, 27) and latent prints (Chapter 25).
- Determine what the perpetrator would have had to touch or manipulate to facilitate the crime, and process these areas.
- Have the victim assist in identifying any changes within the isolation zone that have disturbed items or items introduced to the scene by the perpetrator. *Caution*: The victim's tendency will be to touch items no matter how often you warn him or her. Consider asking the victim to place his or her hands in his or her pockets.
- Examine and process for latent prints all surfaces that might have been touched by suspects. Consider touch DNA. Collect or process out-of-place items.
- If latent prints are recovered, obtain elimination prints from all those who logically had access to the vehicle or area.

Recovered Motor Vehicle—Crime Scene Processing Guidelines

Specific guidance for steps in securing the vehicle, photography, and initial processing procedures is covered in Section I, "Crime Scene Investigation." Section I is applicable to all crime scenes and should be reviewed to ensure no steps are missed.

Establish Perimeter

- Establish the specific location of the vehicle.

- Establish a generous perimeter that includes likely paths of travel to and from the stolen vehicle.
- Include any area where the vehicle may have been stripped for parts. These areas may contain valuable trace evidence, such as cigarette butts, candy wrappings, footwear impressions, etc.

Establishing Context

Abandoned Motor Vehicle

- Does the location indicate a likely area the perpetrators operated in or from (near a certain housing area or commercial district)?
- Is the location remote and indicate that another conveyance was required to leave the area? If so, are there additional tire marks present from this vehicle?
- Are personal effects of the owners still in the vehicle? Can they be discerned from any effects the perpetrators may have left behind?
- Has the vehicle been stripped of only high-dollar items such as stereo equipment?
- Has the vehicle been stripped of all usable parts?

Vehicle Recovered in Control of Suspects

- The perpetrators may claim they discovered the vehicle abandoned or that an intermediary provided it and they did not know it was stolen.
- Multiple suspects may identify each other as the one that stole it; thus, it may be necessary to determine who drove the vehicle.
- It may be necessary to establish the perpetrators' prints or DNA on those unique surfaces involved with the theft of the vehicle and control of the vehicle.

Determine if There Are Any Indications of Forced Entry to the Vehicle

- Establish who has additional keys to the vehicle.
- Establish if an automatic locking code was digitally stolen (intercepted).

Vehicle Processing Guidelines

Note: Latent prints, trace DNA, and other indicators may be present on both the vehicle's exterior and interior. The exterior of the vehicle may undergo incidental contact for a variety of reasons. Focus on the specific exterior areas that would indicate control of the vehicle or theft (e.g., license plate screws if the plates were changed out) and those areas in the interior that demonstrate control of the vehicle (e.g., adjusted mirrors, seat position control knobs, steering wheel, shifters).

- Fully document the vehicle through notes, photography, and sketching.
- Determine what the perpetrator would have had to touch or manipulate to steal the vehicle, and process these areas.
- Examine control surfaces and the driver's seat for perishable evidence, such as clothing fibers, hair, blood, or transfer evidence, to include touch DNA.
- Working from the outside to the inside, focus on the following areas for latent prints and touch DNA:
  - License plate (if changed)
  - Point of entry and areas immediately adjacent
  - Seat adjustment controls
  - Steering wheel
  - Shift controls
  - Mirrors
  - Radio or sound system controls
- Consider taking an electrostatic dust print lift of the brake and gas pedals to see if they match the tread pattern of any suspect's footwear.
- Identify all papers, possessions, trash, and garbage within the car and discern what belongs to the owner and what the perpetrators may have left.
  - Process for DNA.
  - Process for latent prints.
  - Consider the presence of specific information that may provide additional leads (e.g., a fast food receipt, correlating it back to the restaurant's surveillance camera).
- Record measurements of the seat position(s). This may aid in eliminating shorter or taller suspects if multiple suspects are involved.

Stolen Property List

- Inventory all items of value that are missing from the recovered vehicle.
- Obtain a description, VIN number, serial numbers, and unique identifiers when possible.
- Enter vehicle and stolen items into appropriate databases for recovery (e.g., NCIC and pawn shop checks).

Commonly Encountered Evidence

- Friction ridge evidence:
  - Patent prints
  - Latent prints
- Biological evidence:
  - Touch DNA
  - Food, drink, or other sources within the vehicle
- Impression evidence:
  - Toolmarks
  - Footwear impressions
- Physical evidence:
  - Receipts
  - Papers
  - Wrappers
  - Clothing

Vandalism and Malicious Mischief

12

This chapter deals with the discovery and processing of physical evidence involved in the act of intentionally destroying or defacing public property or the property of another.

Initial Actions

Establishing Perimeter

- Connected scenes: Stylized vandalism, or vandalism connected by modus operandi, may be located in various sites throughout a jurisdiction. The locations chosen by the vandals may aid in identifying the perpetrator(s).
- Route of ingress and egress: The vandals must move to and from a location as well as between locations. Footwear impressions, tire marks, and surveillance cameras may aid in identification of people or vehicles.

Legal Concerns

- Determine the legal authority to be present and to conduct a crime scene examination.
- What is the continued authority to remain on scene and collect evidence (e.g., search warrant, consent authorization, no reasonable expectation of privacy)?
- See Chapter 1, "Initial Response," for a detailed explanation of search and processing legal concerns.

Establishing Context

- Youth: Youthful offenders may be involved in vandalism and malicious mischief for no more motivation than "they can." Targets may include schools, the residences of teachers or fellow students, businesses, public property, and abandoned buildings.
- Cultural: Graffiti has emerged as a subculture activity in youth groups. This stylized graffiti is often very artistic and stylized. In

these instances the "artist" will almost always "sign" the work with a personalized graffiti signature. Pay particular attention to recurring symbolisms, as this may lead to connecting various vandalism acts.

- Gangs: Gang-related tagging or graffiti is used to mark territory to indicate incursions into other territories.
- Retribution: Malicious mischief or vandalism in retribution, or retaliation, for a real or perceived wrong will be aimed at the business, organization, or individual that is believed to have caused the wrong. Businesses that have been vandalized and are the sole targets should look to disaffected employees and former employees as possible suspects.
- Some extreme environmental and animal rights activists may choose to cause damage to either the institution, research lab, or business that represents the behavior they protest. These include:
  - Tree spiking by driving metal rods, spikes, or nails into trees to keep foresters from effectively and safely harvesting them.
  - Attacks on research laboratories that are believed to be involved in animal experimentation or industrial polluting may often be linked back to the organized or loosely organized group that sponsored or encouraged it.
  - High-profile personalities may have blood, red paint, or other materials thrown on them at a public venue to demonstrate the individual's opposition to the wearing of furs. These tend to be public, and the identity of the perpetrator is often captured on either professional or individual digital media.

Crime Scene Processing Guidelines

Specific guidance for steps in securing the scene, photography, and initial crime scene procedures is covered in Section I, "Crime Scene Investigation." Section I is applicable to all crime scenes and should be reviewed to ensure no steps are missed.

- Establish if forced entry is a factor and process accordingly (Chapter 9).
- Examine the area leading to and surrounding the damaged area for two- and three-dimensional footwear impression evidence.
- Detailed photography of damage is paramount.
- If a crowd has gathered, photograph and videotape the crowd. Perpetrators may have blended in with the crowd and can later be identified as having been present at the scene.
- Examine damaged area for trace evidence and process (Chapter 28).
- Examine damaged area for toolmarks and process (Chapter 26).

- Examine damaged area and adjacent area for latent prints (Chapter 25).
- A thorough search of the scene and surrounding area may result in the recovery of any tools or implements used to create the damage.

Commonly Encountered Evidence

The following evidence is commonly found at scenes of vandalism and malicious mischief:

- Friction ridge evidence:
  - Patent prints
  - Latent prints
- Biological evidence:
  - Touch DNA
  - Discarded food, drink, or cigarette butts within the surveillance area
  - Bloodstain patterns
- Impression evidence:
  - Toolmarks
  - Footwear impressions
  - Tire impressions
- Trace evidence:
  - Hairs and fibers
  - Paint matches
- Physical evidence:
  - Spray paint cans
  - Discarded lid from spray paint can
  - Stylized handwriting
  - Marking pens
  - Discarded caps from marking pens
  - Nails and spikes (may be processed for DNA/prints)
  - Paint
  - Broken eggshells (may be processed for DNA/prints)

Searches Related to Suspect

Search the suspect's person, home, vehicle, work area, work lockers, possessions, etc., for tools or weapons used to cause the damage or for any items possibly taken from the scene. Also, search for trace evidence linking the suspect to the scene. Remember to obtain control samples.

Fire and Arson Scenes*   13

Arson involves the willful or malicious burning of the property of another, or the burning of one's own property, with intent to defraud.

The interpretation of fire damage is highly specialized and requires special training. Processing of the scene should be done in conjunction with a trained fire investigator. If a trained fire investigator is not available, it is crucial to thoroughly document the scene in a manner that will lend itself to later analysis by a trained fire investigator. This chapter is meant to familiarize the CSI with the terminology, on-scene investigative steps, and procedures for collecting and safeguarding evidence from a fire scene.

NFPA 921 is a guide produced by the National Fire Protection Association that fully details the steps, processes, and procedures for fire and explosive investigations.

Initial Actions

Caution: Fire scenes pose a special risk of danger to the crime scene investigator through weakened structural integrity, toxic fumes/residues, and the risk of thermal injury. It is a good practice to have an experienced firefighter assigned to you to serve as your safety officer. No CSI should enter the scene unless accompanied by a trained firefighter.

Note: Do not enter the scene until active firefighting has been completed. Request that an overhaul of the scene by the fire department be delayed until after scene processing. Ensure that all CSIs assigned to the scene have appropriate safety equipment and training to enter.

Establishing Perimeter

- A perimeter should be established that includes an adequate working and safety zone around the burned area or structure. Possible structural collapse, partial collapse, and falling debris should be

---

* Special thanks to John Lentini, CFI, D-ABC, Scientific Fire Analysis, LLC for his technical assistance and guidance in the preparation of this chapter.

considered when establishing the perimeter. The fire scene perimeter may not necessarily coincide with the safety zone.

- Secondary perimeters should be established on possible routes of ingress and egress from the scene.

Legal Concerns

- Determine the legal authority to be present and conduct a crime scene examination. At some point the exigent circumstances for responding to the scene (e.g., caring for victims) will be over.
- What is the continued authority to remain on scene and collect evidence (e.g., search warrant, consent authorization, no reasonable expectation of privacy)?
- See Chapter 1. "Initial Response," for a detailed explanation of search and processing legal concerns.

Establishing Context

- Was a dog(s) in the home with access to the fire's origin?
  - A large or aggressive dog within the home may help place events into context. If the animal is discovered dead in the scene, have a necropsy (autopsies are only on humans) done to include toxicology and blood gases.
  - If the dog died as a result of the fire, smoke inhalation, etc., consider the perpetrator may be known to the dog, allowing him or her access. An animal that has been killed or incapacitated prior to the fire may indicate a stranger to the home or someone the animal would consider a threat.
- The context of the scene may often be indicated after an initial walk-through or scene survey.
  - A **juvenile fire setter** situation may involve the accidental or experimental (curious) fire lighting that results in destruction and damage far beyond that intended. Matches, paper, combustible materials, and a relatively unsophisticated lighting method are generally observed, and the location of the origin may be a closet or other area isolated from observation.
  - The **juvenile vandal/delinquent** fire setter will often target schools or other properties that have meaning to them as representing the establishment or the social order that they are rebelling against.
  - A fire to **commit fraud** by the owner or one with a financial interest in a property may be indicated when furnishings, office

equipment, high-dollar, or personal items are removed from the location prior to the fire being set. Similar but lower-cost items may have been placed in the scene to give the appearance of an undisturbed scene. Consider that insurance records, tax records, legal liens, bankruptcy, and foreclosure notices affecting the property all may give indications of arson for profit.

- A fire used to **conceal another crime** may be indicated by having high-dollar items (those commonly taken during a theft) absent from the burned structure.
- An **extremist arsonist** uses fire and burning to advance a political, religious, or social agenda. This may include acts of terrorism, burnings during civil unrest/riots, and other circumstances. Consider the nature of the targeted scene.
- A **serial arsonist** or fire setter may be juvenile or adult. The fires will seldom involve theft or removal of property, as the fire itself is the motivation for this crime. Patterns as to the physical locations of the fires and methods of ignition may suggest an offender profile.
- There are a variety of motivations that are involved in fire setting; the above examples are emphasized because they may be indicated from the appearance of the physical scene.

Structural Fire Scene Investigations

Fire Scene Processing Guidelines

Specific guidance for steps in securing the scene, photography, and initial crime scene procedures is covered in Section I, "Crime Scene Investigation." Section I is applicable to all fire scenes and should be reviewed to ensure no steps are missed.

General Considerations

- Photograph and videotape the crowd watching the fire.
- Photograph and record all vehicles in a several-block radius of the fire during fire suppression efforts. Many arsonists will watch the burn.
- If at night, note which houses have lights on and show ongoing activity.
- Search the vicinity and logical egress routes for discarded accelerant containers.
- Consider having an accelerant detection dog work the crowd of bystanders, as the arsonist may be among them.

- Request that the fire department **not** overhaul the scene until after the crime scene investigation.
- Safety is paramount, as structural damage and the presence of hazardous conditions/materials may be encountered.
- When assessing the scene, always begin in the areas of least damage and move toward areas of greatest damage. This often aids the CSI in recognizing the nature of the debris found in the more heavily damaged areas.

Scene Photography

Fire scenes pose a special challenge to the photographer. Within the scene the evidence tends to be varying shades of black against a black background. The use of aperture, shutter, and focus control for depth of field and proper exposure is critical. Detailed photographic procedures and techniques are covered in Chapter 4, "Crime Scene Videography and Photography."

- Fire suppression (active fire) photographs:
  - Do not wait until the fire is extinguished to begin scene documentation. Photograph and videotape the active fire and how it responds to suppression efforts. The amount, density, behavior, and color of the smoke and flames should be photographed. These may prove to be valuable indicators for the fire scene analysis.
  - Ensure color rendition is as precise as possible by using a photographic identifier card with color and gray scale.
  - Take photographs of the crowds and by-standers. The fire setter may be watching the results of his or her efforts.
  - Take photographs of the cars in the immediate neighborhood for a distance of several blocks. The fire setter may have parked nearby. These photographs may be used later in the investigation to determine which cars might be out of place.
- Fire scene photography:
  - Follow the guidelines for technique from Chapter 4, "Crime Scene Videography and Photography."
  - Use the guidelines in Chapter 4 for composing overall, evidence-establishing, close-up, and examination quality photographs.

Documenting Fire Patterns

Fire patterns manifest themselves in a number of ways. All of them assist the fire scene investigator in understanding the flow and behavior of the fire. These fire signs should be generally understood by the CSI and documented as fully as possible, particularly if no fire scene investigator is present during initial crime scene efforts. These signs include:

- Burn patterns: Fire tends to burn up and out. A characteristic burn pattern is the V pattern found on vertical surfaces (Figure 13.1). Another classic pattern is the hot gas layer pattern. Heat rises and a layer of hot gas often builds in the scene; this manifests itself as a horizontal burn mark, below which articles and surfaces demonstrate lesser burn damage.
- Damage patterns: Fire "flows" in a scene and damages articles and the structure in differing ways based upon that flow. Look for signs of burn damage that is greater or lesser on a side. Document these patterns fully (Figure 13.2).
- Smoke and soot patterns: The manner in which smoke and soot is deposited in the scene can be of significance to the fire scene investigator. Note and document differing smoke and soot patterns or areas of "clean burn" (Figure 13.3).
- Char patterns: Structural or dimensional lumber of buildings often demonstrate different levels of burn damage. Photograph the condition of exposed structural lumber, and using a depth gauge, document the depth of the char (Figure 13.4).

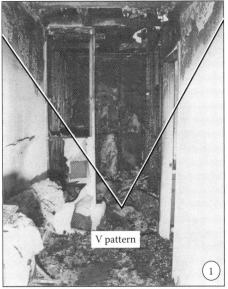 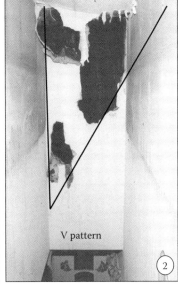

Figure 13.1 "V" pattern indicating likely origin of fire. 1)" V" is demarcated on side walls with thermal damage. 2)"V" is shown on reverse side of wall, demarcated with burn through damage.

Greater thermal damage to the side
facing the origin

Figure 13.2 Burn damage greater on one side indicating side fire burned hottest or longest and indicating likely direction of origin.

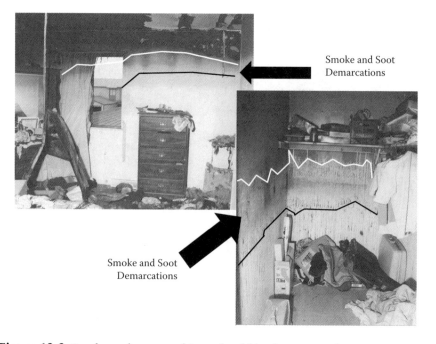

Smoke and Soot
Demarcations

Smoke and Soot
Demarcations

Figure 13.3 Smoke and soot markings should be documented.

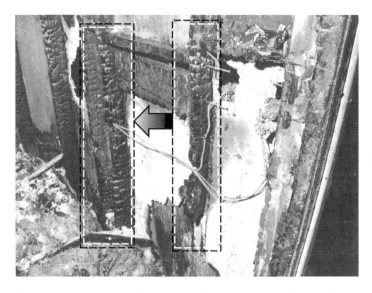

Figure 13.4 Depth of char on dimensional lumber may indicate which area was closest to the origin.

Documenting Indicators of Suspected Area(s) of Origin

- Consideration of the fire patterns in the scene will assist in determining the fire's likely area of origin. All areas of suspected origin should be thoroughly documented. If not properly trained, ensure an arson or fire investigator assists in this step.
- If more than one area of origin is discovered, this is often suggestive of arson. Thus, pay particular attention and document each thoroughly.
- Generally the area of the greatest thermal damage (the area exposed to the fire the longest) will be found near the area of origin (Figure 13.5).
- Fire burns up and out; look for "burn through" of the ceiling. This is often another indicator of area of origin. In the absence of lateral air currents, fire travels upward first before traveling laterally. Thus, ceiling burn through will indicate a longer burn period for the area below (Figure 13.6).
- The area demonstrating the most damage to upper structure is often located over the area of origin.
- The area of origin is often located at the lowest level of the fire damage. Fire tends to spread upward; thus, any indication of low burn should be documented fully.
- As fire burns up and out, it often leaves a characteristic V pattern in soot or fire damage to a wall; the V patterns demonstrate the fire flow and may aid in locating the area of origin as well.
- The greatest depth of charring of wooden structural lumber will often be found near the area of origin.

Figure 13.5 The area of greatest thermal damage tends to be at or near the origin.

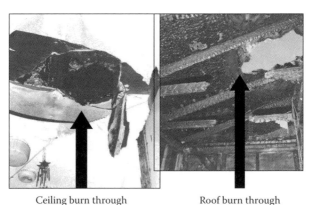

Ceiling burn through   Roof burn through

Figure 13.6 If there is an isolated "burn-through" area of the ceiling or roof, it tends to be over the origin.

Documenting Indicators of the Cause of the Fire

- Once the suspected area of origin is identified, document possible causes for the fire (natural, accidental, incendiary, undetermined).
  - Look for out-of-place tools, electrical appliances, and other things that might have started the fire.
  - Determine which windows, doors, or other openings were closed, opened, or locked.

- Determine if fire or burglar alarms appear to have been tampered with or disabled.
- Note and photograph the position of all circuit breakers serving the structure. A tripped breaker may indicate an electrical fault that led to the fire.
- Be alert to the possibility that the fire was set to conceal another crime (burglary, homicide).
- Look for evidence of substitution of contents. Were old furniture and clothes substituted for new?
- Look for the absence of personal items. Were keepsakes, pictures, important documents, etc., removed from the house?
- Note smoke patterns on top of windows and doorways. This may reveal the direction the fire burned.
- Note and recover items found at the scene that do not belong to the occupant.

Documenting Any Indications the Fire Was Accelerated

- Determine if an accelerant may have been used to increase the ignition time, spread, or speed of the fire.
- If not properly trained, ensure an arson or fire investigator assists in this step.
- A hydrocarbon detector or accelerant dog may be very helpful in this stage of the scene processing.
  - Odors of petroleum products in the debris should be considered suspicious and the debris collected.
  - Look at undersides of doors, chairs, shelves, sofas, and tables. These areas normally are spared direct burn damage unless an accelerant is burning at the floor level.
  - If accelerant is suspected, consider removing sections of wood from floors, walls, and baseboards. They may contain unburned accelerant.
  - Look for evidence of a "trailer" or pour pattern where accelerants were used (e.g., linear burn patterns on the floor where accelerant was used to guide or propagate the fire). Document these completely, with scale for further analysis.
  - Areas of suspected origin and areas of suspected trailers must be excavated completely. This is only accomplished while the fire scene investigator is present and under his or her supervision. As each level of debris is removed, the exposed flooring should be documented photographically (Figure 13.7). Pay particular attention to the removed debris, as it often holds additional burnt evidence.

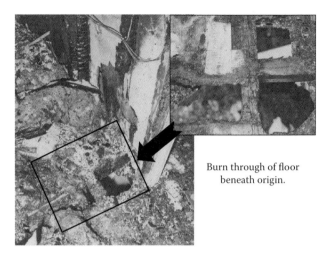

Burn through of floor
beneath origin.

Figure 13.7 Debris is systematically removed and the layers beneath photographed until a clean surface is reached.

Documenting Depth of Charring

- It must be noted if the fire impinged upon a single surface or both sides of the dimensional/structural lumber.
- It must be noted if the structural lumber was directly exposed to the fire or if paneling, sheet rock, etc., covered the lumber at the time of the fire.
    - Search the lumber for nails or drywall screws on the exposed surface. This will indicate sheet rock was likely present at the time of the fire. The offset between the dimensional lumber and head of the screw may provide an indication of the thickness of the sheetrock. Photographically document with scale.
    - Search the lumber for regularly spaced nails. This will indicate that paneling of some type was likely present at the time of the fire. The offset between the dimensional lumber and head of the nail may provide an indication of the thickness of the paneling. Photographically document with scale.
- Using a carpenter's square, complete the square to the thickness of the dimensional lumber on the burned and charred side.
- Using a depth gauge, press it gently into the charred wood until solid wood is found. Measure the depth of the burned-away portion and char from the carpenter's square. Document photographically.
- Repeat the depth of char findings at regular intervals radiating both laterally and above the suspected origin until undisturbed wood is found. Document through sketching and photography.

Sampling, Collecting, and Packaging Fire Scene Evidence

General

- Use only clean, unlined paint or lined (keep control sample) cans or glass jars without rubber liners or seals.
- Nylon collection bags may be used for solid objects or objects of unusual shape or size.
- Never fill a container more than two-thirds full.
- An adhesive-backed activated charcoal strip may be secured to the inside lid of the container. This strip will absorb a sample of any volatile fumes coming from the sample.

Sampling for Accelerants

- Sample any area where a hydrocarbon detector or accelerant canine indicates the possible presence of accelerants.
- Near any suspected area of origin remove wood trim, molding, or threshold molding, and sample and preserve for accelerants that may have leached into cracks and joints.
- Take samples from the suspected origin, but also move just outside of this area and sample as well.
- Consider searching for and collecting evidence (soil and fluids) from under the structure beneath the suspected origin.

Liquids

- Liquid samples should be collected from the runoff liquid that collects at the lowest point near the point of origin.
- Using a syringe, eyedropper, or pipette, draw a liquid sample from the surface of the liquid and place in a clean unlined metal can. Seal tightly.
- The sample may also be soaked into a clean, untreated gauze pad or cotton swabbing and packaged as above.

Solids

- Solid materials, which may have absorbed liquid evidence, should be collected in an unlined or lined (keep control sample) sealed can.
- Solid samples of accelerants are potentially corrosive and should be placed in a glass jar without a glued cap liner or rubber seal.
- Large or irregularly shaped objects may be collected and sealed in nylon bags.

- Always collect a control sample relating to an item of evidence taken. This sample is an unaffected portion of the same surface or object.

Searches Related to Suspect

Search the suspect for burn injuries and the presence of smoke, ashes, and accelerants. Recover clothing, if appropriate. Search the suspect's home and possessions for matches, accelerants, trailer material, motive, and trace materials linking the suspect to the scene

Vehicle Fire Scene Investigations

The same general techniques used for structure fires are employed for vehicle fires. Whenever possible, examine the vehicle in place, at the scene.

General

- Check for information for fires and fire causes for specific vehicles of the same make, model, and year.
- This type of information may be obtained from the Auto Safety Hotline number at 1-800-424-9153.

The Scene

- Search the area surrounding the vehicle for accelerant containers, footprints, and tire marks.
  - Recover soil samples from the owner's footwear as well as alibi samples (where the owner said he or she was when the vehicle fire occurred).
- Search for accelerants that may be found in the soil beneath and around the vehicle.
  - Soil samples should be taken from the ground surrounding the vehicle.
  - Soil samples should be taken from beneath the vehicle.
  - Samples should be collected in unlined metal cans.
  - Control samples should also be taken.

The Vehicle

- Is only the interior or engine compartment burned?
- Exterior survey:

- Look for old tires on a new vehicle. Tires of the wrong size or mismatched tires may be indicative of arson for insurance fraud.
- Is the fuel tank cap absent? Are there adjacent pour patterns? If present, they should be noted and documented.
- Check exterior for pour patterns of flammable liquids that may have splashed on the outside.
- Engine compartment survey:
  - Look for missing engine parts, or indications that the engine has been recently disassembled. This may indicate the owner realized excessive mechanical repairs would be required.
  - If there is doubt as to if the fire started from mechanical reasons, consider a complete inspection of all electrical and mechanical systems by a qualified fire safety engineer.
- Interior survey:
  - Was any equipment removed or replaced with inferior components prior to the fire? This may be indicative of insurance fraud.
  - Was all personal property from the trunk, such as tools, personal equipment, etc., removed prior to the fire?
  - Note position of key and switches, and if windows were up or down.
  - Look for and document any fire signs (e.g., splash patterns of accelerant, V patterns, unexplained low burn).

Fire Scene Evidence

The following evidence is commonly found at fire scenes:

- Friction ridge evidence:
  - Patent prints
  - Latent prints
- Biological evidence:
  - Touch DNA
  - Discarded food, drink, cigarette and butts within the surveillance area
- Impression evidence:
  - Toolmarks
  - Footwear impressions
  - Tire impressions
- Trace evidence:
  - Accelerants
- Physical evidence—debris:
  - Accelerant cans or containers

- Burn patterns
- Charred wood
- Matches

Postblast (Explosive Incident) Scenes
14

The interpretation of explosive scenes is highly specialized and requires special training. Working in conjunction with a trained postblast investigator or with the Bureau of Alcohol, Tobacco, Firearms and Explosives (BATFE) is highly recommended.

Note: It is highly recommended that an explosive ordnance detachment (EOD) team be present to inspect and make safe all such devices prior to processing and collection.

Initial Actions

Caution: It should always be assumed that secondary explosive devices have been set to attack first responders. Extreme caution must be exercised. All explosive scenes should be cleared by EOD personnel.

Establishing Perimeter

- The perimeter of the explosive scene must be set at a minimum of 1½ times the distance from the center of the explosion (seat of blast) to the furthest piece of debris identified.
- This is not necessarily the furthest area of damage; blast wave and shock damage will likely far exceed the distance to the furthest debris from the seat of blast.
- It may be necessary to establish a secondary safety perimeter to ensure the safety of responders and bystanders. The area contained inside of this secondary perimeter will include areas that have falling glass, debris, or demonstrate structural instability.

Legal Concerns

- Determine the legal authority to be present and to conduct a crime scene examination. At some point the exigent circumstances for responding to the scene (e.g., caring for victims) will be over.

- What is the continued authority to remain on scene and collect evidence (e.g., search warrant, consent authorization, no reasonable expectation of privacy)?
- See Chapter 1, "Initial Response," for a detailed explanation of search and processing legal concerns.

Establishing Context

- The context of the scene may provide indicators as to the nature of the bomber, which may be apparent during the initial walk-through or scene survey.
  - A **juvenile bomber** circumstance may involve the accidental or experimental (curious) making of devices that result in destruction and damage far beyond that intended. Gunpowder, matches, PVC pipe, combustible materials, and a relatively unsophisticated detonation method are generally observed, and the location of the origin may be an outside area isolated from observation or in a garage, basement, or other area where the device is constructed.
  - The **juvenile vandal/delinquent bomber** will often target schools or other properties that have meaning to him as representing the establishment or the social order that he is rebelling against. The devices may resemble that of the juvenile bomber or be more sophisticated. Web searches on bomb manufacture or books such as the *Anarchist Cookbook* may be present in written or digital format.
  - An **explosion to commit fraud** by the owner or one with a financial interest in a property may be indicated when furnishings, office equipment, high-dollar, or personal items have been removed from the location prior to the fire explosion. Lower-cost items may have been placed in the scene to replace the more expensive items to give the appearance of an undisturbed scene. Additionally, examination of insurance records, tax records, legal leans, bankruptcy, and foreclosure notices affecting the property may provide indications of arson for profit.
  - An **extremist bomber** uses explosive devices to advance a political, religious, or social agenda. This may include acts of terrorism, burnings during civil unrest/riots, and other circumstances.
  - A **serial bomber** may be juvenile or adult. The explosions will seldom involve theft or removal of property, as the explosion itself is the motivation for this crime. Patterns as to the physical locations of the bombings and the construction of the device itself may suggest an offender profile.

- There are a variety of motivations involved in constructing and detonating bombs. The cited examples are emphasized only as they may be indicated from the appearance of the physical scene.

Crime Scene Processing Guidelines

Specific guidance for steps in securing the scene, photography, and initial crime scene procedures is covered in Section I, "Crime Scene Investigation." Section I is applicable to all crime scenes and should be reviewed to ensure no steps are missed.

Initial Briefing

If possible, seek and debrief someone responsible and objective who witnessed or heard the event. Discuss this information with first responders and investigators who might have additional information about the event.

- Determine when the incident reportedly occurred.
- Determine who had control over the site of the bomb when it went off.
- Determine if other secondary devices are present.
- Determine whether or not anyone videotaped the smoke plume or other effects of the explosion.
- Determine if commercial or government video devices might have recorded the explosion.
- Determine what parties all have already been through the scene (e.g., first responders, witnesses, neighbors).
- Determine if the area has open access to the public or visitors, or if access is generally limited, such as private/guarded property.

Initial Walk-Through

Conduct a scene walk-through, avoiding paths of travel likely used by the perpetrators.

- Note any perishable evidence and document/collect or safeguard it.
- Note any obvious items missing or disturbed.
- Determine area of primary activity to commit the crime.
- Limit the scene through logical progression to determine specifically where the individual might have been to trigger the blast and what he or she would have had to touch.

Blast Scene Mapping (Searching and Evidence Recovery)

A thorough crime scene search must be made for portions of the detonating devices and explosive containers. These are often difficult to identify and may still pose an explosive hazard. The use of an explosives expert is highly recommended.

Any items that seem strange or foreign to the setting should be documented and collected.

Items closest to the origin of the blast may contain explosive residues. These should be documented and collected.

- One of the most effective methods for documenting the location of evidence within a blast scene is using polar coordinates (Figure 14.1).
- The seat of blast (SoB) is searched first and rendered safe.
  - Note any material and its construction found near the seat of blast.
  - Note the size and depth of the crater at the seat of blast.
  - Dirt and debris should be sifted using a ½ in. screen first, and then a ¼ in. screen in an attempt to locate remnants of the device.
- The blast area should be broken down into four 90-degree quadrants covering the full 360 degrees surrounding the seat of blast.
- Quadrants with the most evidence are processed first. All quadrants, however, must be thoroughly searched.

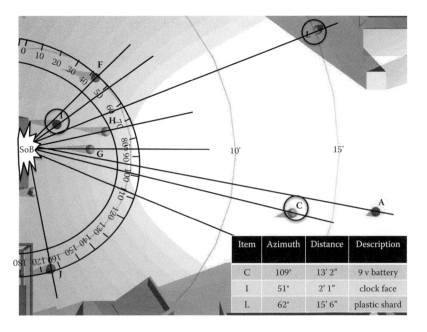

Item	Azimuth	Distance	Description
C	109°	13' 2"	9 v battery
I	51°	2' 1"	clock face
L	62°	15' 6"	plastic shard

Figure 14.1 Example of polar coordinates method on a post-blast scene.

Note: Blasts resulting from exploding dust, gas, or chemicals that are not under pressure may not leave an identifiable seat of blast. If noted early in the scene investigation, the lack of a distinct crater may assist in discerning whether this type of explosion is involved.

Procedure for Mapping

- A surveyor's transit or similar device is set up at the seat of blast (a lensatic compass may be used if necessary) (Figure 14.2).
  - Designate magnetic north as 0 degrees.
  - Zone 1: 0 to 90 degrees.
  - Zone 2: 90 to 180 degrees.
  - Zone 3: 180 to 270 degrees.
  - Zone 4: 270 to 360 degrees.
- Search teams examine the quadrants and mark all items of evidence. It is easiest at this point to use a standard evidence placard.
- Designate each item of evidence on the sketch using the evidence number inside of the following symbols:
- Record the azimuth and distance from the seat of blast for each item of evidence.

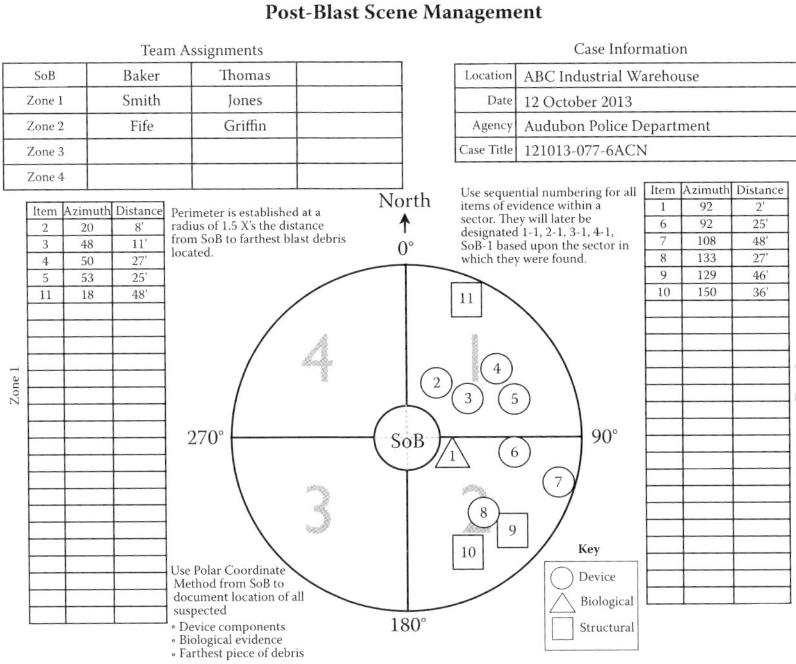

Post-Blast Scene Management

Figure 14.2 Example of a completed post-blast worksheet.

- It is preferable to measure distance from the seat of blast using a sonic or laser measuring device that has been calibrated at the scene.
- Photograph the evidence with an evidence marker.

Collecting the Evidence

- Evidence is collected and grouped by category and zone number.
- Significant evidence is bagged separately. This includes:
  - Body parts/biological material
  - Suspected device components, which are subdivided as:
    - Electrical
    - Wiring
    - Mechanical
- General debris may be packaged together in a bag marked for the zone/quadrant.
- The guidelines provided in Chapter 28, "Trace Evidence at the Scene," should be followed when collecting, sampling, explosive residues, and other trace evidence.

Associated Fire

If fire is involved, as is often the case with explosive devices, refer to processing the arson scene (Chapter 13).

Commonly Encountered Evidence

The following evidence is commonly found at explosive scenes.

Associated with Device and Component Parts

- Friction ridge evidence (be sure to consider any tape used to build the device):
  - Patent prints
  - Latent prints
- Biological evidence:
  - Touch DNA
  - Hairs
- Impression evidence:
  - Toolmarks

Postblast Debris

- Timing devices
- Explosive devices
- Electrical devices
- Explosive containers
- Wiring and connectors
- Batteries
- Circuit boards
- Body parts
- Unidentified biological material

Evidence of an accelerated fire or explosive residue must be handled carefully. It is best to detect, sample, and collect in conjunction with a trained postblast or fire investigator. Liquids or solids may still be highly flammable, shock sensitive, or toxic.

Explosive Evidence Collection Guidelines

- Use only clean, unlined paint or lined (keep control sample) cans or glass jars without rubber liners or seals.
- Nylon collection bags may be used for solid objects or objects of unusual shape or size.
- Never fill a container more than two-thirds full.
- An adhesive-backed activated charcoal strip may be secured to the inside lid of the container. This strip will absorb a sample of any volatile fumes coming from the sample.

Sampling for Explosive Residue

- Sample any area where an explosives detector or bomb canine indicates the possible presence of explosives.
- Take soil and other samples for potential explosive residue near the seat of blast.
- Sample from both the seat of blast and just outside of the seat of blast.
- Remaining vertical surfaces near the seat of blast sometimes retain blast residues and should be checked and sampled.
- Sampling may be conducted by either seizing the item on which the residue is deposited or vigorously swabbing the surface with several swabs moistened with distilled water.

Collecting and Packaging

Liquids

- Using a syringe, eyedropper, or pipette, draw a liquid sample from the surface of the liquid and place it in a clean, unlined metal can. Seal tightly.
- The sample may also be soaked into a clean, untreated gauze pad or cotton swabbing and packaged as above.

Solids

- Solid materials, which may have absorbed liquid evidence or been exposed to explosive residue, should be collected in an unlined or lined sealed can.
- Solid samples of accelerants explosive residue are potentially corrosive and should be placed in a glass jar without a glued cap liner or rubber seal.
- Large or irregularly shaped objects may be collected and sealed in nylon bags.
- Always collect a control sample relating to any item of evidence taken.

Crimes against Persons

Aggravated Assault

15

Aggravated assaults are generally defined as assaults that cause serious bodily injury or involve the use of a weapon. They involve any level of assault if the intent is to commit robbery or rape.

Initial Actions

Establishing Perimeter

- The assault scene may be easily discernable in instances where there was a struggle and bloodshed. Additionally, spent bullet cases, discarded medical debris from emergency medical services (EMS), and other physical findings may help define the location of the final assault.
- Blood trails may be followed to their origin to better locate the initial stages of the assault.
- If the threat of violence rather than violence itself was employed (such as in an armed robbery), there may be very little physical evidence present. The specific scene will have to be established by victim and witness statements as well as any video coverage of the area. Video may indicate specific items the perpetrator touched for the possible recovery of DNA, footwear, and fingerprint impressions.
- The body of the victim is in itself a valuable scene. Trace evidence transfer of hairs and fibers, DNA transfers in blood, saliva, or other body fluids, and possible touch DNA or even fingerprints may be present and recoverable from the body of the victim.

Legal Concerns

- Determine the legal authority to be present and to conduct a crime scene examination. At some point the exigent circumstances for responding to the scene (e.g., caring for victims) will be over.
- What is the continued authority to remain on scene and collect evidence (e.g., search warrant, consent authorization, no reasonable expectation of privacy)?

- See Chapter 1, "Initial Response," for a detailed explanation of search and processing legal concerns.

Establishing Context

- **Domestic assault:** Physical assault that takes place within a family or with an intimate partner. The victim may be hesitant to identify the attacker and will often present at the hospital or medical facility with injuries inconsistent with the "accident" he or she states is the cause.
- During or as a precursor to **sexual assault:**
  - **Stranger rape:** In stranger rape situations it is vital for the attacker to gain immediate compliance of the victim. If through ambush or deception, there comes the point when overwhelming force or the threat of that force is made to gain compliance.
  - **Acquaintance rape:** As the victim's level of consent for social or intimate interaction is exceeded, the perpetrator may find it necessary to gain continued compliance through force or the threat of force.
- **Retribution or retaliation-based assault:** These crimes often involve spontaneous eruptions of violence as the result of a perceived wrong or slight.
- **Criminal enterprise assault:** These assaults involve retaliation for failure to meet financial obligations or to abide by the criminal enterprises rules (e.g., gambling debts, loss of drugs, getting "jumped out" of a gang).
- **Hate crime assault:** When the victim is chosen as a result of his or her race, sex, religion, sexual orientation, national identity, etc. Often derogatory language epithets, slurs, and insults are associated with the attack.

Crime Scene Processing

Processing the Scene

Consideration should be given to securing the scene and delaying its processing until information from the medical examination and victim interview is available. Specific guidance for steps in securing the scene, photography, and initial crime scene procedures is covered in Section I, "Crime Scene Investigation." Section I is applicable to all crime scenes and should be reviewed to ensure no steps are missed.

- Ensure documentation is begun by notes, sketching, and photography. This is an ongoing process.
- Paths of entry, exit, and the area of the incident should be examined for two- and three-dimensional footwear or tire impressions (Chapter 26).
- If forced entry was used, refer to burglary and housebreaking crime scene processing (Chapter 9).
- Note the location of and safeguard any perishable evidence.
- Process surface and evidence for biological, touch, and trace evidence (Chapters 27 and 28).
- Any debris left by emergency medical personnel should be documented as to its location.
- Document any bloodstain patterns (Chapter 31).
- Consider processing or protecting items of evidence recovered for future latent print examination.
- Search for, examine, and recover any weapons used.
  - If a weapon cannot be found, conduct an expanded search of the area focusing upon the likely path of retreat, to include dumpsters, bodies of water, and roofs of buildings.
  - Search for, examine, and recover items associated with the weapon, such as spent cartridge cases, bullets, etc.
  - Bullets may travel through or ricochet off of a variety of objects, including the victim, before reaching their final resting place. Document these thoroughly through photography and seize if possible. Prior to seizing the item, document the precise location of the bullet defects through the mapping technique described in Chapter 32. Defects or markings left by the bullet may provide valuable indicators as to the bullet's path of travel.
  - Bullets should not be dug out from objects, but rather, the object or portion of the object containing the bullet should be collected.
- If restraints were used (e.g., ropes, belts, tape, clothing) to bind the victim, these items should be seized and protected for the recovery of trace and other evidence. Knots and overlapped areas of tape should not be cut through or untied.
- Search for, examine, and recover any other items that might link a suspect to the crime or crime scene.
- In robberies, any notes passed by the suspect should be protected for fingerprints, indented writing, and handwriting analysis (Chapter 16), as well as fingerprints and touch DNA.
- Process appropriate areas for the presence of latent prints (Chapter 25).
- Blunt and sharp weapons may retain blood or body tissues that are not readily visible and should be packaged appropriately (Chapter 27).

Examination of the Assault Victim

Have victim examined by a medical doctor to document injuries and collect evidence. Specific indicators and items to look for in injuries are covered in Chapter 21, "Injuries Commonly Associated with Violent Crime." Any statements made to medical personnel concerning the assault should be thoroughly documented.

- Obtain any evidence recovered during the examination.
  - Collect a blood sample for testing for drugs and alcohol.
- Collect clothing worn by the victim at the time of attack.
  - Arrange for a change of clothing for the victim.
  - Have the victim disrobe while standing on a clean paper or a hospital sheet. Be sure to collect the sheet or paper as evidence.
  - Place each item of clothing into separate paper bags.
  - If clothing is bloodstained, air-dry at the office in an area separate from the suspect's clothing.
- Take color photographs (without and with a scale) of injuries.
  - The use of a color card will allow for more accurate color rendition on final photographs of the injuries.
  - Photos of individual injuries should also be taken with the camera parallel to the body surface, close-up, with a scale on the same plane as the injury being photographed.
  - Consider ultraviolet or infrared photography. These methods may enhance the visibility of a patterned injury or older bruising.
  - Injuries should be photographed over several days.
- Ask the doctor for any opinions on what type of weapon might have caused the injuries. Determine if the injuries are consistent with the victim's account of the assault.
- Search for pattern injuries that may be able to be tied back to other evidence (e.g., a ring on the hand of the attacker or other implement in the attacker's possession).
- If victim was able to mount any level of defense, consider fingernail scrapings or swabbing rings or associated jewelry of the victim for possible DNA from the perpetrator.
- Bite marks should be processed as soon as possible (Chapter 26).
- Consider the use of gunshot residue (GSR) testing, if appropriate.
- Obtain copies of all associated medical reports.

Examination of Suspect

In addition to processing the suspect in the same manner as the victim:

- Search the suspect for weapons used in the crime.
- Any statements made to medical personnel concerning the assault should be thoroughly documented.
- Examine the suspect thoroughly for injuries he or she may have sustained during the assault.
- Obtain fingernail scrapings.
- Search for other evidence that might link the suspect to the crime scene.
- In robberies search the suspect for items belonging to the victim.

Commonly Encountered Evidence

- Bloodstains
- Spent cartridge cases
- Bullets
- Knives
- Blunt force weapons
- Broken bottles or glass
- Friction ridge evidence
- Touch DNA
- Medical debris
- Firearms

Robbery from an Individual

16

The key to a physical investigation of these crimes is pinpointing the location of the incident. If the threat of violence rather than violence itself was employed, there may be very little physical evidence present with the exception of possible footwear and fingerprint impressions. The procedures listed below may or may not apply to all situations. Those portions that are pertinent should be considered.

Initial Actions

Consideration should be given to securing the scene and delaying its processing until information from the medicolegal examination and victim interview is available. Specific guidance for steps in securing the scene, photography, and initial crime scene procedures is covered in Section I, "Crime Scene Investigation." Section I is applicable to all crime scenes and should be reviewed to ensure no steps are missed.

Establishing Perimeter

- **Surveillance location** is the location from which the perpetrator observed the behavior and activities of potential victims. A search of the general area should be made to determine whether or not this occurred. Likely physical evidence might include items touched or discarded by the suspect, as well as footwear or fingerprint evidence.
- **Ambush area** is where the initial contact is made to abduct or accost the victim for the purpose of robbery. This is where the robbery started, even if it continued elsewhere. It is also a likely place to search for and collect physical evidence, if any is present.
- **Transportation/conveyance** is any vehicle or other conveyance used to transport the victim from the ambush location to another location where the actual robbery took place, or to a location where the victim was released.
- **Release location** is where the victim was released after the robbery was completed. It may be the same as the ambush area itself, if the robbery was a quick action and the victim was not transported elsewhere.

- **Dump location** is where the perpetrator dumped items associated with the robbery that were unwanted (e.g., uniquely identifying or items of low value). This may include the wallets or purses, or identification cards, while the cash and credit cards are maintained.
- **Suspect's dwelling**, if not the site of the robbery, may contain valuable physical evidence as to the planning and carrying out of this or other robberies. Any tools, instruments, or weapons used in the robbery may be located here, as well as items of value taken from the victim(s) and not yet disposed of or sold.

Legal Concerns

- Determine the legal authority to be present and to conduct a crime scene examination. At some point the exigent circumstances for responding to the scene (e.g., caring for victims) will be over.
- What is the continued authority to remain on scene and collect evidence (e.g., search warrant, consent to search, no reasonable expectation of privacy)?
- See Chapter 1, "Initial Response," for a detailed explanation of search and processing legal concerns.

Establishing Context

The site of a strong-armed robbery, where brute force was used to take items of value from the victim, may yield different physical evidence from a location where the suspect committed an armed robbery with a weapon.

- If actual violence, rather than the threat of violence, was used, refer to Chapter 15, "Aggravated Assault," when processing the scene.
- If the weapon was discharged, refer to Chapter 15, "Aggravated Assault," Chapter 21, "Injuries Commonly Associated with Violent Crime," and Chapter 32, "Documenting and Processing the Shooting Scene."

Strong-Armed Robbery

- The threat or actual use of physical violence is key in identifying physical evidence from this scene.
- If actual physical violence was utilized, transfer evidence (e.g., hairs, fibers, touch DNA) may be present on both the suspect and victim. Bloodstain pattern evidence may be present to both identify the scene and help reconstruct the actions at the scene (Chapter 31).
- Patterned injuries may be present on the victim that may assist in identifying any jewelry (e.g., rings on the suspect's hand when he or she struck the victim) or other implements used during the attack.

Armed Robbery

- In an armed robbery, the investigator will likely be searching for the actual weapon used as well as stolen items.
- If the victim was pistol whipped, patterned injuries may help identify the weapon used. It is likely there will also be transfer evidence, such as hairs, fibers, skin, blood, or touch DNA, on the weapon.
- If blood was shed at the scene, refer to Chapter 31, "Documenting and Processing Bloodstain Patterns at the Scene."
- When other crimes are committed during the event, such as aggravated assault against the victim, the investigator should review that chapter of the book for additional guidance.

Crime Scene Processing Guidelines

- Ensure documentation is begun by notes, sketching, and photography. This is an ongoing process.
- Paths of entry, exit, and the area of the incident should be examined for two- and three-dimensional footwear or tire impressions (Chapter 26).
- If forced entry to the area of the robbery was used, refer to burglary and housebreaking crime scene processing (Chapter 9).
- Note the location of and safeguard any perishable evidence.
- Process surfaces and objects for biological and trace evidence (Chapters 27 and 28).
- Any debris left by emergency medical personnel should be documented as to its location. It may be necessary to interview emergency medical personnel and other first responders (include police officers) in detail to determine what alterations of the scene they made.
- Document any bloodstain patterns (Chapter 31).
- Consider processing or protecting items of evidence recovered for future latent print examination.
- Search for, examine, and recover any weapons used. Again, this may be the immediate area of the robbery or additional sites. If a weapon cannot be found, conduct an expanded search of the area focusing upon the likely path of retreat, to include dumpsters, bodies of water, and roofs of buildings. The suspect's vehicle and residence should also be considered.
- Search for, examine, and recover items associated with the weapon, such as cartridge cases, bullets, etc.
- Bullets may travel through or ricochet off a variety of objects, including the victim, before reaching their final resting place. Document these thoroughly and seize if possible. The defects and markings left

by the bullet may provide valuable indicators as to the bullet's path of travel. Bullets should not be dug from objects, but rather, the object or portion of the object containing the bullet should be removed and collected, leaving the bullet untouched if possible (Chapter 32).

- If restraints were used (e.g., ropes, belts, tape, clothing) to bind the victim, these items should be seized and protected for the recovery of trace and other evidence. Knots and overlapped areas of tape should not be cut through or untied.
- Search for, examine, and recover any other items that might link a suspect to the crime or crime scene. This should include surveillance cameras covering the area(s) involved and potential debris discarded in garbage containers by the perpetrator.
- Any notes passed by the suspect should be protected for fingerprints, indented writing, handwriting analysis, fingerprints, and touch DNA.
- Process appropriate areas for the presence of friction ridge evidence prints (Chapter 25).
- Blunt and sharp weapons may retain blood or body tissues that are not readily visible and should be packaged appropriately (Chapter 27).

Examination of Robbery Victim if Assaulted during Incident

- Have victim examined by a medical doctor to document injuries and collect evidence (Chapter 21).
- Any statements made to medical personnel concerning the assault should be thoroughly documented.
- Obtain any evidence recovered during the examination.
- Collect fingernail scrapings as well as head hair combings and pluckings from the victim as standards.
- Collect blood from the victim for comparison with blood at the scene or on clothes.
- Consider blood testing for drugs and alcohol.
- Arrange for a change of clothing for the victim.
- Collect clothing worn by the victim at the time of attack.
- Have the victim disrobe while standing on a clean paper or a hospital sheet. Be sure to collect the sheet or paper as evidence.
  - Place each item of clothing into separate paper bags.
  - If clothing is bloodstained, air-dry at the office in an area separate from the suspect's clothing.
- Take color photographs (without and with a scale) of injuries.
  - The use of a color card will allow for more accurate color rendition on final photos.

- Photos of individual injuries should be taken with the film/CCD plane parallel to the victim's body surface. Document close-up and with a scale.
- Consider ultraviolet or infrared photography. These methods may enhance the visibility of pattern injuries or older bruising.
- Photographs of injuries should be repeated over several days to show changes.
- Ask the doctor's opinion as to what type of weapon might have caused the injuries. Determine if the injuries are consistent with the victim's account of the assault or weapons found at the scene or in the possession of the suspect.
- Bite marks should be processed as soon as possible (Chapter 26).
- Consider the use of gunshot residue (GSR) testing, if appropriate.
- Obtain a copy of all associated medical reports.
- Consider obtaining elimination fingerprint samples, if appropriate.

Examination of Suspect

Process the suspect in the same manner as the victim if any direct contact was made. Document any statements made to medical personnel concerning the assault.

- Search for weapons used in the crime on the subject's body and in any areas of his or her control.
- Search for other evidence that might link the suspect to the crime scene and the victim.
- Bite marks should be processed as soon as possible (Chapter 26).
- Look for any evidence of injury to the suspect that might have been described by the victim.
- In robberies, search the suspect for items belonging to the victim.
- Take major case fingerprints, and a blood sample for DNA determinations, if appropriate.

Additional Searches

- All items reported as stolen by the victim(s) should be searched for and recovered where possible.
- Search areas along a suspected path of egress by the suspect (to include dumpsters and roofs) commonly used for the disposal of nonvalue items such as a purse, wallet, or backpack.

- Perpetrators have been known to use a prepaid mailing envelope and simply drop the stolen items in the nearest mailbox. If there is any indication of this MO, a mail cover should be considered and coordinated through the Postal Inspection Service.
- NCIC and pawn shop searches are also effective in recovering stolen items.
- Storage units, the residence, garage, and outbuildings controlled by the suspect should be searched.
- All recovered items should be fully documented, and then packaged and preserved as described in the appropriate chapter covering that type of evidence.
- Search for any weapon reported to or suspected of having been used. These may include firearms, knives, or other items.
- As with nonvaluable items, if the perpetrator believed that he or she might be apprehended or stopped while fleeing, weapons may have been discarded along his or her egress route. Consider searching nearby dumpsters, rooftops, sewer grates, and bodies of water.
- Once recovered, all efforts should be made to preserve biological, friction ridge, or touch DNA that may link the weapon to the perpetrator and suspect.
- Robberies are frequently planned with a specific location chosen in advance. Search for a likely surveillance area(s) and process for footwear, friction ridge evidence, or trash (e.g., cigarette butts, gum, pistachio shells) that may have been discarded by the perpetrator.
- Any items associated with surveillance or ambush should also be searched for and recovered.
- Seek out and check surveillance video at these sites as well.
- If footwear or tire mark impressions were noted and documented at the scene, potential shoes or tires should be searched for and recovered.

Stolen Property List

- Inventory all items that were taken during the robbery.
- Obtain descriptions, photographs, serial numbers, and unique identifiers of stolen items when possible.
- Enter into appropriate databases for recovery (e.g., NCIC, pawn shop checks).

Commonly Encountered Evidence

- Friction ridge evidence:

- Patent prints
- Latent prints
- Biological evidence:
  - Touch DNA
  - Discarded food, drink, or cigarette butts within the surveillance area
  - Bloodstain patterns
- Impression evidence:
  - Toolmarks
  - Footwear impressions
  - Tire impressions
- Physical evidence—weapons:
  - Weapons
  - Bullets
  - Bullet cases
- Physical evidence—debris:
  - Receipts
  - Papers
  - Wrappers

Robbery from a Business

17

The key to a physical investigation of these crimes is pinpointing the location of the incident. If the threat of violence rather than violence itself was employed, there may be very little physical evidence present, with the exception of possible footwear and fingerprint impressions. The procedures listed below may or may not apply to all situations. Those portions that are pertinent should be considered.

Initial Actions

Specific guidance for steps in securing the scene, photography, and initial crime scene procedures is covered in Section I, "Crime Scene Investigation." Section I is applicable to all crime scenes and should be reviewed to ensure no steps are missed.

Establishing Perimeter

- The perimeter needs to be established quickly in order to safeguard all physical evidence that would link the suspect(s) to the scene.
- The perimeter of the scene should include the exterior of the building in such a manner as to protect areas of entry and exit used by the perpetrator(s).
- Interior areas of the business where the robber moved and conducted the robbery.

Legal Concerns

- Determine the legal authority to be present and to conduct a crime scene examination. At some point the exigent circumstance for responding to the scene (e.g., caring for victims) will be over.
- What is the continued authority to remain on scene and collect evidence (e.g., search warrant, consent authorization, no reasonable expectation of privacy)?
- See Chapter 1, "Initial Response," for a detailed explanation of search and processing legal concerns.

Establishing Context

- The specific intent of the perpetrators is to rob the business. This places the dynamic events generally in the area of the tellers, cash registers, high-value items (such as jewelry), or safes.
- Individuals present at the time of the robbery may also be targeted; however, they are generally incidental to the actual targeting of the business.
- Robberies may include personal injuries to victims, or they may be void of actual physical injury.
- The scene investigator should consider the possibility of employee involvement in the robbery when talking to witnesses and victims and processing the scene.
- Robbery of a financial institution such as a bank is somewhat different than robbery of other businesses. For instance, a dye pack might be used by a bank, and surveillance cameras are of more frequent use. However, the scenes of all types of businesses should be worked in a methodical manner, as described below.

Crime Scene Processing Guidelines

- Ensure documentation is begun by notes, sketching, and photography. This is an ongoing process.
- In commercial robberies, ensure any notes passed by the suspect are protected for fingerprints, indented writing, touch DNA, and handwriting analysis.
- Paths of entry, exit, and the interior area of the incident should be examined for two- and three-dimensional footwear or tire impressions (Chapter 26).
- If forced entry was used, refer to burglary and housebreaking crime scene processing (Chapter 9).
- Note the location of and safeguard any perishable evidence.
- Process surfaces and objects for biological and trace evidence (Chapters 27 and 28).
- If a physical assault or weapon was used that resulted in injuries, any debris left by emergency medical personnel should be documented as to its location.
- Document any bloodstain pattern evidence (Chapter 31).
- Search for, examine, and recover any weapons used.
  - If a weapon cannot be found, conduct an expanded search of the area focusing upon the likely path of retreat, to include dumpsters, bodies of water, and roofs of buildings.

- Search for, examine, and recover items associated with the weapon, such as bullets, cartridge cases, etc.
- Bullets may travel through or ricochet off of a variety of objects, including the victim, before reaching their final resting place. Document these thoroughly and seize if possible. The defects and markings left by the bullet may provide valuable indicators as to the bullet's path of travel.
- Bullets should not be dug from objects, but rather the object or portion of the object should be collected.
- Blunt and sharp weapons may retain blood or body tissues that are not readily visible and should be packaged appropriately.
- If restraints were used (e.g., ropes, belts, tape, clothing) to bind the victim(s), these items should be seized and protected for the recovery of trace and other evidence. Knots and overlapped areas of tape should not be cut through or untied.
- Search for, examine, and recover any other items that might link a suspect to the crime or crime scene.
  - Examine close-circuit TV or similar surveillance video from the business involved.
  - Seek out and examine close-circuit or similar surveillance video from neighboring businesses or public cameras that would cover the approach or egress paths taken by the perpetrators.
- Determine whether victims or witnesses captured still or video images of the suspect or his or her activities of the event, and request consent to retrieve those images.
- Consider a separate search of the suspect's vehicle or residence to recover stolen items, weapons, clothing worn, and any other physical evidence that might link him or her to the scene.

Evidence of Injury

Examination of Assault Victim

- Have victim examined by a medical doctor to document injuries and collect evidence.
- Any statements made to medical personnel concerning the assault should be thoroughly documented.
- Obtain any evidence recovered during the examination.
- Collect fingernail scrapings as well as head hair combings and pluckings from victim as standards.
- Collect blood from the victim for comparison with blood at the scene or on clothes.

- Consider blood testing for drugs and alcohol.
- Arrange for a change of clothing for the victim.
- Collect clothing worn by the victim at the time of attack.
- Have the victim disrobe while standing on a clean paper or a hospital sheet. Be sure to collect the sheet or paper as evidence.
- Place each item of clothing into separate paper bags.
- If clothing is bloodstained, air-dry at the office in an area separate from the suspect's clothing.
- Take color photographs of injuries, without and with a scale.
- The use of a color card will allow for more accurate color rendition on final photo prints.
- Photos of individual injuries should also be taken with the film/CCD plane of the camera parallel to the victim's body surface, close-up, with a scale.
- Consider requesting ultraviolet or infrared photography. These methods may enhance the visibility of pattern injury or older bruising.
- Photographs of injuries should be repeated over several days to document changes.
- Ask the doctor's opinion of what type of weapon might have caused the injuries. Determine if injuries are consistent with the victim's account of the assault.
- Bite marks should be processed as soon as possible (Chapter 26).
- Consider the use of gunshot residue (GSR) testing, if appropriate.
- Obtain a copy of all associated medical reports.

Examination of Suspect

- Process the suspect in the same manner as the victim. Document any statements made to medical personnel concerning the assault.
- Search for weapons used in the crime.
- Search for other evidence that might link the suspect to the crime scene and the victim.
- Bite marks should be processed as soon as possible (Chapter 26).
- In robberies, search the suspect for items belonging to the business and/or victim.

Commonly Encountered Evidence

Every commercial robbery scene will be different when it comes to the physical evidence involved, but it may involve any of the following:

- Items/money stolen during the robbery.

- Latent fingerprints left by the suspect(s). Elimination prints from others present may be required as well.
- Footwear or tire mark impressions. Elimination footwear or tire marks may be required.
- Toolmarks and the tools used when forced entry was involved.
- Biological fluids or trace evidence if physical assault, shooting, or similar events occurred that resulted in injury. Blood or saliva samples may be needed from victims and others for elimination purposes if DNA evidence from the scene is examined.
- Bullets or cartridge cases expended during the event.
- Clothing of the suspect(s).
- Money (dye) pack used by financial institutions.
- Video/surveillance tapes that have recorded the presence or activities of the suspect(s).
- Any items used to bind, quiet, or otherwise restrict the activities of victims.
- Cell phones from victims or witnesses used to capture photos of the suspect(s).

Carjacking

18

Carjackings differ from the simpler stolen vehicle or grand theft auto case in that there is usually an act of force or threat of force involved. This is much like the difference between robbery of the person and simpler theft/ larceny. Therefore, there is sometimes a direct contact between suspect(s) and victim(s), and sometimes not. It follows then that there may or may not be injuries to either party. Occasionally, the driver or passenger(s) is taken (kidnapped) along with the vehicle.

Initial Actions

Establishing Perimeter

There may be two scenes involved in a carjacking event:

- The scene of the carjacking itself.
  - This scene is where the actual contact with the driver/owner occurred and the vehicle was taken. It is this scene to which the information provided in this chapter is applicable.
  - A perimeter should be established around this area in such a manner that allows the investigator to locate and collect any physical evidence that would be associated with the event while keeping others away from the scene.
- The scene where the vehicle is located.
  - The vehicle may be found abandoned, at the suspect's residence, or another location.
  - A perimeter should be established that allows the investigator to locate and collect all pertinent physical evidence while keeping third parties away from the scene.
  - The condition of the vehicle can range from its original condition when stolen to completely destroyed by fire or wreckage.
  - The vehicle should be processed as a recovered stolen vehicle, as discussed in Chapter 11. If it is damaged by fire, the guidance provided under "Vehicle Fire Scene Investigations" in Chapter 13 should be consulted.

- There may be additional evidence found at this type of scene (a vehicle) not covered in these chapters. This might include personal items stolen from the victim(s) at the time of the carjacking, weapons used to consummate the carjacking, or other personal items left in the vehicle by the suspect(s).

Legal Concerns

- Determine the legal authority to be present and to conduct a crime scene examination. At some point the exigent circumstances for responding to the scene (e.g., caring for victims) will be over.
- What is the continued authority to remain on scene and collect evidence (search warrant, consent to search, no reasonable expectation of privacy)?
- See Chapter 1, "Initial Response," for a detailed explanation of search and processing legal concerns.

Establishing Context

Although carjacking is a federal crime under some circumstances, some states do not have a codified statute for carjacking, since it involves different crimes already on the books. Depending on the individual circumstances, a given event may have elements of various crimes, such as robbery, assault, aggravated assault, kidnapping, theft/larceny, motor vehicle theft (grand theft auto), etc. Therefore, the reader is advised to determine which types of these crimes are involved and process the scene as recommended in those specific areas of the book.

Crime Scene Processing Guidelines

If physical injuries occurred during the robbery, consideration should be given to maintaining the scene until information from the medical examination and victim interview is available. Specific guidance for steps in securing the scene, photography, and initial crime scene procedures is covered in Section I, "Crime Scene Investigation." Section I is applicable to all crime scenes and should be reviewed to ensure no steps are missed.

- A quick interview of the victim(s) will help to determine the extent of the search for physical evidence.
- The scene is often a parking space, pavement, or other road surface and the immediate area around it.

- Once the perimeter is determined and cordoned off, look for broken glass if the victim or witnesses indicated this occurred.
- Look for footwear evidence if nearby surfaces offer the likelihood of one or more suspects leaving them behind. This is particularly important if the perpetrator(s) is suspected to have surveilled the victim(s) or laid in wait to ambush them.
- Evidence related to an ambush/surveillance site might also include items discarded by the suspect(s), such as drinking containers, food wrappers, cigarette butts, etc.
- Search for tire mark evidence if another vehicle was used indirectly in the carjacking (perpetrator dropped off by someone else).
- If any victim or suspect was injured in such a manner that blood-staining occurred, search the road surface for this type of evidence and any related trace evidence.
- Search for any surveillance cameras that might have covered the event and other nearby cameras that might have captured images of the arrival or departure of the suspect(s).
- Question the victim(s) and any witnesses to see if they captured images of the suspects on their phone cameras, and ask for consent to seize those images.

Evidence of Injury

- Should the victim(s) have been injured during the carjacking, have the victim examined by a medical doctor to document injuries and collect evidence.
- Any statements made to medical personnel concerning the assault should be thoroughly documented.
- Obtain any evidence recovered during the examination.
- Collect fingernail scrapings as well as head hair combings and pluckings from the victim as standards.
- Collect blood from the victim for comparison with blood at the scene or on clothes.
- Consider blood testing for drugs and alcohol.
- Arrange for a change of clothing for the victim.
- Collect clothing worn by the victim at the time of attack.
- Have the victim disrobe while standing on a clean paper or a hospital sheet. Be sure to collect the sheet or paper as evidence.
- Place each item of clothing into separate paper bags.
- If clothing is bloodstained, air-dry at the office in an area separate from the suspect's clothing.
- Take color photographs of injuries without and with a scale.

- The use of a color card will allow for more accurate color rendition on final photo prints.
- Photos of individual injuries should also be taken with the film/CCD plane of the camera parallel to the victim's body surface, close-up, with a scale.
- Consider requesting ultraviolet or infrared photography. These methods may enhance the visibility of pattern injuries or older bruising.
- Photographs of injuries should be repeated over several days to show changes.
- Ask the doctor's opinion as to what type of weapon might have caused the injuries. Determine if injuries are consistent with the victim's account of the assault or weapons found at the scene or in the possession of the suspect.
- Consider the use of gunshot residue (GSR) testing, if appropriate.
- Obtain a copy of all associated medical reports.
- Consider obtaining elimination fingerprint samples, if appropriate.

Commonly Encountered Evidence

- Friction ridge evidence:
  - Patent prints
  - Latent prints
- Biological evidence:
  - Touch DNA
  - Discarded food, drink, or cigarette butts within the surveillance area
  - Bloodstain patterns
- Impression evidence:
  - Footwear impressions
  - Tire impressions
- Physical evidence—motor vehicle:
  - Biometric—seat position, control position, mirror positions
  - Friction ridge—control surfaces
  - Touch DNA—control surfaces
- Physical evidence—weapons:
  - Weapons
  - Bullets
  - Cartridge cases
- Physical evidence—debris:
  - Receipts
  - Papers
  - Wrappers

Kidnapping and Missing Persons

19

While kidnappings often involve the extortion of money from the victim's family, kidnapping can also be the precursor to other crimes, such as sexual assault or murder. The family of the victim is often distraught and can be less than helpful at the scene. With missing persons, the situation can be that of a runaway, a child that has simply lost his or her way, people lost in open or wilderness locations, those with mental issues or the elderly that cannot remember where they are or were, or something more sinister that turns into a kidnapping. In a confirmed child abduction, immediately consult agency policy for issuance of an America's Missing: Broadcast Emergency Response (AMBER) Alert.

Initial Actions

Establishing a Perimeter

Primary Scene
- The victims themselves are often a scene and a valuable source of information as to the type of physical abuse and the type of weapon or implement used to consummate the abduction and cause any injury.
- Kidnappings can occur from any conceivable location, to include the victim's residence, vehicle, or from a business or the street.
- While one might not immediately connect the missing person case to an actual scene, it is nonetheless very important to treat it as such, as noted below.

Secondary or Ancillary Scenes
- Ancillary scenes may include areas where the victim is later found. These can vary from the street where someone was allowed to go free to the suspect's residence or even a death scene.
- Social media accounts may provide documentation of the abductor callously bragging about instances of kidnapping, extortion, or other related criminal acts.

Legal Concerns

- Determine the legal authority to be present and to conduct a crime scene examination. At some point the exigent circumstances for responding to the scene (e.g., caring for victims) will be over.
- What is the continued authority to remain on scene and collect evidence (e.g., search warrant, consent search, no reasonable expectation of privacy)?
- See Chapter 1, "Initial Response," for a detailed explanation of search and processing legal concerns.

Establishing Perimeter

- Often a kidnapping or missing persons report will not involve an identifiable crime scene.
- Through follow-up interviews, determine if there is a viable scene that needs to be processed.
- The act may have taken place on a street, playground, or the home by an estranged parent or in other circumstances that do not leave significant physical evidence.
- Thorough neighborhood canvassing and interviews may provide the only details as to the actual act and its location.
- If it is suspected that a struggle was involved, the area of the struggle should be processed in the same manner as described in "Processing the Scene" in Chapter 15.

Establishing Context

Through initial reports from family, friends, or coworkers, attempt to determine the most likely type of crime involved as soon as possible.

Kidnapping
- Extortion
- Incident to sexual crime or murder
- Politically motivated
- Hostage

Missing Person
- Vulnerable Adult
- Vulnerable child
- Lost
- Runaway

Crime Scene Processing Guidelines

Specific guidance for steps in securing the scene, photography, and initial crime scene procedures is covered in Section I, "Crime Scene Investigation." Section I is applicable to all crime scenes and should be reviewed to ensure no steps are missed.

- When conducting a missing persons investigation (children and elderly), check the residence, neighborhood, and surrounding areas for potential hiding spots, wells, abandoned vehicles, and buildings. Consider abandoned kitchen appliances that could trap a child or adult, and prevent him or her from getting loose.
- If kidnapping is involved, a ransom note may be involved or left as a recorded message on the answering machine or included with the incoming mail.
- Additionally, in a missing persons investigation a note of intent to leave home or run away may be present.
- These should be collected and processed as questioned documents to ascertain their authenticity.
- A thorough search of the victim's personal effects, residence, and location where last seen should be conducted for possible leads and evidence. This may also assist in the identification of friends/relatives, recent telephone numbers called, or places frequented.
- Obtain the most recent photograph of the victim.
- Consider the collection of known samples of head hair from the victim's residence (e.g., hairbrush, pillow) and his or her toothbrush (for epithelial skin cells). These should be seized and packaged as possible secondary sources of DNA identification (Chapter 27). *Note*: If not handled tactfully, this could have adverse emotional impact on the victim's relatives.
- Consider seizing unwashed clothing belonging to the victim(s) that could later be used by dog handlers if a canine search is deemed appropriate. Such clothing should be packaged in a manner to protect the scent of the person who wore it.
- If any video surveillance is used at or near the area/residence where the abduction occurred, review and seize any memory/recording device.
- If the kidnapping is suspected to have been accomplished by unknown persons or someone who has not been present at the residence prior to the incident, conduct a latent fingerprint examination early in the scene investigation. Priority areas include doorknobs,

phones, and any items that seem to have been moved or disturbed during the kidnapping.

- Areas of egress other than paved roads may leave physical evidence, to include footwear and tire impressions. These areas should be thoroughly examined before other persons have the opportunity to inadvertently damage the evidence.
- If the kidnapping occurred while the victim was in a vehicle, or if a vehicle suspected to have been used in transporting the victim is recovered, it should be processed as the recovery of a stolen vehicle, with the added focus of recovering evidence that might show that the suspect or victim was present in the vehicle. A search for blood or other indicators of injury should be considered.

Evidence of Injury

The scene may show signs of an injury to the victim, or the party reporting a kidnapping may indicate that there were injuries involved. If so, the scene should be processed in a manner similar to that for an aggravated assault.

- Bloodstains should be documented and collected in accordance with Chapter 31.
- A search should be made for any weapons that were reportedly used. This search might need to be expanded beyond the immediate area of the abduction.
- A search for trace and biological evidence beyond bloodstains should be made as well. Those items should be collected in accordance with the guidance provided in Chapters 27 and 28.
- Any damages to furnishings or other indicators of a struggle should be well documented.

Commonly Encountered Evidence

- Items used for binding or quieting an individual
- Weapons used to threaten or injure a victim
- Notes left by runaways or kidnappers
- Clothing torn from the victim and left behind
- Signs and evidence from a physical struggle during the abduction
- Secondary sources of DNA identification, as noted above

Rape and Sexual Assault

20

Rape and sexual assault cover a wide range of criminal offenses. Rape is generally defined as sexual penetration or contact that is forced or coerced. This may include vaginal, anal, or oral penetration. These are not limited to male-on-female assaults and may be perpetrated by either sex upon either sex. Common contact includes:

- Penis to vagina
- Penis to anus
- Mouth to vagina
- Mouth to anus
- Mouth to penis
- Mouth to breast
- Mouth to scrotum
- Scrotum to mouth
- Finger (digit) to vagina
- Finger (digit) to anus
- Object to vagina
- Object to anus

Initial Actions

Establishing Perimeter

Primary Scene
The primary scene includes the physical location of the assault as well as the body and clothing of the victim and perpetrator.

- The primary scene is generally the physical location where the assault took place. This may be in a car, bathroom, bedroom, alley, etc.
- The body of the victim is a primary scene. It may contain trace, fiber, biological, or friction ridge evidence.
- The body of the perpetrator is also a primary scene. It too may contain trace, fiber, biological, or friction ridge evidence.

Secondary Scenes

Secondary scenes include, but are not limited to:

- Any location where the perpetrator may have conducted surveillance to choose a victim.
- The location of the initial ambush/contact if the victim was moved prior to the sexual assault.
- Any location where either the perpetrator or victim cleaned up after the sexual assault.
- The residence of the perpetrator where he or she might have secret tools, weapons, or souvenirs associated with the sexual assault.
- Any conveyance used by the perpetrator to transport the victim from the ambush/contact site to the sexual assault site.

Legal Concerns

- Determine the legal authority to be present and to conduct a crime scene examination. At some point the exigent circumstances for responding to the scene (e.g., caring for victims) will be over.
- What is the continued authority to remain on scene and collect evidence (e.g., search arrant, consent authorization, no reasonable expectation of privacy)?
- See Chapter 1, "Initial Response," for a detailed explanation of search and processing legal concerns.

Establishing Context

Stranger Rape

- Victim selection:
  - May be elaborate stalking of a particular victim based upon idealized fantasy by rapist. May be based on body type, hairstyle, hair color, race/ethnicity, clothing, or profession/trade.
  - May be elaborate surveillance based upon ideal location and independent of specific victimology. May require a setting by a lake, in an alley, office building after hours, etc.
  - May be completely disorganized with little preparation or selection, based upon inability to control impulses. When the impulse becomes irrepressible, he will choose a victim and location with little thought or planning. The victim and location are of convenience.
- Victim control:
  - Ambush: Speed and violence of attack leave the victim little time to mount any level of resistance. Initial force followed rapidly by complete intimidation.

- Deception: Allows access to victim in a secluded location followed by an ambush that is typically fast, violent, and overcomes resistance rapidly through force, threat of force, and intimidation.
- Barriers and strategies when dealing with the victim:
  - Victim is often completely overwhelmed physically and emotionally.
  - The surprise, speed, and violence of the attack may leave the victim with extensive physical injuries and psychological trauma.
  - Victim may feel guilt at not having seen the attack coming or not having been careful enough.
  - The overwhelmingly priority is to ensure the victim's physical safety.
  - Victim may not voluntarily acknowledge all physical acts perpetrated on him or her due to humiliation or social upbringing.
- Unique scene indicators:
  - Secondary scene: Location of ambush.
  - Secondary scene: Location of surveillance/observation.
  - Attacker may have come with prepared kit.

Acquaintance Rape

- Victim selection:
  - Victim known to perpetrator.
  - Some prior or present level of social interaction.
  - May be engaged in some level of consensual social relationship or intimate relationship.
- Victim control:
  - Perpetrator has legitimately gained position or location of relative privacy.
  - Victim has accepted position of privacy.
  - Consensual social or physical contact is withdrawn or exceeded.
  - Control maintained through intimidation.
  - Control maintained through verbal threats or coercion.
  - Physical force used as necessary to gain compliance.
  - Resignation on part of victim—futility.
- Barriers and strategies when dealing with the victim:
  - Emotional barriers: Trust, betrayal, judgment.
  - Omission of details (e.g., preceding consensual behavior)
  - Omission of voluntary intoxication or recreational drug use before the incident.
  - Build rapport, build trust, be patient.
  - Establish:
    - Specific physical acts, consensual and nonconsensual.

- Victim's physical reaction to assault (e.g., resistance, verbal resistance).
- The factors will provide a context to consider when approaching the various scenes.
- Unique scene indicators:
  - Consider safeguarding fragile evidence and then holding scene until after statements are taken.
  - This allows the focus to narrow and to emphasize what physical evidence may be used to deconflict victim's and suspect's statements.
  - Look for possible souvenirs taken from victim (e.g., panties, a picture, photographs).

Drug-Facilitated Sexual Assaults

- Victim selection:
  - Victim may be an acquaintance or stranger.
  - Victim may already be mildly intoxicated. The effects of the drug may not be as noticeable to bystanders.
  - Victim may be a recreational drug user, lowering his or her sexual inhibitions.
  - Victim is often alone or has inattentive friends.
- Victim control:
  - The drug causes a state mimicking alcohol intoxication.
  - Greatly reduced social and sexual inhibitions.
  - Unconscious or inability to physically respond to assault.
  - Amnesia of the assault.
- Barriers and strategies when dealing with the victim:
  - If still under effects of drug, obtain a urine sample immediately.
  - Victim will be confused and uncertain as to what happened or even if he or she was assaulted.
  - Victim may report that his or her clothing is on wrong, or that he or she feels sticky or sore in the genital area.
  - Victim may have only a partial recollection of the events.
- Delays in reporting:
  - Victim may have been unconscious for hours.
  - Victim may have heard about assault from others.
  - Victim may have heard about a sex tape involving her.
- Unique scene indicators:
  - Often photographs or recordings of the assault are taken by the perpetrator(s); look for any media, cameras, or video systems.
  - Witnesses may have been present and captured aspects of the assault on personal cameras and phones.
  - Additional drugs may be present on the suspect or in his car, apartment, or clothing.

- Drugs commonly associated with facilitated sexual assaults include GHB, ecstasy, ketamine, rohypnol, and alcohol.

Crime Scene Processing Guidelines

Specific guidance for steps in securing the scene, photography, and initial crime scene procedures is covered in Section I, "Crime Scene Investigation." Section I is applicable to all crime scenes and should be reviewed to ensure no steps are missed.

- Consideration should be given to securing the scene and delaying its processing until information from the medicolegal examination and victim interview is available.
- Ensure documentation is begun by notes, sketching, and photography. This is an ongoing process.
- Paths of entry, exit, and the area of the incident should be examined for two- and three-dimensional footwear or tire impressions (Chapter 26).
- If unlawful entry or forced entry was used, refer to burglary and housebreaking crime scene processing (Chapter 9).
- If a physical assault with injury occurred in addition to the sexual assault, refer to aggravated assault crime scene processing (Chapter 15).
- Note the location of and safeguard any perishable evidence.
- Items such as clothing, bed linens, rugs, car seats, etc., may contain evidence of hair, broken fingernails, blood, semen, and fibers. Process these areas for biological or trace evidence (Chapters 27 and 28).
- Utilize an alternate light source (ALS) to fluoresce saliva, urine, and semen stains. Some fibers may also fluoresce.
- Pay special attention to bathrooms, as suspects and victims often clean up after a sexual assault. The drain trap and trash cans are areas where physical evidence may be found.
- If the victim has washed clothing, bedding, etc., from the assault, consider cleaning the lint trap of the dryer for trace evidence.
- If the victim has changed clothing prior to examination, both the panties worn at the time of the incident and those worn directly after the incident should be seized. This would include any panty liners, tampons, or feminine napkins used to absorb vaginal drainage. *Note*: If the victim is a male, appropriate undergarments should be collected.
- Process logical areas based upon victim's statement for impression and latent print evidence.

Evidence of Injury

Minimizing Cross-Contamination of Evidence

- Do not transport the victim and suspect in the same vehicle.
- Do not keep them in the same waiting area (even at different times).
- Do not have them examined in the same hospital room (even if at different times).

Examination of Sexual Assault Victim

- On drug facilitated sexual assaults, a urine sample should be obtained as soon as possible, even if done outside the confines of a medical facility.
- Locate an established medical facility with a sexual assault response team (SART). The examination will most likely be conducted by a sexual assault nurse examiner (SANE).
- Arrange for the medicolegal examination of the victim using a prepared victim sexual assault kit approved by your servicing crime lab. A CSI should be present at the facility to prebrief the nurse examiner on the scene findings and resolve any evidentiary issues. This may include specialized services such as processing the victim for latent prints.
- This examination should be done before any detailed interview, if the victim is in need of medical attention, or when any evidence can be lost because of a delay.
- Any statements made to medical personnel concerning the assault should be thoroughly documented.
- Evidence associated with a sexual assault is very fragile and should be collected as soon as possible.
- Discuss the sexual assault examination with the attending medical professional before the examination.
- Provide the details of the allegation to the doctor.
- Consider leaving the room during the medical examination.
- Advise the doctor of the possibility of cross-contamination when examining both the suspect and victim.
- Ask the doctor to scan victim's body with an ultraviolet (UV) lamp to look for seminal fluid and fibers.
- Ask the doctor to microscopically examine vaginal or anal swabbing, or both, for motile sperm.

Evidence of Additional Physical Assault

- Take color photographs (without and with a scale) of injuries.
- The use of a color card will allow for more accurate color rendition on final photo prints.

- Photos of individual injuries should also be taken with the film/CCD plane of the camera parallel to the body surface, close-up, with a scale on the same plane as the injury.
- Consider requesting ultraviolet or infrared photography. These methods may enhance the visibility of pattern injury or older bruising.
- Injuries should be photographed over several days.
- Ask the doctor's opinion as to what type of weapon might have caused the injuries. Determine if the injuries are consistent with the victim's account of the assault.
- Bite marks on a sexual assault victim should be processed as soon as possible (Chapter 26).
- Obtain a copy of all associated medical reports.

Examination of Sexual Assault Suspect

- Ensure appropriate legal requirements have been met for a legally permissible search.
- Generally, if less than 24 hours has elapsed since the reported incident, arrange for a complete medicolegal examination of the suspect using a prepared sexual assault examination kit approved by the servicing crime lab.
- Ensure complete documentation (notes, sketches, and photography) of any physical injuries.
- Ensure complete documentation of any identifying marks (e.g., tattoos, scars, abnormal anatomical characteristics).
- Generally, if more than 24 hours has elapsed since the time of the reported incident, arrange for a medicolegal examination of the suspect using a prepared sexual assault examination kit approved by your servicing crime lab. This should include, at a minimum, combed and plucked pubic and head hairs, blood, and saliva.
- Any statements made to medical personnel concerning the assault should be thoroughly documented.
- Collect the clothing the suspect was wearing during the incident. Use the procedure described for victims.
- If the suspect has condoms in his possession, seize them for possible later analysis against any questioned condoms.
- Bite marks on a sexual assault suspect should be processed as soon as possible (Chapter 26).

Examination of a Third Party

- Consider if any third party exists with whom the victim may have had sexual relations and who could have contributed evidence collected in the victim's physical examination.

- The third party should submit to a medicolegal examination using a prepared sexual assault examination kit approved by the servicing crime lab. This should include plucked pubic and head hairs, blood, and saliva.

Commonly Encountered Evidence

- Friction ridge evidence:
  - Patent prints
  - Latent prints
- Biological evidence:
  - Blood/semen
  - Saliva
  - Urine
  - Feces
  - Touch DNA
  - Discarded food, drink, or cigarette butts within the surveillance area
  - Bloodstain patterns
- Impression evidence:
  - Toolmarks
  - Footwear impressions
  - Tire impressions
  - Bite marks
- Physical evidence—weapons:
  - Weapons
  - Bullets
  - Cartridge cases
- Physical evidence—debris:
  - Condom
  - Rags (for cleaning up afterwards)
  - Clothing
  - Receipts
  - Papers
  - Wrappers

Injuries Commonly Associated with Violent Crime

21

A disadvantage from an investigative standpoint with nonfatal injury or wounding is the inability to have it evaluated and thoroughly documented by a forensic pathologist. Nonfatal injuries and wounds are quickly altered through medical intervention, and in many cases valuable forensic evidence is lost. If at all possible, photographs of the injury prior to medical intervention should be taken when appropriate.

Manual Strangulation (Throttling)

This is caused by pressure of a hand, arm, or other limb against the neck, causing compression of the neck. This may be seen in aggravated assaults and sexual assaults.

Injury in Context

- Most frequently encountered in domestic assaults, intimate partner assaults, and sexual assaults.
- Throttling is almost always an intentional act intended to cause serious bodily harm. It may be accidental in the instances of sexual activities involving hypoxyphilia.
- Generally, there is a disparity in strength between the assailant and the victim, or the victim could have been incapacitated prior to being strangled.

The Scene

- Look for signs of struggle; manual strangulation does not instantly incapacitate the victim.
- Rugs may be displaced if under the victim's feet at the time of strangulation, and other items within reach may be disturbed.

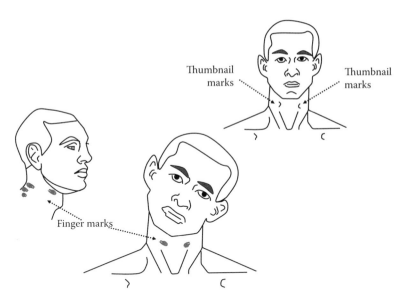

Figure 21.1 During manual strangulation the victim's own fingernails or the attacker's fingers may leave a pattern injury on the skin.

The Victim

- Externally, the skin of the victim may take on a bluish hue due to the increased amount of poorly oxygenated blood in the system.
- Evidence of a struggle may be evident, often seen as bruising and defensive scratches around the neck caused by the victim attempting to break an attacker's hold. Scrapings found under the nails of the victim might provide useful information about the attacker. The attacker may likewise be linked to the victim (Figure 21.1).

Blunt Force Injury

Blunt force injuries associated with assaults are produced by blows or falls. They may also occur when a victim is run over, struck, or dragged behind a motor vehicle. They result in abrasions, contusions, lacerations, and fractures. These are frequently encountered during aggravated assaults or stranger rape/sexual assaults.

Injury in Context

- Blunt forces tear, crush, and shear tissues. Blunt forces are transmitted by objects that have relatively broad or rounded edges.
- The pattern and appearance of blunt force injuries vary depending on the amount of force, the location of the wound, and the type of weapon.

- Blunt force trauma can also cause skeletal fractures, if sufficient force is used.
- Abrasions, contusions, and lacerations are the three general types of blunt force injuries.
- A blunt force injury can display any combination of these types of injuries.

The Scene

- Weapons may have fingerprint, blood, hair, or tissue evidence on them.
- Bloodstain evidence should be thoroughly documented.

The Victim

- Weapons may leave identifiable injury patterns (Figure 21.2).
- Patterns of the weapon may be imparted to the skin, and are referred to as pattern abrasions or a patterned injury.
- The injury pattern may suggest the type of weapon used.
- Close-up photography of injuries, without and with scales (held on the same plane as the injury), is essential to the proper evaluation of wounds. Consider UV and infrared (IR) photography.

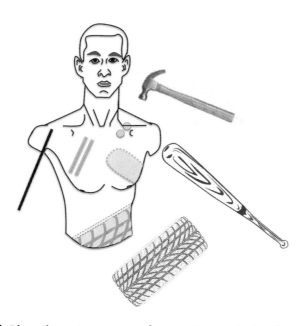

Figure 21.2 Blunt force trauma may leave pattern injuries that give an indication of the weapon or shape of the weapon used. A metal rod leaves parallel bruising with a void area the approximate width of the rod.

- While there may be significant internal injuries, an abrasion may be the only visible injury.
- Contusions (bruises) do not necessarily reflect the intensity of the blow. Bruises may or may not transmit a pattern of the object that caused them.
- Lacerations may be external, or internal involving the tearing of organ tissues.
- Trace evidence transfer is possible between the weapon and the victim. Paint, debris, or fragments of the weapon may be found in the wound. Hair, blood, or fibers from the victim may be found on the weapon.
- The size and shape of the laceration can sometimes suggest the type of weapon used.

Sharp Force Injury

Sharp force injury during assaults results in cutting injuries known as incised, stab, or chopping wounds. The weapon involved may be a knife, ice pick, screwdriver, broken bottle, hatchet, or almost any edged object.

Injury in Context

- Evaluation of the wound can provide information about the type of weapon used.
- Triangular stab wounds are generally made with a single-edged weapon.
- Diamond-shaped stab wounds are generally made with a double-edged weapon.
- Wound patterns and their frequency may provide assistance in determining a motive.

The Scene

- Recovery of the weapon may yield fingerprint evidence, hairs, and fibers, along with blood and tissue evidence.
- If the weapon has a broken or chipped tip or edge, the broken-off piece may be present in the wound or underlying bone. Check with the attending physician to see if any weapon part was removed and collect it.
- The suspect's and victim's clothing may provide bloodstain, trace, and serological evidence.
- Bloodstain evidence should be thoroughly documented.

- If the weapon is not readily apparent, the wounds themselves may give an indication as to the type of weapon used. (Guidelines are listed below in "The Victim.")

The Victim

- Incised wounds are defined as sharp force wounds that are longer than they are deep. The length and depth of the wound will not provide specific information about the weapon.
- Close-up photography of injuries is essential to the proper evaluation of wounds.
- Incised wounds are often sustained by persons defending themselves from knife attacks. These wounds are most commonly located on the forearms, palms, fingers, and backs of the hands and can be quite severe. These types of wounds are usually referred to as defensive injuries.
- Stab wounds are defined as sharp force wounds that are deeper than they are long.
- Hilt marks from where the handle of the knife impacted the skin may be evident in stabbing injuries where the blade fully penetrated the victim (Figure 21.3).
- The width of a blade (measured across from sharp edge to dull edge) cannot be measured exactly, as the knife may have been drawn through the injured tissues (Figure 21.4).
- The shape of a stab wound is dependent upon the shape of the instrument and lines of Langer. Lines of Langer are the elastic fibers in the

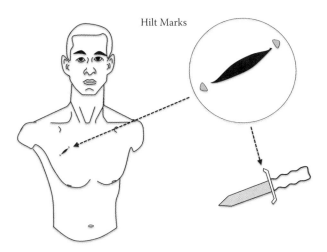

Hilt Marks

Figure 21.3 "Hilt" marks may leave a pattern injury on the skin.

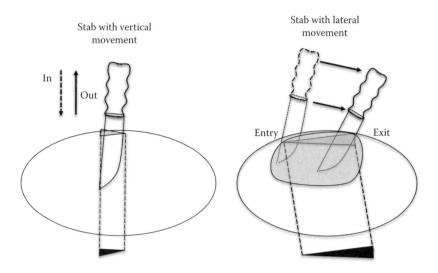

Figure 21.4 It is difficult to determine the width of the blade based upon an examination of the resulting injury.

skin that run in the direction that the skin is being stretched over the body.

- Stab wounds tend to gape if the stab is across or perpendicular to the lines; they will gape less if the stabs are parallel to the lines (Figure 21.5).
- After a knife has been shoved into the victim, the twisting of the knife or the struggling of the victim when it is removed can cause Y- or L-shaped wounds.
- Paired stab wounds (or other multiples) may be the result of scissors, forks, etc.
- Paired wounds with a consistent distance of separation between the paired stabs are indicative of a weapon like a fork (Figure 21.6).
- Paired wounds where the separation between paired stabs varies are indicative of a weapon like scissors (Figure 21.6).

Chopping Injury

Chopping wounds demonstrate a combination of both blunt and sharp force injuries. The typical weapon employed might be an axe, hatchet, or machete.

Injury in Context

- Chopping injuries are generally present in multiple clusters (not a single blow).

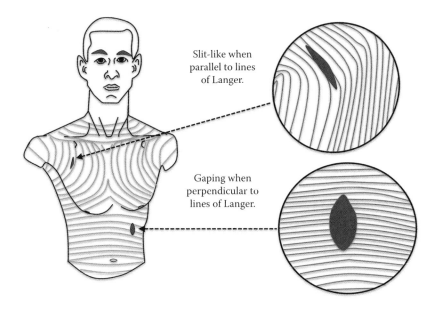

Slit-like when parallel to lines of Langer.

Gaping when perpendicular to lines of Langer.

Figure 21.5 Lines of Langer.

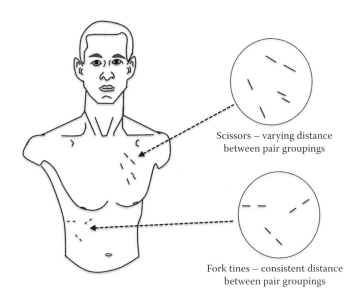

Scissors – varying distance between pair groupings

Fork tines – consistent distance between pair groupings

Figure 21.6 Paired wounds—fork and scissors stabs.

- Associated bloodstain patterns in the scene may help determine victim and attacker positions during the attack.

The Scene

- Chopping wounds are usually caused by common objects that are sharp and heavier than household knives. Look for an axe, machete, meat cleaver, boat propeller, etc.
- Bloodstain evidence should be thoroughly documented.

The Victim

- Weapons may leave identifiable injury patterns.
- The injury pattern may suggest the type of weapon used.
- Close-up photography of injuries, without and with scales (held on the same plane as the injury), is essential to the proper evaluation of wounds. Consider UV and IR photography.
- While there may be significant internal injuries, including fractures, an external abrasion may be the only visible injury.
- Patterns of the weapon may be imparted to the skin, and are referred to as pattern abrasions or patterned injury.
- Resulting contusions (bruises) do not necessarily reflect the intensity of the blow. Bruises may or may not transmit a pattern of the object that caused them.
- Resulting lacerations may be external, or internal involving the tearing of organ tissues.
- Trace evidence transfer is possible between the weapon and the victim. Paint, debris, or fragments of the weapon may be found in the wound. Hair, blood, or fibers from the victim may be found on the weapon.
- The size and shape of the laceration can sometimes suggest the type of weapon used.

Gunshot Wounds

When a handgun or rifle is discharged, flame, smoke, a bullet, and burned and unburned powder exit the barrel. Gunshot wounds have many different appearances that are dependent upon the proximity of the weapon to the target and the bullet's direction of travel. Common characteristics of handgun and rifle wounds are described below.

Injury in Context

- The distance between the muzzle of the weapon and the victim (range of fire) may often be determined by the presence of soot, powder particles, and other indicators at the wound site or on the clothing covering the wound site. This may aid in determining if the shot was fired from a distance, intermediate distance, close range, or with the muzzle in contact with the victim.
- Dynamic movement of the victim at the time the shot was fired may be determined through alignment of the bullet defect in the skin with the bullet defect in the clothing. This may be useful in determining if at the time of the shot the victim turned away from the shot, turned toward the weapon, or was bending, sitting, or standing naturally.
- Range of fire and dynamic movement are useful in determining the veracity of the suspect, witness, or victim's statement as to the circumstances surrounding the shooting.

The Scene

- Thoroughly document and map all bullet defects at the scene (Chapter 32).
- Thoroughly document and map all spent cartridge cases at the scene (Chapter 32).
- Thoroughly document and map all bloodstain patterns at the scene (Chapter 31).
- Based on victim, suspect, or witness statements, examine and sample any surfaces that would have been adjacent to the weapon when it discharged for gunshot residue.
- Based on the victim, suspect, or witness statements, examine any possible intermediate targets that the bullet may have passed through before striking the victim.
- Examine recovered bullets to determine if it is likely that they deflected from another surface prior to striking the victim or passed through an intermediate object.
- Utilizing trajectory analysis, integrate the above data to determine the likely shooter and victim positions at the time of the event.

The Victim

- Recover any bullets from medical personnel who were associated with the victim.

- Examine recovered bullets to determine if it is likely that they deflected from another surface prior to striking the victim or passed through an intermediate object.
- Have a board-certified forensic pathologist examine the wound site or photographs of the wound site to determine if it is an entrance or exit wound.
- Have a board-certified forensic pathologist examine the wound site to determine if it is a contact, close-range, intermediate, or distant wound.
- Have the clothing covering the wound site examined by a ballistics examiner to attempt to determine range of fire.

Entrance Wounds

- Most entrance wounds, no matter what the range of fire, are surrounded by a reddish zone of abraded skin.
- Fibers from clothing may be driven into the wound.
- Entrance wounds resulting from a ricochet or the round striking an intermediary target may be irregular in shape.
- For more details on entrance wounds, see the descriptions based upon effects of distance on gunshot wounds.
- It is not possible to determine a bullet's trajectory through the body from examination of the entrance wound alone.

Exit Wounds

- Exit wounds are usually more irregularly shaped than entrance wounds.
- Exit wounds are usually larger than entrance wounds and, with few exceptions, do not have an abrasion ring.
- As the bullet travels through the body, it may either tumble, deform as it strikes objects, or both, resulting in a more irregular and larger shape than that of the entry wound.
- The size and shape of the exit wound are often dependent on the body area from which the bullet exits. In slack skin the wound tends to appear smaller and slit shaped. In areas where the skin is stretched across a hard surface, such as bone, the exit wound will often appear larger and more irregular.
- In some circumstances, an exit wound may have an abrasion ring and a regular shape. These wounds are known as shored exits. This may be seen in cases where the injured person was up against a hard surface, such as a wall or floor, or wearing constrictive clothing, such as a bra or belt. In these instances, the hard surface or clothing supports the skin, keeping it from tearing into an irregular shape.

- Bullets may sometimes be found just under the skin, partly protruding from the skin, or loose in the clothing around the exit wound.

Effect of Distance on Gunshot Wounds

Contact Gunshot Wounds

When the muzzle of a gun is held against the body at the time of firing, gas, soot, powder, and metallic particles from the bullet are shot into the wound tract along with the bullet.

- The flesh around the wound is burned by hot gases and blackened by soot. Soot is characterized by being able to be washed off. This differs from stippling (tattooing), which is the burned and unburned powder that becomes lodged into the skin and cannot be washed off.
- Muscle surrounding the entrance wound may have a cherry-red color due to carboxyhemoglobin formation from the carbon monoxide in the muzzle gas.

Close Gunshot Wounds

- Close gunshot wounds fall between contact and intermediate-range wounds. In these cases, the muzzle of the weapon is not in contact with the skin, but is held a short distance away.
- Near-contact entrance wounds are surrounded by a wide zone of powder and soot that may overlay blackened, seared skin.
- Near-contact wounds with handguns usually occur at ranges less than several inches. This will vary depending on the caliber, ammunition, and barrel length.

Intermediate-Range Gunshot Wounds

- In this wound, the muzzle of the weapon is held away from the body, but is close enough for powder particles to be projected into and onto the skin, yet far enough away that the soot does not reach the skin.
- Powder tattoo marks are produced by the impact of powder grains on the skin. Tattooing consists of reddish brown to orange-red punctate (small dot or point) lesions surrounding the entrance wound (Figure 21.7).
- The distance between the muzzle of the gun and the target is important because it affects the appearance of the soot and powder particle distribution. As the range between the muzzle and the target increases, the size of the area of soot blackening increases, and the density of the soot on the body decreases until it becomes so faint that you cannot identify exactly where the soot begins or ends.

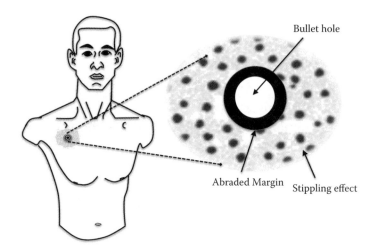

Figure 21.7 Stippling or "tattoo" pattern.

- As the distance between the gun muzzle and target increases, the density of the powder particles will decrease until few particles adhere to the target surface. This seldom extends more than several feet from the muzzle.

Distant Gunshot Wounds
- When a gun is fired from a distance, the only marks on the target are those produced by the bullet penetrating the skin. The muzzle of the weapon is held far enough away so that neither soot nor unburned powder reaches the target. Without the soot or powder particles, there are no indicators of distance between the gun and target.
- The only visible characteristics of the wound may be an abrasion ring and the defect can occur in a little as a few feet from the muzzle.
- A distant-range wound may be difficult to distinguish from an intermediate-range wound in certain circumstances. For instance, an intermediate-range gunshot wound may look like a distant-range wound if something, such as clothing, comes between the gun and the body, preventing soot and unburned powder from reaching the skin. Only by careful examination of the facts of the case (e.g., was the victim clothed at the time of the shooting?) will you be able to correctly identify a particular gunshot wound.

CSI Wound Documentation Concerns
- Many of the characteristics described will be destroyed or marred by medical intervention to the living victim.

- The CSI should note and document the nature of the wounds to whatever extent is possible, without adversely impacting medical intervention itself.
- This will often require taking photographs of the wounds under dynamic conditions (e.g., during medical intervention at the scene or ER room) at distances greater than those generally considered appropriate for evidence photography. However, it is better to have some documentation than no documentation.

Child Sexual Assault or Abuse

22

Child sexual assault involves the sexual abuse of a child or inappropriately exposing or subjecting a child to sexual contact, activity, or behavior. The behavior does not necessarily have to be between an adult and child, as coerced sexual contact between children for the sexual gratification of a third party also falls under this category.

Initial Actions

Determine the Scene and Establish a Perimeter

- Sexual assault and sexual assault with abduction may involve a variety of scenes:
  - **Surveillance location** is the location from which the perpetrator observed the behavior and activities of potential victims.
  - **Ambush area** is where the initial contact is made to abduct the victim for the purpose of sexual assault.
  - **Transportation/conveyance** is any vehicle or other conveyance the victim is transported in from either the ambush location to the assault location or the assault location to the dump location.
  - **Assault location** is where the child is sexually assaulted or exploited. This may be the same area where he or she is kept if a continuing series of assaults take place during the abduction.
  - **Dump location** is where the child is left when the sexual abuse and exploitation are complete. It is seldom that the child is left alive, but he or she may be left in a condition where his or her demise is imminent.
  - **Suspect's dwelling**, if not the assault site, may contain valuable documentary and physical evidence as to the planning and carrying out of the assaults. Additionally, child pornography will often be present in either print or digital media formats.
- Sexual abuse will involve a variety of scenes:
  - **Abuse location** is that place where the abuse most often takes place. It may be the child's bedroom, the bathroom, a workshop, office, or basement, in the car, or almost any other place where the perpetrator may seek privacy with the child without undue suspicion.

- The **child's room**, even if not the location of the abuse, may contain valuable evidence. The room may contain bedding or discarded clothing, or toys that contain semen or other biological stains.
- The **abuser's room**, even if not the location of the assault, may contain valuable evidence. The perpetrator may have discarded clothing or towels with biological stains (vaginal, fecal, or seminal). There may be indications of cleanup in the master bathroom. The abuser may hide sex toys, special clothing, or souvenirs from or associated with the abuse in this area.
- **Electronic media** of the perpetrator may contain Internet searches, website histories, etc., with images of child pornography or relating to child pornography. Additionally, specific images, chats, or other communications and media documenting the specific abuse of the victim may be present. *Note*: Many gaming consoles have the ability to store files and are often overlooked during searches.
- Production of pedophilic media:
  - The **soundstage or set** may be simple or elaborate. It could be an elaborate set with a bed, bondage, or other paraphernalia and high-tech audio and video recording devices and editing capabilities. It may also be as simple as a handheld video recorder, perhaps with a tripod.
  - All **digital (or film) media recording devices** and associated equipment should be seized at either the soundstage/set or at an editing office, residence, or business of the perpetrator. This includes gaming consoles that may have digital media storage capabilities.

Legal Concerns

- Determine the legal authority to be present and conduct a crime scene examination. At some point the exigent circumstances for responding to the scene (e.g., caring for victims) will be over.
- What is the continued authority to remain on scene and collect evidence (e.g., search warrant, consent to search, no reasonable expectation of privacy)?
- See Chapter 1, "Initial Response," for a detailed explanation of search and processing legal concerns.

Establishing Context

- **Familial sexual assault/abuse:** The familial abuser is a family member or close friend of the family that utilizes his or her access and the trust of the victim inherent in their relationship to target, cultivate, and abuse the victim.

- This is seldom a single-occurrence crime, but rather a continuing series of abuse that stops only when the crime becomes known to law enforcement, or the victim "ages out" of the targeted age range of the abuser and is replaced by a new victim.
- Older siblings have often been victims of abuse as well, whether reported or not.
- Oftentimes the spouse is aware of the abuse but has minimized it or taken steps to protect the child (almost always ineffective) from further abuse.
- Scenes are generally found within the family residence.

- **Preferential sexual assault/abuse:** This may be a neighbor, youth leader, coach, or any other adult that is able to cultivate a relationship with the child initially based on trust.
  - That trust may be followed by deception or imparting shame on the abused and creating sufficient psychological roadblocks in the child's way that they do not disclose the abuse.
  - The victim may have been cultivated from a dysfunctional family unit where the abuser's attention and gifts are sufficient to prevent disclosure of the abuse.
  - This type of abuser seldom has a single victim. Instead, a series of victims have been cultivated and are often run concurrently.
  - Scenes are generally located in areas where the abuser feels safe (e.g., an area that the abuser can control either short term or long term).

- **Failed sexual assault abduction:** This is almost always stranger based and involves the abduction of the child specifically for the purpose of sexual abuse.
  - The abductor either intends to cultivate the child through a series of abuse and conditioning to be a long-term victim or intends a shorter duration cycle of abuse that will end with the child's murder.
  - In both of these cases the abduction/abuse cycle is somehow disrupted with the recovery of the live child.
  - Scenes may be those of convenience (e.g., an abandoned home) or under the direct control of the abuser.

- **Production of pedophile media and materials** involves an individual that creates, produces, and distributes child pornography.
  - May be as simple as a camera, tripod, and computer with web access and a single victim.
  - May be as complex as a soundstage/set, professional cameras, lighting, and editing equipment and the recruitment of multiple victims.

- Scenes are almost always areas under the primary control of the abuser, allowing significant privacy.
- **Child offender:** The child offender may range from a juvenile serial offender to a child or juvenile that is just curious and experimenting with intimate contact and touches. It is vital to determine the extent of the behavior and frequency of the behavior.
  - **Scenes are often public locations** (e.g., parks and playgrounds) or areas where the juvenile has isolated contact with the child.

Crime Scene Processing Guidelines

Sexual Assault Scenes

Do not rush to process the crime scene. A medicolegal examination and a thorough interview by a specially trained forensic interviewer of the victim (as is age appropriate) should be accomplished before the crime scene search. The victim, suspect, and witness statements should be considered when processing the scene. Have the police secure the scene until it is time to conduct the search.

Specific guidance for steps in securing the scene, photography, and initial crime scene procedures is covered in Section I, "Crime Scene Investigation." Section I is applicable to all crime scenes and should be reviewed to ensure no steps are missed.

- Consideration should be given to securing the scene and delaying its processing until information from the medicolegal examination and victim interview is available.
- Ensure documentation is begun by notes, sketching, and photography. This is an ongoing process.
- Paths of entry, exit, and the area of the incident should be examined for two- and three-dimensional footwear or tire impressions (Chapter 26).
- If unlawful entry or forced entry was used, refer to burglary and housebreaking crime scene processing (Chapter 9).
- If a physical assault with injury occurred in addition to the sexual assault, refer to aggravated assault crime scene processing (Chapter 15).
- Note the location of and safeguard any perishable evidence.
- Items such as clothing, bed linens, rugs, car seats, etc., may contain evidence of hair, broken fingernails, blood, semen, and fibers. Process these areas for biological and trace evidence (Chapters 27 and 28).
- Consider use of an alternate light source (ALS) to fluoresce saliva, urine, and semen stains. Some types of fibers also fluoresce.

- Pay special attention to bathrooms, as suspects and victims often clean up after a sexual assault. The drain trap and trash cans are areas where physical evidence may be found.
- If the victim has washed clothing, bedding, etc., from the assault, consider cleaning the lint trap of the washer and dryer for trace evidence.
- If the victim has changed clothing prior to the examination, the underwear or diaper worn at the time of the incident and directly after the incident should be seized. Depending on the victim's age, this might include any panty liners, tampons, or feminine napkins used to absorb vaginal drainage. *Note*: If the victim is a male, appropriate undergarments should be collected.
- Process logical areas based upon victim's statement for impression and latent print evidence.

Failed Sexual Assault/Abduction

Child abduction for the purposes of sexual assault in most instances is followed by murder. Failed sexual assault/abduction will cover those instances where the child escapes from the abduction or when the child is abducted for the purpose of becoming a long-term sexual captive of the perpetrator, and is freed. The CSI focus will be on the abduction scene, the scene where the sexual assault occurs, and the scene were the victim is discovered.

Missing Child Report

- In the early stages this may be a missing child investigation. Check the residence, neighborhood, and surrounding areas for potential hiding spots.
- Additionally, in a missing persons investigation, a note of intent to leave home or run away may be present. These should be collected and processed as questioned documents to ascertain their authenticity.
- A thorough search of the victim's personal effects, residence, and place last seen should be conducted for possible leads and evidence, identification of friends/relatives, telephone numbers, places frequented, etc.
- Identify and search all social media accounts and computers that the child utilized.
- Obtain most recent photograph of victim.
- Consider the collection of the toothbrush of the victim and known samples of head hair from the victim's residence (e.g., hairbrush, pillow). These should be taken and packaged as secondary sources of DNA for possible future DNA identification. *Note*: If not handled tactfully, this could have significant adverse emotional impact on the victim's relatives.

Abduction Scene

Often a kidnapping or missing persons report will not involve an identifiable scene. The act may have taken place on a city street, playground, or other public area. In these instances, thorough neighborhood canvassing and interviews may provide the only details as to the actual scene. If it is suspected that a struggle was involved, the area of the struggle should be processed in the same manner as any violent assault scene.

- In a confirmed abduction, immediately consult agency policy for issuance of an AMBER Alert.
- All available video of the suspected abduction location and avenues of approach and egress from the scene must be immediately seized and reviewed.
- Through both logical scene analysis and a review of videotapes determine if the suspect handled anything for processing of latent prints and touch DNA.
- Through both logical scene analysis and a review of videotapes determine if the suspect would have left any items suitable for DNA processing (cigarette butts, chewing gum, etc.).
- Through both logical scene analysis and a review of videotapes determine if the suspect would have left any two- or three-dimensional footwear impressions or tire marks.
- Through both logical scene analysis and a review of videotapes determine if the suspect would have dropped or discarded (such as in waste cans) any items that might be used to identify him or her.

Assault Scene

If a scene is identified where it is suspected the victim was held and sexually assaulted, process the scene as follows:

- Ensure documentation is begun by notes, sketching, and photography. This is an ongoing process.
- If the alleged perpetrator is not a member of the household, paths of entry, exit, and the area of the incident should be examined for two- and three-dimensional footwear or tire impressions.
- Items such as clothing, bed linens, rugs, car seats, etc., may contain evidence of hair, blood, semen, and fibers. Process these areas for biological and trace evidence.
- If items of clothing, bedding, etc., have been laundered, and the suspect does not live in that residence, consider removing the lint from the washer and dryer for possible trace evidence.
- Use an ALS for detection of biological evidence and fibers.

- Pay special attention to bathrooms, as suspects may clean up after a sexual assault. Washcloths, towels, and tissues may contain biological evidence residue.
- Any clothing, particularly underwear or diapers worn by the victim at the time of the incident, should be seized.
- If the alleged perpetrator is not a member of the household, process logical areas for impression and latent print evidence.
- Search for all evidence that corroborates or refutes witnesses' or suspects' statements.

In addition:

- Thoroughly search for biological staining, particularly semen and blood.
- Identify any item that could have been used to restrain the child; examine for DNA, fingerprints, or trace evidence.
- Identify any item that could have been used to gag the child; examine for DNA, fingerprints, or trace evidence.
- If the residence is occupied by adults only, search for and seize any age-inappropriate items (e.g., children's toys, clothing).
- Search for cameras and recording devices.
- Search for a hidden area containing souvenirs from this and other victims.
- Look for any evidence of social media accounts and search all known accounts for evidence of contact with children.
- Computer-related evidence, such as website histories, searches for child pornography, or related material, may be present.

The Pedophile and Production of Pedophile Media and Materials

Identify the location of the soundstage or set. This may be an elaborate setup in a basement, spare bedroom, or warehouse, or as simple as home digital video recorder, tripod, and lights.

- It is critical to get 360-degree ceiling and floor photographic coverage of the entire set.
- Unique identifiers (e.g., wallpaper pattern matching at seams) may be used to tie the set into child pornography videos and video clips that have been released.
- All props, children's toys, bedspreads, etc., must be thoroughly photographed for the same reason.
- If possible, establish the camera angle. This may be identified through the presence of fixed tripods or tripod impressions in carpet.

Videotape the scene with a similar camera and lens to establish field of view and perspective.
- Thoroughly process this area as a sexual assault scene (Chapter 20).

Extended searches should include outbuildings, sheds, garages, automobiles, attics, basements, storage facilities, post office boxes, and work space. Look for the following types of evidence:

- Camera equipment and video equipment intended for taking, producing, or reproducing photographic images, including, but not limited, to cameras (instant developing and otherwise), video production, photographic printing, lenses, enlargers, photographic papers, film, chemical, and anything else described by the victim.
- Phone books, phone registers, calendars, correspondence, and papers with names, addresses, or phone numbers that identify the victim or any other juvenile. This information may be located on computer hard drives, disks, or other media storage devices. Such information may be encrypted on a computer. Remember, common gaming consoles may be used to store significant amounts of digital data.
- Photographs, movies, slides, videotape, computer images, negatives, drawings, and undeveloped film that identify the victim or any other juvenile or adult. Such information may be encrypted on the storage media.
- Computers, thumb drives, storage devices, and disks intended for recording, producing, or transferring photographic images, data, or correspondence related to the victim.
- Correspondence, diaries, calendars, and other writings; tape recordings; or letters relating to any juveniles or adults that tend to show the identity of juveniles and adults, and sexual conduct between juveniles or adults. This information may be saved on computer hard drives or disks. It may also be encrypted on the storage media.
- Magazines or books depicting nudity or sexual activities of juveniles or adults, as well as collections of newspaper, magazine, and other clippings of juveniles that demonstrate a particular sex and age preference of the suspect. This may include materials involving child erotica, "art" collections, dance, ballet, gymnastics, cheer leading, etc. Such information may be encoded on a computer.
- Sexual aids or sex toys, such as rubber penises, dildos, vibrators, lubricants, condoms, and bondage gear.
- Articles of personal property (e.g., locks of hair, panties, barrettes), toys, drawings, and anything else described by the victim or played with, belonging to, or made by the victim.

- Safe deposit box keys, bank statements, billings, and checks that show the location and identity of safe deposit boxes and storage facilities of any person involved in the sexual exploitation of children through molestation, child pornography, or prostitution. The items may be found in file cabinets, mail envelopes, or items of mail.
- Indicators of occupancy, consisting of articles of personal property that establish the identity of the person or persons in control of the premises where the sexual assault occurred, including, but not limited to, rent receipts, canceled mail, keys, utility bills, and telephone bills. *Note*: This can be important if occupancy is questioned or disputed.
- Evidence of membership in a pedophile organization such as North American Man-Boy Love Association (NAMBLA), Rene Guyon Society, Diaper Pail Fraternity (DPF), etc. This can be in the form of newsletters, check stubs, and credit card receipts from dues payments, bills for membership dues, application paperwork, phone records, etc.
- Evidence of computer site visitations to areas depicting or advertising adult pornography meant to simulate child pornography. This must be accomplished by a qualified computer forensic investigator.
- Evidence of the suspect's participation in legitimate youth organizations and activities.
- The suspect's work records and time sheets.
- Peepholes, drop ceilings, and hidden cameras and compartments.

Sexual Abuse Scene

In all instances of child sexual assault or sexual abuse the victim is examined thoroughly by a properly trained medical team familiar with both sexual assault response team (SART) protocols and pediatric sexual assault/abuse.

Examination of the Victim

- If necessary, the victim should be transported to the nearest medical facility for treatment of life-threatening injuries. If there are no life-threatening injuries, attempt to have the victim treated at the nearest medical facility with a sexual assault response team (SART).
  - Notify attending medical personnel that the victim is suspected of having suffered a sexual assault or sexual abuse.
  - Coordinate for the collection of evidence by a sexual assault nurse examiner (SANE) or by another medical professional with SART training.

- Inform the attending physician or nurse examiner of any allegations, suspicions, or scene indications of vaginal or anal penetration (penile, digital, or other), recent oral penetration, fondling, biting or other physical injuries, etc. If physical evidence is known to be on the body, this should be pointed out to the examiner.
- Discuss swabbing for "touch DNA" on areas the body was likely to have been handled to facilitate the sexual assault or movement of the victim. This must be done prior to substantial manipulation by medical personnel.
- Request an examination of the body, with and without clothing, using an alternate light source (ALS) for detection of biological fluids or other trace evidence, such as lubricants, lotions, fibers, and hairs. Refer to Chapter 27, "Biological Evidence at the Scene."
- If an ALS is not available, a UV light should be used. These are commonly used at the medical facilities and referred to as woods lamps.
- Discuss the sexual assault examination with the SART examiner before the examination; ensure the examination is conducted using a prepared victim sexual assault kit approved by the servicing crime lab.
- Evidence associated with a sexual assault is perishable and should be collected as soon as possible.
- Ensure that the victim's clothing, to include diapers or other disposable undergarments, is collected, protected for trace evidence, and separately packaged.
- An examination using a colposcope may be helpful in finding microscopic injuries in the vagina and anus. This instrument can be used to better view bruises, tears, and scars. A camera can be attached to the colposcope, allowing for excellent documentation.
- If vaginal penetration is alleged or suspected, have the condition of the hymen evaluated and documented.

Evidence of Additional Physical Assault

- Take color photographs (without and with a scale) of injuries.
- The use of a color card will allow for more accurate color rendition on final prints.
- Photos of individual injuries should also be taken with the film/CCD plane of the camera parallel to the body surface, close-up, with a scale held on the same plane as the injury.
- Consider ultraviolet or infrared photography. These methods may enhance the visibility of pattern injury or older bruising.
- Injuries should be photographed over several days.
- Ask the doctor's opinion as to what type of weapon might have caused the injuries. Determine if the injuries are consistent with the victim's account of the assault.

- Bite marks should be processed as soon as possible (Chapter 26).
- Obtain copies of all associated medical reports.

Examination of Sexual Assault Suspect

- Generally, if less than 24 hours has elapsed since the reported incident, arrange for a medicolegal examination of the suspect using a prepared sexual assault examination kit approved by the servicing crime lab.
- Ensure complete documentation (notes, sketches, and photography) of any physical injuries.
- Generally, if more than 24 hours has elapsed since the time of the reported incident, arrange for a medicolegal examination of the suspect using a prepared sexual assault examination kit approved by your servicing crime lab. This should include, at a minimum, combed and plucked pubic and head hairs, blood, and saliva.
- Any statements made to medical personnel concerning the assault should be thoroughly documented.
- Collect the clothing the suspect was wearing during the incident. Use the procedure described for victims.
- If the suspect has condoms in his possession, seize them for possible later analysis against any questioned condoms.
- Bite marks should be processed as soon as possible (Chapter 26).

Commonly Encountered Evidence in Sexual Assault and Abuse

Abuse

- Biological evidence (semen, saliva, blood, fecal)
- Trace evidence (hairs and fibers)
- Soiled undergarments
- Toys or stuffed animals with biological materials present
- Inappropriate children's toys, videos, etc., in a home with no children
- Child erotica or pornography

Additional Evidence of Assault

- Ties, rope, gags
- Bondage equipment
- Objects for sexual penetration

Additional Evidence of Production of Child Pornography

- Digital cameras
- Digital video recording equipment
- Tripods
- Photographer's lighting
- Computers with editing software

Special Note: Sexual Assault Victim Interview: The interview of a child victim of sexual abuse or assault is a highly specialized area. Only those trained in forensic interview techniques for children should conduct this interview. Interviews conducted by nontrained personnel may jeopardize the validity of future interviews.

Child Physical Abuse
23

Child physical abuse involves the intentional harm of a child or infant by inflicting physical harm or suffering. This may take the form of inappropriate discipline, beatings, or confinement. This chapter will focus on nonfatal child abuse.

Initial Actions

Establish Perimeter

Primary Scene
- The children themselves are a scene and a valuable source of information as to the type of physical abuse and type of weapon or implement used to cause the injury and the duration of the abuse.
- The primary abuse location is generally set in a location within the home, in the parent's bedroom, the child's bedroom, or may it occur at any location when and where the abuser chooses.

Secondary or Ancillary Scenes
- Ancillary scenes may include areas where the child is confined or kept after the abuse or as a continuing part of the abuse. Ropes, chains, animal cages/kennels without associated animals, and locks on the outside of bedroom or closet doors may indicate these areas.
- The child's room, even if not the location of the abuse, may contain valuable evidence. The child may have gone to bed and continued to bleed or have discharge from wounds.
- The abuser's room, even if not the location of the assault, may contain valuable evidence. The perpetrator may have discarded clothing with bloodstains from the child. There may be indications of cleanup in the master bathroom. There may be an established location where implements of the abuse (e.g., belts, wooden spoons, paddles, electric wires, coat hangers) are kept. The child may be responsible for retrieving these items for the abuser when a "discipline" session is to be initiated.
- Social media accounts may provide documentation of extended absences or callously brag about or document instances of abuse.

- Medical records of treatment for prior injuries are critical to the child abuse investigation and may be located within the home. It is possible that records will be in several children's names, all of the same approximate age, as the abuser attempts to avoid curiosity and concern from the healthcare providers. Additionally, multiple physicians and medical facilities may have been used to avoid detection of repetitive abuse.

Legal Concerns

- Determine the legal authority to be present and to conduct a crime scene examination. At some point the exigent circumstances for responding to the scene (e.g., caring for victims) will be over.
- What is the continued authority to remain on scene and collect evidence (e.g., search warrant, consent, no reasonable expectation of privacy)?
- See Chapter 1, "Initial Response," for a detailed explanation of search and processing legal concerns.

Establishing Context

- Child physical abuse is often at the hands of a primary caregiver.
- Babysitters, nannies, aunts, uncles, or even family friends may also be in a position to abuse the child or infant.

Crime Scene Processing Guidelines

Do not rush to process the crime scene. A medicolegal examination and a thorough interview of the victim (as is age appropriate) should be accomplished before the crime scene is searched. The victim, suspect, and witness statements should be considered when processing the scene. After conducting a sweep for perishable evidence, secure the scene until it is time to conduct the search.

Specific guidance for steps in securing the scene, photography, and initial crime scene procedures is covered in Section I, "Crime Scene Investigation." Section I is applicable to all crime scenes and should be reviewed to ensure no steps are missed.

General Guidelines

- Ensure documentation is begun by notes, sketching, and photography. This is an ongoing process.

- Conduct an initial walk-through and note the location of, and safe-guard, any perishable evidence.
- Process for biological and trace evidence such as blood and pulled hair (Chapters 27 and 28).
- Any debris left by emergency medical personnel should be documented as to its location.
- Document any bloodstain patterns (Chapter 31).
- Consider processing or protecting items of evidence recovered for future latent print or touch DNA examination (Chapters 25 and 27).
- Search for, examine, and recover any other items that might link a suspect to the crime or crime scene or corroborate the victim's, suspect's, or witnesses' version of events.

Weapons or Disciplinary Tools/Devices
- Seize items believed to have been used to inflict injury (e.g., weapons, belts, coat hangers, wire, cords). These items often leave a distinct patterned injury on the victim. Safeguard these items for friction ridge and DNA evidence.
- If the object associated with the injury cannot be found, conduct an expanded search of the area focusing upon likely hiding places or places where the items may have been dumped.
- If restraints were used (e.g., ropes, belts, tape, clothing) to bind the victim, these items should be seized and protected for the recovery of trace, friction ridge, and DNA evidence.
  - Knots and overlapped areas of tape should not be cut through or untied.
  - Knots may often be examined by an expert to determine the skill level required to tie them or if the particular knot is used in a specific trade or occupation. This may help narrow the suspect pool when multiple suspects have access to the victim.
- An unkempt home, dirty living conditions, and lack of child's toys or furnishings may be indicative of child neglect. Child physical abuse and neglect often go hand in hand. If scene indicators are present, consider documenting and processing the scene for child neglect as well.

Burns, Scalds, Immersion Burns
- Measure the temperature of hot water from the faucet in cases involving scalds, splash, or immersion burns. Also, note the temperature setting of the hot water heater. These procedures and steps are detailed in Appendix O for the immersion burn worksheet.
- Look for items that are consistent with patterned burn injuries on the child.

- Look for the victim's skin on the surface of objects (e.g., iron, cookware) used to dry-burn the victim. A single burn may be accidental; multiple burns, especially at different stages of healing or of a repetitive nature (clusters of cigarette burns), are indicative of abuse.

Examination of Child Abuse Victim

- Arrange for a medicolegal examination of the victim. If the victim is in need of medical attention, do this before the interview. This examination is best done by a pediatrician or other medical personnel with specialized child abuse training, such as a forensic nurse examiner.
- Any statements made to medical personnel concerning the abuse should be thoroughly documented.

During the Medical Examination

- Request full-body x-rays to look for old and new bone injuries. Be sure that the person holding the child during the x-ray series does not cover the ends of the child's long bones with the hands. Tell the person to grasp the child by the fingers or toes. The ends of long bones often contain small fractures indicative of nonaccidental trauma.
- Ask the doctor or radiologist to date any observable injuries.
- Document and photograph any injuries, to include bruises and bite marks.
  - Take color photographs (without and with a scale) of injuries.
  - The use of a color card will allow for more accurate color rendition on final prints.
  - Photos of individual injuries should also be taken with the film/CCD plane of the camera parallel to the body surface, close-up, with a scale.
  - Consider ultraviolet or infrared photography. These methods may enhance the visibility of pattern injuries or older bruising.
  - Injuries should be photographed over several days.
- Bite marks should be processed as soon as possible (Chapter 26).
- Fully document and collect the victim's clothing, including undergarments, as they may contain evidence.

Additional Questions for the Physician

- What type of implement might have caused the injuries?
- Are injuries consistent with the care provider's account of the incident?
- Are the injuries likely to be the result of an accidental or inflicted trauma?
- If the actual weapons or items suspected of having inflicted the injuries are available, ask the physician to compare them with the injuries.

If not, when the weapon or implement is discovered, return to the physician for an opinion. Ensure the item is protected for the preservation of friction ridge evidence and touch DNA prior to handling.
- Is it possible to date (even roughly date) fractures and bruising? If not, can it be determined if they occurred at different times?
- Recommend that the examining physician opine to one of the following diagnoses in the medical report:
  - No evidence of physical abuse by history or examination.
  - History and physical examination compatible with child physical abuse.
  - History supportive of child physical abuse with normal physical examination.
  - History is negative for child physical abuse, but the examination is supportive of abuse.
- Obtain a copy of all associated medical reports.

Medical Records Review

A thorough review of all medical records must be conducted in any case where physical child abuse is suspected.

- Any statements made to medical providers by parents or care providers concerning this injury or past injuries should be thoroughly documented.
- To avoid detection of multiple incidents of abuse, different medical facilities may have been used. Insurance records, Medicaid records, and medical bills located at the scene may lead to the discovery of the various healthcare providers.
- Injuries documented during autopsy, healing burns, or particularly old fractures may have no medical record associated with them, as treatment was not sought to avoid detection.
- If the child is daycare or school age, check the school for a record of frequent absences or frequent reports of accidents from home. If present, they should be documented.

Commonly Encountered Evidence in Child Abuse Scenes

- Biological evidence (saliva, blood, feces)
- Trace evidence (hairs and fibers)
- Soiled and bloodstained clothing/undergarments
- Ties, rope, gags
- Cages, locks

- Objects for discipline/punishment
  - Electric cord
  - Coat hangers
  - Paddles
  - Sticks
  - Rods

Special Note: Child Victim Interview: The interview of a child victim of abuse or neglect is a highly specialized area. Only those trained in forensic interview techniques for children should conduct this interview. Interviews conducted by nontrained personnel may jeopardize the validity of future interviews.

Child Neglect

24

Child neglect involves the infliction of harm upon a child or infant by failing to provide sufficient food, clothing, shelter, or medical care to ensure the child is able to thrive in a healthy manner. There are certain medical conditions that will result in a child's or infant's failure to thrive, but these may be identified through a thorough scene and medical examination/evaluation. This chapter will focus on nonfatal child neglect.

Initial Actions

Establishing Perimeter

Primary Scene
- The children themselves are scenes and valuable sources of information. A thorough medical examination, evaluation, and treatment may be necessary to rule out congenital causes of failure to thrive. Additionally, the duration and extent of the neglect may be indicated through the physical examination.
- The home, to include the kitchen, food storage areas, child's room, bathroom, and play area, is examined to determine if there are sufficient quantities of age-appropriate food, clothing, hygiene products, and toys.

Secondary or Ancillary Scenes
- Social media accounts may provide documentation of extended absences or callously brag about or document indifference and neglect.
- Seek out and evaluate records such as bank accounts, cable TV, cellular phone service, and other bills that might indicate that the neglect was not solely the result of financial need.
- Medical records documenting the child's health, growth, and medical history may also be located within the home.

Legal Concerns

- Determine the legal authority to be present and to conduct a crime scene examination. At some point the exigent circumstances for responding to the scene (e.g., caring for victims) will be over.
- What is the continued authority to remain on scene and collect evidence (search warrant, consent, no reasonable expectation of privacy)?
- See Chapter 1, "Initial Response," for a detailed explanation of search and processing legal concerns.

Establishing Context

- Child neglect is almost exclusively in the domain of the primary caregiver(s).
- The adults responsible for the home setting, providing food, clothing, and shelter, are almost exclusively responsible for neglecting the child or infant.
- Other parties may facilitate the neglect through indifference, failing to act in the child's interest, or failing to bring their concerns to child protective agencies or law enforcement.
- An exception to the above is when the primary caregiver is also the subject of abuse and forced into a neglect situation. An example of this may be the long-term kidnap victim who has borne a child during her captivity.

Crime Scene Processing Guidelines

Do not rush to process the crime scene. A medicolegal examination and a thorough interview of the victim (as is age appropriate) should be accomplished before the crime scene is searched. The victim, suspect, and witness statements should be considered when processing the scene. After conducting a sweep for perishable evidence, secure the scene until it is time to conduct the search.

Specific guidance for steps in securing the scene, photography, and initial crime scene procedures is covered in Section I, "Crime Scene Investigation." Section I is applicable to all crime scenes and should be reviewed to ensure no steps are missed.

General Guidelines

- Ensure documentation is begun by notes, sketching, and photography. This is an ongoing process.

- Conduct an initial walk-through and note the location of and safeguard any perishable evidence.
- If there is any indication of physical abuse, also process in accordance with Chapter 23, "Child Physical Abuse."
- Consider processing or protecting items of evidence recovered for future latent print or touch DNA examination (Chapter 27).
- Search for, examine, and recover any other items that might link a suspect to the crime or crime scene or corroborate the victim's, suspect's, or witnesses' versions of events.

The Scene

- It is advisable to examine the scene in conjunction with a state or local child welfare professional.
- An unkempt home, dirty living conditions, and lack of child's toys or furnishings may be indicative of child neglect. Child physical abuse and neglect often go hand in hand. Document the general living conditions. Specific aspects of the child's living conditions to document include the following.

Overall Residence and Living Conditions
- Dirty or filthy living environment
- Evidence of poor housekeeping
- Overcrowded living conditions
- Inadequate child safety measures taken
- Lack of items normally associated with child care
- Infestation by roaches, other insects, and vermin

Living/Sleeping Area of Child
- Dirty or filthy.
- Lack of or inappropriate bed or bedding.
- Lack of or inappropriate clothing.
- Failure to properly dispose of soiled diapers, clothing, etc.
- Presence of roaches, insects, or vermin. Consider turning off the lights in the child's room, wait about 10 minutes, and turn the lights back on. Photograph any insects or vermin present in the room.

Food Preparation/Eating Area
- Dirty or filthy
- An excess of unclean dishes and cooking supplies
- Leftover food not properly disposed of
- Presence of roaches, insects, or vermin

Kitchen Cupboards, Pantries, Refrigerator
- Lack of appropriate foods for the child.
- Insufficient quantities of food for the child.
- Presence of spoiled or rotting food.
- Overall cleanliness of food storage and preparation areas.
- Note and document any contrasting conditions (e.g., a presence of plenty of adult food, cigarettes, or alcohol products).

Note: After thorough photographic documentation, consider seizing an appropriate number of items to give a representative sample of the living conditions.

Examination of Child Neglect Victim

- Arrange for a medicolegal examination of the victim. If the victim is in need of medical attention, do this before the interview. This examination is best done by a pediatrician or other medical personnel with specialized child abuse training.
- Any statements made to medical personnel concerning the abuse should be thoroughly documented.
- Document insect bites or other bites indicative of infestation within the living environment.
- Document severe diaper rash, untreated sores, or other indicators of failure to provide basic hygiene.
- Examine diapers or undergarments; determine if entomological evidence (maggots) is present that would indicate prolonged time between changes. Collect entomological evidence as directed in Chapter 29.

During the Medical Examination
- Ensure steps are taken to exclude any congenital conditions or disease that may result in the child's failure to thrive.
- Request an examination of the child for any signs of physical abuse.
- Document and photograph any injuries, to include bruises and bite marks. Bite marks may be from insects, rodents, pets, or people.
  - Take color photographs (without and with a scale) of injuries.
  - The use of a color card will allow for more accurate color rendition on final photo prints.
  - Photos of individual injuries should also be taken with the film/ CCD plane of the camera parallel to the body surface, close-up, with a scale.

- Consider ultraviolet or infrared photography. These methods may enhance the visibility of pattern injury or older bruising.
  - Injuries should be photographed over several days.
- Insect, rodent, or other bite marks should be processed as soon as possible (Chapter 26).
- Fully document and collect the victim's clothing; it may contain evidence, such as blood, entomological evidence, etc.

Additional Questions for the Physician

- If the child/infant demonstrates a failure to thrive:
  - Is there a disease, genetic disorder, or other medical condition that would result in or exacerbate this condition?
  - Are there medical indications that may indicate the duration of the neglect?
- Are there indications of absence of routine medical care?
  - Excessive decay, rot of teeth
  - Open sores with no indication of treatment or care
  - Untreated rashes or other skin conditions
  - Serious injuries that healed without medical intervention, such as fractures or cuts/lacerations (e.g., bones misaligned or no indication of stitches or medical treatment)
- Are injuries or healed injuries present that might indicate physical abuse? If so, process in accordance with Chapter 23, "Child Physical Abuse," as well.
- Are there indications of a failure to maintain basic hygiene needs?
  - Child is filthy.
  - Child's clothing is filthy.
  - Indications of repeated wear without laundering of clothing or undergarments.
  - Presence of insect larvae or pupae in the child's clothing.
  - Infestation of fleas or head lice.
- Thorough photographic documentation of the child as he or she first presents (prior to cleaning) is essential.
- Recommend that the examining physician note in his or her medical report one of the following diagnoses:
  - No evidence of neglect by history or examination.
  - History and physical examination compatible with child neglect.
  - History supportive of child neglect with normal physical examination.
  - History is negative for child neglect, but the examination is supportive of neglect.

- Obtain copies of all associated medical reports.
- Request or obtain follow-up reports of the child's improvement or lack thereof while under medical supervision.

Medical Records Review

A thorough review of all medical records must be conducted in any case where physical child neglect or abuse is suspected. Look for:

- Any statements made to medical providers by parents or care providers concerning their ability to properly care for the child should be thoroughly documented.
- Medical records indicating successful treatment while in a health professional's care and subsequent failure to thrive while in a caregiver's care should be documented. Insurance records, Medicaid records, and medical bills located at the scene may lead to the discovery of the various healthcare providers utilized by the caregiver.
- Prior history or documented instances where neglect or abuse where suspected.
- Reports or prior "unattended child" incidents made by authorities (e.g., police, schools).

Commonly Encountered Evidence in Child Neglect

The child neglect scene differs from others, as there is seldom specific evidence of neglect. Rather, a documentation of the living conditions as a whole is required. The following items may be present at the scene:

- Deadbolts or other locks on outside of interior doors
- Inappropriate foodstuffs
- Inappropriate bedding
- Dirty/filthy clothing
- Indications of insect or rodent infestation
- Biological, trace, and entomological evidence

Special Note: Child Victim Interview: The interview of a child victim of abuse or neglect is a highly specialized area. Only those trained in forensic interview techniques for children should conduct this interview. Interviews conducted by nontrained personnel may jeopardize the validity of future interviews.

Evidence Processing and Documentation

IV

Friction Ridge Evidence 25

Latent prints consist of friction ridge prints from fingerprints, palm prints, or footprints located at the scene of a crime. They are generally processed by chemical or physical means to allow for visualization, photography, and collection. Any chance friction ridge prints found at a scene are often referred to as latent prints; technically it is correct to categorize them as:

- **Latent** (not readily visible): This category makes up the bulk of prints at a scene. They require physical or chemical development to make them visible.
- **Patent** (visible): These prints can be seen because they are made in some sort of contaminant (e.g., blood, dust, ink, oil, etc.), which contrasts with the substrate on which they are found.
- **Plastic** (three-dimensional): These prints are impressed into items such as putty, soap, or other pliable material.

A friction ridge evidence worksheet is provided in Appendix F. It will assist in keeping friction ridge recovery efforts organized and properly documented.

Prints at the Scene

General

- It is usually necessary to photograph and sketch the scene prior to examining items for prints, as the processing for prints may involve the moving of items.
- It is generally best to process for prints after biological and trace evidence has been processed.
- It is best to use a systematic search for prints. Do not skip from one area to another.
- Remember to examine items inside other items found at the scene (e.g., the batteries inside a flashlight left behind, the magazine inside a weapon, or food and containers inside a refrigerator from which prints are developed on the door).

- Elimination prints should be taken from persons with legitimate access to the area.

Detecting Prints

Oblique Lighting

- The use of reflected light (such as that from a flashlight) held at a low oblique angle is helpful in locating prints (Figure 25.1).
- Varying the angle and direction of the light will assist in locating prints.

Note: Even if prints are not readily visible when using reflected light, they may still be present, and the area should still be dusted or further processed for prints.

Reflected Ultraviolet Imaging System (RUVIS)

- RUVIS utilizes a shortwave UV light source combined with an imaging system that enhances UV light.
- RUVIS can see the reflected UV even in bright ambient light.
- RUVIS may be able to visualize undeveloped prints on nonporous surfaces.
- RUVIS is a nontouch technology. Visualized prints must be photographed through the RUVIS imager; they cannot be lifted, as they are in effect unprocessed. After imaging the print can be processed using standard techniques and a lift attempted.

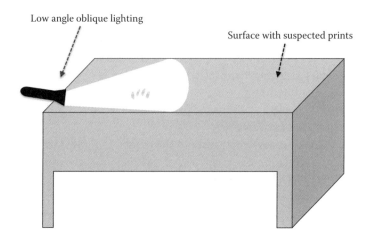

Figure 25.1 Locating latent prints with oblique lighting.

Figure 25.2 Photographing a print when first visible and then when fully developed.

Alternate Light Sources
- Occasionally fingerprints will inherently fluoresce.
- A general crime scene search wavelength of about 450 nm with orange goggles is appropriate for this search.

Photography of Prints (Figure 25.2)
- Always photograph a print as soon as it becomes visible. Do not overpowder the print.
- Fill the frame of the camera viewfinder with the print; 1:1 photography is preferred.
- Use a scale in the photograph.
- Be sure to take the photograph with the film/CCD plane of the camera oriented parallel to the surface where the print is located.
- Be aware of depth of field problems associated with prints on items with curved surfaces or other three-dimensional surfaces.

DNA Considerations
- Be aware of the potential for cross-contamination of touch DNA through the use of reusable fingerprint brushes and powders.
- The issue can be resolved through two approaches:
  - Ensure all DNA collection efforts precede any fingerprint recovery efforts. In this instance there is no requirement for disposable fingerprint brushes.

- Use disposable fingerprint brushes. Always use fresh fingerprint powder from the container, and never return used powder to the container.

Prints on Nonporous Surfaces

Items that do not absorb moisture, such as plastics, glass, metal, etc., are considered nonporous and can generally be processed at the scene.

Print Stabilization with Superglue® Fuming (Cyanoacrylate) (Figure 25.3)

- Superglue fuming on scene is the most effective way to stabilize a latent print before processing and lifting. Superglue also stabilizes any touch DNA that may be present in the print.
- Portable items may be fumed on scene in a portable fuming chamber, or surfaces can be covered and glued in place (e.g., using a makeshift plastic chamber to cover a doorknob and fuming inside it).
- Entire rooms, vehicle interiors, vehicle exteriors, or larger surfaces may be fumed with creative larger makeshift containers.

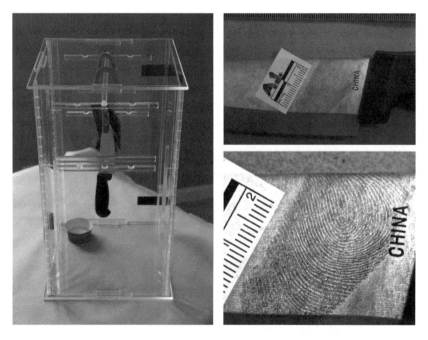

Figure 25.3 Superglue® fuming of evidence in portable chamber. Polymerized print may then treated with powders or dye stains.

- Commercial portable fuming chambers may be used on the scene. An expedient chamber may also be constructed for on-scene processing or large items of evidence. As an example, larger items of evidence may be fumed in a large plastic trash can with locking lid.
- The size of the fuming chamber, ambient temperature, and humidity will affect how much glue is used. The amount used and the time the item is exposed to fumes in field applications are based on experience.
- Cotton balls soaked in a solution of baking soda and water (1 lb of baking soda dissolved in 1 gal of water) and then thoroughly air-dried will act as a catalyst and accelerate the reaction. These are prepared ahead of time and stored in a large plastic bag with the crime scene supplies.
- A small aluminum tin is placed in the bottom of the chamber, and several cotton balls are placed in the tray. At least 10 to 15 drops of Superglue are dripped onto the cotton balls. The reaction should be visible within moments, as the cotton balls will begin to emit visible fumes. The chamber is then sealed.
- A black fingerprint card with a print applied to its surface is placed in the chamber where it can be readily viewed as a test print.
- Items of evidence should never be overfumed. As soon as the test print is lightly visible as a white print on the black fingerprint card, stop the fuming. Remove the evidence from the fuming chamber, allow the items to set up for a few minutes, and then photograph any visible prints and package the evidence.

Caution: Superglue fumes are very irritating to the eyes and lungs. Be cautious when working near the fumes. Do not utilize field-fuming techniques if wearing contact lenses. Ensure good ventilation when using Superglue.

Developing

- Generally nonporous items at the scene will be processed with fingerprint powders either before or after Superglue fuming.
- Once a technique is chosen, if possible, place a test print on the item and attempt to develop it. Place the test print on an area not considered likely to contain fingerprint evidence (e.g., if confronted with a coffee mug of unknown composition, obtain a similar mug from the back of a cabinet, place prints on it, and process it as a test).
- Contrast: Choose a color of powder that will contrast with the color of substrate being examined (dark powder on light surfaces, light powder on dark surfaces).

- Surface: Standard powders applied with a fiberglass brush can be used on most nonporous surfaces.
- Magnetic powders applied by a magnetic brush should be used on nonferrous items.

Note: A surface may be checked for magnetic properties by touching it with the magnetic wand in an area less likely to damage any potential print, prior to the application of powder.

- If in doubt about how to process an item, consider:
  - Contacting the servicing forensic laboratory for guidance
  - Removing the item and forwarding it to a laboratory for processing

Recovering Latent Prints from Nonporous Surfaces

- Photograph prints once they become visible; do not overpowder. Once photographed, use standard lifting tape to lift the developed print from the surface. Recover the tape and lift and secure as evidence.
- Prints on curved and textured surfaces may be recovered using standard tape, but gel lifters and polyethylene tape generally recover more ridge detail.
- The tape with the lifted print is placed on a white or black card, contrasting the color of powder used.
- On the backside of the card should be annotated the time, date, and investigator's initials, the item from which the print was taken, and a sketch of its relative location on the item.

Note: If the print is not successfully lifted, the photograph may become your evidence.

Packaging

- When seizing items that have not yet been processed or stabilized with Superglue techniques, it will be necessary to secure them in such a way that they cannot move within a container and no other items can rub against them in transit. Always consider protecting the print by Superglue fuming the item on scene.
- Do not place unprocessed items in plastic bags or containers.
- Clearly label the container or tag "Preserve for Latent Prints."

Prints on Porous Surfaces

Items that would absorb moisture, such as paper, unfinished wood, etc., are best photographed, seized, protected, and forwarded to a lab for further processing, as they may require advanced chemical means to develop prints.

Packaging

- When seizing items that have not yet been processed, it is necessary to secure them in such a way they cannot move within a container and no other items can rub against them in transit.
- Papers that are being preserved for both latent prints and questioned document examination may be placed in a clear document protector or paper envelope. The advantage to the document protector is that the document may be photographed or photocopied without having to handle it in and out of the envelope.
- Clearly label the container or tag "Preserve for Latent Prints."

Chemical Development of Latent Prints

Prints on Wet Surfaces

- If possible, wet surfaces should be air-dried and processed in the manner recommended for that particular surface.
- If a wet, nonporous surface must be processed for prints immediately, MOS_2 (Wet Print®) may be used.
- MOS_2 (Wet Print) is sprayed on the wet surface, allowed to stand for about a minute, and then gently rinsed off.
- The print is then photographed; be sure to include examination quality photographs.
- Once the print is thoroughly dried it can then be lifted with standard lifting tape.
- If the surface cannot be dried, use standard lifting tape and squeegee it across the print with the edge of a credit type card. The print is then lifted and applied to a white backing card.

Prints in Blood

- Patent prints in blood on nonporous surfaces may be treated with various dye stains.
- The print is photographed before any development. Be sure to include examination quality photographs.

- Biological sampling of the blood in the print can be accomplished in any area of the stain where ridge detail is obscured.

Amido Black (Figure 25.4)

- Amido Black is available as either an aqueous (water-based) dye stain or an alcohol-based dye stain. The alcohol-based dye stain is the more effective treatment; however, the aqueous-based one is easier to travel with and mix at the scene.
- The bloody prints are treated with a fixing solution. This solution is sprayed or washed over the print and allowed to stand for about a minute. On a vertical surface an absorbent paper towel may be taped over the suspected print and saturated.
- The Amido Black is mixed according to instructions and either sprayed on or washed over the surface with the bloody prints. On a vertical surface an absorbent paper towel may be taped over the suspected print and saturated.
- Ensure areas around the print where continued ridge detail or impression is possible are covered. The dye will stain visually undetectable quantities of blood and often develop considerably more of the print than was originally visible.
- The dye stain is allowed to saturate the blood for about a minute.
- The excess Amido Black is gently rinsed with water.
- The print is allowed to completely dry.
- The print is photographed again. Be sure to include examination quality photographs. Photography is the best method of documentation.
- If at all possible, collect the surface.
- If this is not possible, attempt to lift the print with a gel lifter.

Prior to chemical enhancement

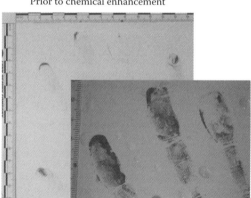

After chemical enhancement

Figure 25.4 Print in blood before and after treatment with Amido Black.

Hungarian Red

- Hungarian Red is an aqueous-based dye. The dried, stained print may show further detail if excited with a green alternate light source (ALS).
- The bloody prints may be treated with a fixing solution. This solution is sprayed or washed over the print and allowed to stand for about a minute. On a vertical surface an absorbent paper towel may be taped over the suspected print and saturated.
- The Hungarian Red is mixed according to instructions and either sprayed on or washed over the surface with the bloody prints. On a vertical surface an absorbent paper towel may be taped over the suspected print and saturated.
- Ensure areas around the print where continued ridge detail or impression is possible are covered. The dye will stain visually undetectable quantities of blood and often develop considerably more of the print than was originally visible.
- The dye stain is allowed to saturate the blood for about a minute.
- The excess Hungarian Red is gently rinsed with water.
- The print is allowed to completely dry.
- The print is photographed again; be sure to include examination quality photographs. The best method of documentation is photography using a green (520–560 nm) ALS. Use of the ALS may show enhanced detail.
- If at all possible, collect the surface.
- If this is not possible, attempt to lift the print with a gel lifter.

Leucocrystal Violet (LCV)

- LCV is available as alcohol based and uses hydrogen peroxide to cause a reaction with the heme molecule in blood. LCV may be mixed at the scene from a prepackaged kit.
- The shelf life, once mixed, is relatively short, and the solution should be used within a day or two and then discarded.
- The advantage of LCV over Amido Black is that it does not require rinsing after application.
- The LCV is mixed according to instructions and either sprayed on or washed over the surface with the bloody prints. On a vertical surface an absorbent paper towel may be taped over the suspected print and saturated.
- Ensure areas around the print where continued ridge detail or impression is possible are covered. The dye will stain visually undetectable quantities of blood and often develop considerably more of the print than was originally visible.
- The excess LCV may be blotted from the surface with an absorbent paper towel.

- The print is allowed to completely dry.
- The print is photographed again; be sure to include examination quality photographs.
- If at all possible, collect the surface.
- If this is not possible, attempt to lift the print with a gel lifter.

Prints in Oil or Grease

- Patent prints in oil or grease on nonporous surfaces may be treated with Sudan Black in either an aqueous (water-based) or mixed ethanol (alcohol-based) preparation.
- The dye will stain the fatty components of sebaceous sweat and produce a blue-black image. It is less sensitive than other stains, but is recommended for prints in oil or grease.
- The item with potential oily or greasy prints is immersed in a tray filled with the Sudan Black–ethanol mixture.
- For surfaces that cannot be immersed in a tray, the following procedure applies:
  - The Sudan Black is mixed according to instructions and either sprayed on or washed over the surface with the prints. On a vertical surface an absorbent paper towel may be taped over the suspected print and saturated.
  - Ensure areas around the print where continued ridge detail or impression is possible are covered. The dye will stain visually undetectable quantities of blood and often develop considerably more of the print than was originally visible.
  - The dye stain is allowed to saturate the print for about a minute.
  - The excess Sudan Black is gently rinsed with water.
- The print is allowed to completely dry.
- The print is photographed again. Be sure to include examination quality photographs. This is the best method of documentation.
- If at all possible, collect the surface.
- The use of Sudan Black is a messy process and can interfere with other subsequent forensic examinations.

Prints on the Skin

Latent or patent prints on the skin may occur as the result of robbery, assault, sexual assault, or homicide. In each of these cases the perpetrator may grasp the body with ungloved hands and, as such, create opportunities for prints to be transferred.

Patent (Visible) Prints on the Skin
- If the print is patent (visible), it should be immediately photographed. Examination quality photographs with scale are critical.
- The contaminant that made the print should be identified if possible. This might include blood, grease, oil, lotions, paint, etc.
- Oil-based contaminants are not likely to dry and flake, but they are prone to smearing with handling.
- Bloody prints may dry and become subject to flaking, or they may be obscured or destroyed during movement and transportation or by continued blood flow.

Latent Prints on the Skin
Detection
- Latent prints on the body are very difficult to visualize even with oblique lighting or the use of an alternate light source.
- If sufficient force was used, bruising or discoloration patterns may indicate likely areas. This might include visible finger marks on the neck of someone who was strangled.
- The bruising or discoloration from these types of injury may also be visible through infrared video or photography.
- These prints are generally located by using a lifting technique on the most likely area for deposition and recovery.
- The most likely area for deposition is determined by examining the body in the context of the scene.
- If the victim has been moved or dragged, determine the most likely area that would have been grasped by the perpetrator.
- The most likely surface for recovery is smooth hairless surfaces such as the neck, inner arms, thighs, and inner ankles.

Transfer Lift Method (Figure 25.5)
- The area identified as the most likely to have prints that could be recovered must be cooled to approximately 75 degrees Fahrenheit. This may be accomplished with a small battery-operated fan blowing across the skin's surface.
- The transfer medium may be a thick piece of glass, polished metal, or metal mirror. The transfer medium is warmed to approximately 85 degrees Fahrenheit. This may be accomplished by placing a medical quick-heat pack against its surface or a commercially available hand warmer pack.
- The transfer medium is then rocked across the cooled surface with firm pressure. It is important not to smear the area where a print might be located.

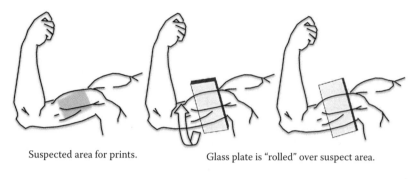

Suspected area for prints.   Glass plate is "rolled" over suspect area.

Plate is held up to light to visualize any transferred prints.

Figure 25.5 Transfer lift method for suspected latent fingerprints on skin.

- The transfer medium may then be manipulated under a light to see if the image of a print transferred to its surface.
- If the image of a print is visible (with or without visible ridge detail), the transfer medium should be Superglue fumed to preserve the print as well as any touch DNA that may have been transferred.

Superglue Fuming of Human Skin
- In the case of a deceased victim, human skin can be superglued just like other surfaces.
- This can be done on scene or under more controlled conditions at the morgue.
- Consult and obtain authority from the medical examiner before attempting any Superglue effort of a deceased victim, whether on scene or at the morgue.
- Superglue fuming cannot be attempted on live victims.

Impression Evidence

26

Toolmarks and Bite Marks (Three-Dimensional Impression Evidence)

These are three-dimensional impressions that result when a hard object (e.g., tool—screwdriver, hammer, or wire cutters, or teeth) comes into contact with a softer substance. The resulting marks may yield both class and individualizing characteristics of the object that made them. Bite marks may be associated with assaults, sexual assault, gags or items forced into a victim's mouth, or food eaten at the scene. Toolmarks may be present at locations of any forced entry. An impression evidence notes worksheet is provided in Appendix G that will assist in keeping impression evidence recovery efforts organized and properly documented.

General

- Impressions also yield the possibility of transfer of trace evidence, such as saliva, paint, metal chips, etc.

Caution: The tool suspected of causing an impression should never be placed into the mark to see if it fits. This will create a potential for cross-contamination of trace evidence and likely alter the impression itself.

Detection

- At the scene carefully examine areas of forced entry or damage where tools may have come into contact with softer objects.
- Oblique lighting may assist in locating subtle, shallow marks.

Photography (Figure 26.1)

- Toolmarks should be photographed in place prior to any processing. Subsequent processing and recovery of these impressions may destroy or alter them. Bite marks in skin or items of food should be considered fragile and processed expeditiously, as they may quickly fade.

Figure 26.1 Photographing tool marks.

- The camera should be tripod mounted with a shutter remote and the film/CCD plane of the camera parallel to the impression.
- The impression should fill the frame of the viewfinder.
- If in bright sunlight, the impression may need to be shaded for proper photography.
- The initial photographs should be without scale.
- Place an appropriate scale (e.g., American Board of Forensic Odontology (ABFO), L scale) adjacent to the impression for subsequent photographs. Ensure the scale is on the same plane as the impression.
- After the initial photographs, large items of trace evidence such as paint chips or metal fragments that are not embedded in the impression may be carefully removed and seized as trace evidence (Chapter 28).
- Low-angle oblique lighting will assist in highlighting the impression.
- Using an off-camera flash or strong flashlight, direct the light at a low angle across the impression. Use a flashlight first to help determine the most effective flash angle.
- Photograph the impression with the oblique lighting from each side of the impression.
- Be aware of depth of field requirements for three-dimensional impressions.

Figure 26.2 Casting tool marks.

Processing/Casting Toolmarks (Figure 26.2)

- Whenever possible, the item containing the impression should be seized if it would not damage the impression.
- If this is not practical, after detailed photography the impression may be cast.
- Casting should be done with silicone rubber casting compound such as Mikrosil®, following the directions supplied by the manufacturer.

Processing Bite Marks, Special Considerations

- For bite marks on the skin of a living individual, in which the skin is broken, seek medical attention.
- Bite marks in living individuals are perishable and will fade quickly, so process as soon as possible.
- Photograph as described above.
- Swab both the inside and outside of the dental arch for possible DNA from the suspect (Figure 26.3).
- Photograph the bite mark again. Consider infrared (IR) or UV lighting (Figure 26.4).
- Consider rephotographing the mark over time.
- Cast the mark, if possible.

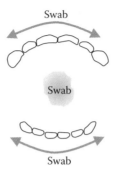

Figure 26.3 Swabbing dental arch of a bite mark for DNA evidence.

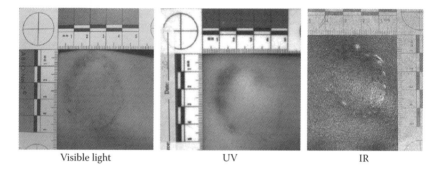

Figure 26.4 Visible, UV and IR photography of bite marks. (Photographs courtesy of Greg Golden, DDS, Chief Odontologist, San Bernardino County Sheriff's Coroner Division.)

- If the mark is in a food item, do not allow the item to dry out. Photograph and cast it as soon as possible.

Footwear and Tire Impressions (Three-Dimensional Impression Evidence)

General

- It is important to keep in mind that law enforcement actions on scene may obscure impression evidence left by the suspect. All attempts should be made to use paths of travel not likely used by the suspect until those areas have been examined.
- It is advisable to keep unessential personnel out of the scene and to wear protective footwear while processing the scene. The use of new clean "booties" by crime scene personnel each time they enter/reenter the scene will minimize further contamination.

- Thorough measurements and documentation of the distances between impressions, as well as their relationship to each other, may provide valuable information as to the gait of the individual, wheel base or axle length of the vehicle, etc.
- Casting impressions in mud, sand, snow, or underwater require specialized techniques. Learn and practice appropriate methods for the local area in advance of any need.

Caution: Do not reapproximate the item suspected of having made the impression to the impression itself. This will create the potential for cross-contamination of trace evidence and likely alter the impression itself.

Detection

- Three-dimensional prints should be fairly obvious on initial inspection of likely areas in the scene.
- Oblique lighting may be helpful in locating more shallow impressions.

Photography (Figure 26.5)

- Impressions should be photographed in place prior to any processing. Subsequent processing and recovery of these impressions will destroy or alter them.

Figure 26.5 Photographing footwear impression evidence.

- The camera should be tripod mounted with a shutter release remote and the film/CCD plane of the camera parallel to the impression.
- The impression should fill the frame of the viewfinder.
- If in bright sunlight, the impression may need to be shaded for proper photography.
- Initial photographs should be without scale.
- Place an appropriate scale (e.g., L scale) adjacent to the impression for subsequent photographs. Ensure the scale is on the same plane as the impression.
- After initial photographs, large items (twigs, leaves, etc.) that are **clearly** not embedded in the impression and appear nonevidentiary may be carefully removed. If there is any doubt if they are or are not embedded, leave them in place and cast as is.
- Low-angle oblique lighting will assist in highlighting the impression.
- Using an off-camera flash or strong flashlight, direct the light at a low angle across the impression. Use a flashlight first to help determine the most effective flash angle.
- Photograph the impression with the oblique lighting from each side of the impression.
- Be aware of depth of field requirements for three-dimensional impressions.

Processing/Casting (Figure 26.6)

- Whenever possible, the item containing the impression should be seized if it would not damage the impression. If this is not practical, and after detailed photography, the impression may be cast.
- Dental stone or die stone is recommended as a casting agent. These substances require no reinforcement, show better detail than plaster of paris, do not shrink, and will set up even underwater.
- The casting material is typically mixed in a large (gallon size) Ziploc® bag.
- The Ziploc bags should be prepackaged with approximately 2 lb of casting material. One bag should be sufficient for one footwear impression. Much larger quantities are required for tire marks.
- Add 12 oz of water (a clean soda can full) to the powder and mix thoroughly by kneading the bag (this is a general guideline; refer to manufacturer's instructions for exact mixing directions).
- The resulting mixture should be adjusted until it is about the consistency of pancake batter.

Note: Framing is not necessary with these materials unless unusual terrain conditions exist (e.g., impression on an inclined surface like a hillside).

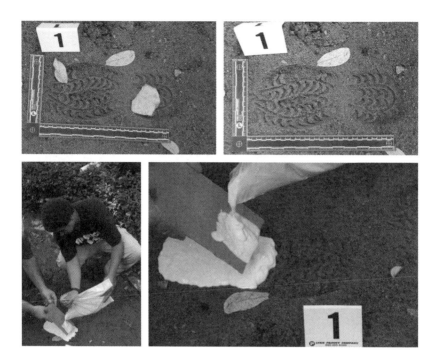

Figure 26.6 Casting footwear impressions: 1) Photograph impression. 2) Remove obvious (non-embedded) contaminants. 3) Pour dental or dye stone using a buffer to help direct the spread and prevent impactin impacting the impression with the pouring stone.

- The mixture should be poured to the side of the impression and allowed to run into the impression. Alternatively, an item can be used to act as a baffle, allowing the mixture to flow gently onto the impression.
- The impression should be completely covered in the first pour. An additional mixture may be added to the first in order to obtain a thickness of about 3/4 to 1 in.
- Once the cast sets, an indelible marker is used to mark the caster's initials, the date/time, and a north arrow directly on the back of the cast.
- The cast should be allowed to set completely before removal. This should take approximately 30 minutes.
- Once removed, leave all adhering sand, dirt, or other particles on the cast surface. Cleaning will be done at the laboratory.
- Allow the cast to air dry for 24 to 48 hours before preparing it for transport to the lab.

Casting Underwater (Figure 26.7)

- Impression evidence under standing or slow-moving water may be cast in place.

Figure 26.7 Casting footwear impressions underwater. Powdered dental stone is poured down the PVC pipe and deposited at impression level or, using a flour sifter, dental stone is dispersed over the surface of the water and allowed to drift down into the impression.

- Impressions should be photographed with a scale at the same depth as the impression.
- A polarizing filter for the lens will reduce reflection from the surface of the water.
- A strong waterproof flashlight (or dive light) may be used to apply oblique lighting. *Note*: Any excessive movement of the water may stir up the bottom and obscure the print.
- Using a flour sifter, the dental/die stone is sifted so that it floats down and covers the print.
- Several layers are built up this way and allowed to partially harden.
- Once the initial layer is set, place a frame around the existing cast.
- Once several sifted layers are built up, mix dental/die stone in a slightly thinner mixture than normal.
- Pour this mixture through the water so it settles within the frame and onto the hardening cast.
- Allow to completely dry; this may take several hours.
- Carefully work your fingers under the edge of the cast.
- Slowly and carefully work back and forth and along the length of the cast until it is free.
- Do not clean off any mud or other matter adhering to the cast.

- If casting in shallow salt water, be aware that the dental stone will harden and set up more quickly.

Impressions in Snow

- **Primary method:** Spray the snow with commercially available spray wax. This fixes the impression in the snow, provides a contrasting color, and insulates it from the casting material.
- **Secondary method:** Using a flour sifter, sift two or three light coatings of dry dental/die stone into the impression and moisten each coating with a fine mist of water.
- Casts in very cold weather may take considerable time to harden. If in an open area that will not be disturbed, vehicles may be moved over the cast to protect it while drying. The catalytic converter/exhaust system will provide warmth to help set the cast.

Impressions in Sand/Dust

- It is very easy to damage the detail of a three-dimensional footwear impression in sand or dust.
- The impression should be photographed first.
- The impression is then fixed by spraying hair spray or a substance sold commercially for this purpose. The can is held in such a way to allow the sprayed material to fall onto the impression via gravity instead of the force of the spray being applied directly to the impression.
- The spray should be allowed to set up/harden.
- After being photographed, the impression can be processed as ordinary three-dimensional impressions in dirt. The use of a baffle or allowing the casting material to flow slowly and indirectly onto the impression is of utmost importance.
- Use a thinner mix of casting material for the initial layer to ensure the material flows easily across the loosely bound sand.

Special Considerations for Tire Marks

Follow the same procedures as for footwear impression, but with the following considerations:

- Tire marks should be cast in approximately 1½ ft sections and encompass a length of about 6 ft (for standard car tires) to 9 ft (for larger/truck tires) to ensure the entire circumference of the tire is cast.
- The full depth of a tire mark should be cast, as important detail is often contained on the sidewall.

- Due to the volume of casting material used, be cautious and ensure the cast is completely dry before removal. The cast will be warm to the touch while drying. Use this as an indicator. Do not attempt to lift until the cast is completely cool.
- The cast is marked with initials, date, item number, and north indicated with an arrow prior to lifting.
- Carefully work your fingers under the edge of the cast.
- Slowly and carefully work back and forth and along the length of the cast until it is free.
- Do not clean off any dirt or other matter adhering to the cast.

Packaging

- Package in separate cardboard containers.
- Ensure the cast is secured and will not slide back and forth within the container.

Footwear and Tire Impressions (Two-Dimensional Impression Evidence)

Two-dimensional impressions, or dust prints, occur when the dust or contaminant on a suspect's footwear or tire is transferred to the surface being walked upon. They may also be present on the clothing or body of the victim when a stomping occurs. These prints are very fragile and should be considered perishable evidence and receive priority processing.

Detection

- As with fingerprints, areas likely used by the suspect should be examined. Start with the point of entry; areas to, around, and from the point(s) where physical evidence is found, and points of exit should all be examined with oblique lighting.
- Likewise, hard outdoor surfaces may also contain two-dimensional impressions. These may need to be processed quickly to avoid loss due to environmental factors (rain, snow, etc.).
- The use of powerful oblique lighting (at very low angles to the surface) will greatly assist in locating two-dimensional impressions.
- Impressions that may not be readily visible or even made visible by oblique lighting may still actually exist. If there is any reason to believe dust prints are present, consider screening the area with an electrostatic dust print lifter.

Oblique Lighting Visualization
- Darken the room or dim the lights, if possible.
- A strong white light is held at about a 10- to 15-degree angle, so it skims across the floor or other surface being searched.
- Starting at the doorway or entrance to the scene, search your way in.
- Mark the location of all two-dimensional evidence as it is revealed to avoid its accidental obliteration.

Mirror and Oblique Lighting
- Clear a path by the oblique lighting method, or make access to the scene from the opposite side.
- Using a long rectangular mirror, hold it at the far end of the search area with the longest edge of the mirror parallel to the floor.
- Lean the mirror forward toward the search area at about a 5- to 10-degree angle. The best angle may be found by moving it back and forth while visualizing for prints.
- The searcher uses the same oblique lighting technique discussed above, but looks into the mirror to visualize the two-dimensional prints.
- Once this technique is practiced and mastered, it is very effective for visualizing two-dimensional prints.

Photography (Figure 26.8)
- Impressions should be photographed in place as soon as they are visualized. The subsequent processing and recovery of these impressions may destroy or alter them.
- The camera should be tripod mounted with the film/CCD plane of the camera parallel to the print.
- The print should fill the frame of the viewfinder.
- Low-angle oblique lighting will assist in highlighting the print.
- Photograph both without and with scale.
- Seize the item if possible.
- An electrostatic dust print lifter, gelatin lifter, or wide tape may be used to lift the print from a hard surface.

Processing Dry Impressions
Electrostatic Dust Print Lifter (Figure 26.9)
- The metallic film from the dust print lifter is placed black side down over the suspected two-dimensional impression.
- The unit's charging lead is placed onto the metallic top surface of the film. (Follow manufacturer's instructions for safety and procedure.)

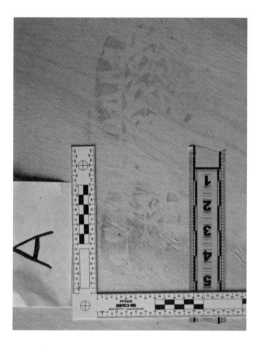

Figure 26.8 Photographing 2-D impression evidence.

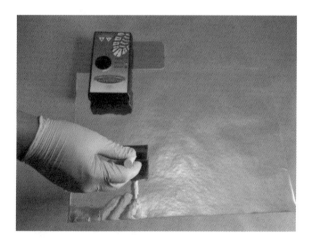

Figure 26.9 Use of the electrostatic dust print lifter.

- The unit's grounding lead is placed on a metal ground plate that is near, but not touching, the metallic film.
- Do not touch any part of the grounding plate or film during operation.
- The unit is powered up starting at the lowest setting, gradually increasing power until the film begins to adhere to the surface. Continue increasing power until the film is tightly adhered to the surface.
- Using the wooden handled rubber roller (provided with kit), gently roll out the film across the suspected print, ensuring tight contact.
- Reduce power.
- Turn the unit off and remove it from film.
- Release any residual static charge (if provided with a static wire) or allow the film to lie in place for a minute, and then carefully lift the film from the surface.
- Turn the film over carefully and inspect with oblique light for two-dimensional impression.
- Photograph any evident impressions in darkness with the camera on a tripod. Fill the viewfinder frame with the impression and use timed exposures of 5, 10, 15, and 20 seconds.
- During exposure time move the beam from a flashlight completely across the image at a very low angle of oblique lighting (Figure 26.10).
  - Do not pivot the flashlight back and forth; this will cause a hot-spot where the light originates.
  - Make certain when moving the light back and forth that the beam comes completely off the film as it passes from left to right, this will prevent the edges from becoming burned out.

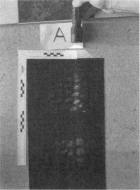 

Light is moved back and forth during timed exposure.   Results in a highlighted 2-dimensional impression.

Figure 26.10 Photographing dust print lifts by painting with light.

- It is possible, though not recommended, to secure the completed metallic film in a box. As the static charge dissipates over time, the dust impression may no longer adhere to the film. The best method for preservation is photography.

Stati-Lift® Dust Print Lifter

- This is similar to the electrostatic dust print lifter in that it uses static electricity; however, the metallic film comes with a static charge already present. It does not require a power source and may be safely used on a living body (e.g., stomp marks, tire marks).
- The film is pulled away from its plastic cover sheet; this creates the static charge and exposes the black film surface.
- The black side of the film is laid carefully over the suspected impression.
- The film is carefully rolled out with a 4 in. rubber roller.
- The film is turned over and immediately photographed; do not replace the plastic cover sheet yet.
- Turn film over carefully and inspect with oblique light for two-dimensional impression.
- It should be photographed the same as with the electrostatic dust print lifts.
- After photography, replace the plastic cover sheet.

Gel Lifter (Figure 26.11)

- Choose a gel lifter that will contrast in color with the suspected contaminant.
- A plastic cover sheet protects the gel. Carefully pull off the plastic cover sheet and expose the gel.
- The gel side of the matrix is laid carefully over the suspected impression.
- The film is carefully pressed into the surface with a 4 in. rubber roller.
- The gel is then lifted and turned over for inspection. Do not replace the plastic cover sheet yet.
- Carefully inspect for impressions. If an impression is evident, photograph.
- If not readily apparent, search with oblique light for the two-dimensional impression.

Tape Lift

- If other means are not available, the two-dimensional impression may be lifted with tape and placed on a contrasting card.
- Apply a base layer of tape below the short axis of the impression.
- Carefully, using the widest tape available, run a strip of tape, overlapping the base layer, the full length of the impression.

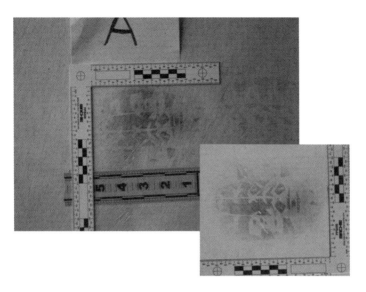

Figure 26.11 Using gel lifters for 2-D impression evidence developed with black magnetic power.

- Repeat as many times as necessary, allowing each piece of tape to overlap at least ¼ in. with the piece beside it.
- When the entire impression has been taped, gently lift the tape, starting with the base tape at the side of the overlapping run that was laid first.
- Lift all of the tape as a single piece and apply it to a contrasting surface card.

Processing Moist Impression

Two-dimensional moisture impressions occur when the impressing surface moves something wet (e.g., puddles, dew on grass) and then comes in contact with a dry firm surface. This print is very transitory and should be photographed immediately upon discovery (Figure 26.12). The print will only be visible as long as the moisture has not evaporated. These prints are very fragile and should be considered perishable evidence and receive priority processing.

Caution: If the print is believed to have been made by a transfer of blood or oily contaminant, collect a sample and use a chemical staining method such as Amido Black or Sudan Black. (Refer to latent print chemical enhancement in Chapter 25.)

- In all other cases immediately photograph the print to demonstrate the spatial relationship and orientation of the print to the scene.

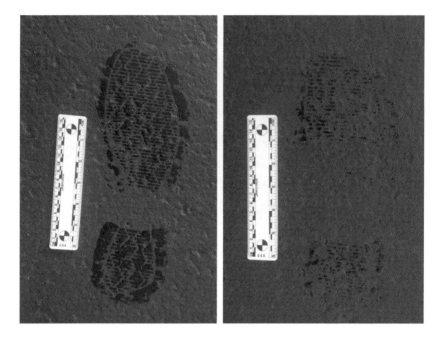

Figure 26.12 Documenting highly perishable moisture prints for 2-D impression evidence. Photograph on right taken two minutes after photograph on left. Expediently photographed with iPhone camera.

- Immediately photograph the print at 90 degrees, filling the frame of the viewfinder with the impression.
- Depending upon the nature of the surface the print is found on, it can be processed either wet or dry.
- If the surface is smooth and nonporous, utilize a dry processing method.
- If the surface is rough or textured, utilize wet processing method.

Processing—Dry
- Continue to photograph the print with scale, as the print disappears.
- Once the print is dry, process the surface like a latent print, with contrasting powder.
- After development with fingerprint powder, photograph without and with scale.
- Lift the developed print with gelatin lifter or wide tape.

Processing—Wet
- Using a good contrasting fingerprint powder, lightly powder the wet print. Do not overpowder.

- Once developed, cast the area in the same manner as a three-dimensional cast, using dental stone. This will require placing a small tab (e.g., a piece of strong tape, a tongue depressor) at one edge of the cast. This tab is used to assist in levering up the dental stone after it is dry.

Packaging

- If the item itself is collected, it must be packaged in such a manner as to avoid having the print contact any item of the packaging, etc.
- The gel lift or tape lift should be secured in a cardboard box.

Biological Evidence at the Scene

27

Biological evidence is found at the scene, on the body, and on clothing of the victim or perpetrator. Biological evidence is a valuable source in determining physical presence or contact as well as actions within a scene. Handling biological fluids and stains is hazardous due to bloodborne pathogens. Hepatitis B virus (HBV) and human immunodeficiency virus (HIV) are of particular concern. Treat all biological fluids as sources of bloodborne pathogens. See Appendix A for safety instructions and the use of universal precautions. A biological evidence notes worksheet is provided in Appendix H that will assist in keeping biological evidence recovery efforts organized and properly documented.

Nuclear DNA

A significant portion of the biological evidence recovered is in the form of physical observable material (e.g., stains, liquids, or particulates that contain cellular material holding the nuclear DNA). This DNA comes from any cell containing a nucleus; however, certain cells do not have a nucleus (e.g., mature red blood cells). The method of evaluating this material is constantly changing and becoming more and more sensitive. In forensic work these methods have evolved from restrictive fragment length polymorphism (RFLP) to polymerase chain reaction (PCR) to current techniques of short tandem repeats (STRs). Recognition and collection are covered in the "Biological Fluids and Stains" section of this chapter. The sensitivity of these techniques, however, has led to the ability to recover what is generally referred to as touch DNA.

Touch DNA

Touch DNA refers to an incidental transfer of genetic material (DNA) when an object is handled, touched, or brushed up against. The DNA of the person may be transferred through shed skin cells or body fluids.

Detection

- The touch transfer is latent, not visible to the naked eye.
- Its possible location, and therefore collection point, is determined through an analysis of the evidence in the context of the dynamics of movement within the scene.
- Touch DNA should be expected to co-reside with latent or patent fingerprint impressions. Obvious locations at the scene would be at points of entry or where items of physical evidence had to be manipulated by the perpetrator.
- Obvious locations on the victim may include the upper arms, wrists, or ankles of a victim that was dragged, or the inner thighs or breasts of a sexual assault victim.
- Other locations may be less obvious, but all possible locations of touch DNA on the victim should be thoroughly examined.
- Nothing precludes collection of both DNA and fingerprint evidence.
- Touch DNA can be sampled from areas associated with latent fingerprint transfer by swabbing areas that lack **any** ridge detail. Swab the areas surrounding the print, or areas of relief (e.g., edges, textured aspects of the object that will not hold ridge detail). If the investigator can see a fingerprint impression, but it is obviously smeared and lacks ridge detail, there is strong possibility that touch DNA could be retrieved from that surface.

Preservation and Collection

- Cyanoacrylate (Superglue®) fuming for the preservation of latent prints serves a dual purpose, as it also preserves touch DNA. This is an ideal method for preserving both possible prints and DNA on weapons.
- Touch DNA may be collected by swabbing the suspected transfer area with multiple swabs moistened with distilled or sterile water. The swabs should be rubbed over the suspected area for at least 15 seconds.
- Do not use standard cotton swabs for touch DNA collection. As the swab is rubbed against the area, the cotton tends to degrade and fall off. This is the very area of the swab that most likely holds the genetic material. Swabs made of rayon or polyester are the better collection method.
- Alternatively, typical small tape tabs (e.g., Post-it sticky notes) can be used if the area to be sampled is dry. The tabs are pressed against the area to be sampled and submitted for evaluation. The adhesive has no known detrimental effect on the DNA itself.

Mitochondrial DNA (mDNA)

Mitochondrial DNA is different from nuclear DNA in that it is found in all cell mitochondria. Mitiochondria exist in great numbers in all cells. Mitochondrial DNA, however, is a shared trait in a familial tree, and is passed through the maternal side of the family. Thus, it is not as specific and represents only a class characteristic. It is, however, viable evidence and may be probative in any investigation, particularly in identification of missing persons.

If nuclear DNA evaluation is not possible due to degradation of samples or insufficient nuclear DNA material, mDNA should be considered.

Biological Fluids and Stains

Biological fluids such as blood, semen, saliva, and urine may be left at the scene or on the body of the deceased. These stains may be either wet or dry, or in some cases pooled.

Detection (Figure 27.1)

- Visual detection may be supplemented with strong oblique lighting. This is the least effective method.

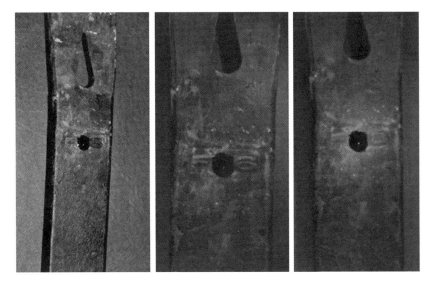

Figure 27.1 A drop of blood on a pry-bar. White light (left), blue light with orange filter (center), UV light (right).

- Ultraviolet lighting (100–400 nm) often fluoresces semen, urine, and occasionally saliva. Use caution when exposing any area believed to contain DNA to extended exposure to ultraviolet light, as UV light does have a detrimental effect on the genetic material. Longwave (315–400 nm) UV is preferred over shortwave (100–280 nm) UV light.
- Semen, saliva, and urine will fluoresce when exposed to an alternate light source (ALS) tuned to 450–485 nm and viewed through orange goggles.
- Blood, however, does not fluoresce when exposed to alternate wavelengths of light. It absorbs all light and appears black or dark. Blood is best visualized when exposed to 415 nm of light and viewed through yellow goggles. The appearance of the stain will be like a dark hole in the background material, and the resulting contrast should allow the investigator to visualize and photograph the blood better.

Scene Analysis

- Typically, the presence of a stain in the appropriate scene context is sufficient to indicate it is biological. If a stain looks like biological staining, and is in an area where biological staining would be expected, it should be processed and collected. A presumptive test is not necessary.
- Occasionally stains may appear in such a context that their biological origin or forensic significance is questioned.
- Presumptive test kits are available that may be used on scene to establish a stain is blood, semen, or saliva. This does not confirm that it is a human sample, but it may assist the CSI in deciding what stains should be sampled (Figure 27.2).
- Human-specific test kits are also available for field use. These allow the stain to be confirmed as human blood, human semen, or human saliva at the scene (Figure 27.3).

Collection of Biological Stains

Biological evidence is usually encountered in one of four conditions:

- Dry: Contains no moisture, crusty.
- Wet: A damp stain or area of biological staining.
- Liquid: A pooled area of biological fluid.
- Tissue: An actual piece or fragment of tissue.

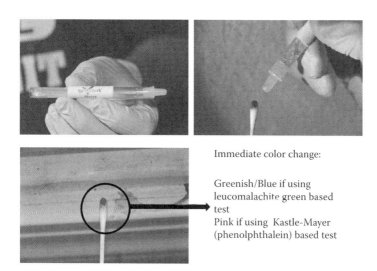

Figure 27.2 Presumptive blood test.

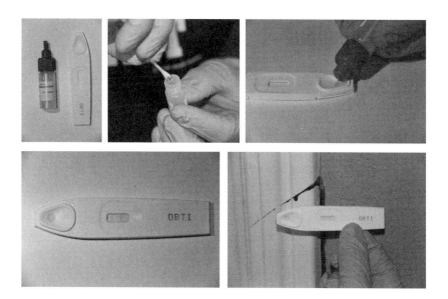

Figure 27.3 Presumptive blood test, human (primate) specific. Positive indicated by parallel blue lines, one at the control (C) position and the other at the test (T) position.

General

- All stains should be thoroughly documented and photographed prior to collection. Include close-up photography, both without and with scale. *Note*: If you are illuminating with UV light, remove any skylight or UV protective filter from the lens or the camera will not capture the image.
- As collection efforts move from one stain the next, the potential for cross-contamination should be minimized. Use either disposable instruments for collection or instruments that have been cleaned in a 10% household bleach solution for 5 minutes. In addition, two pairs of gloves should be worn, with the outer pair changed between unassociated stains or samples.
- Use a marker pen to circle any suspected wet semen observable on sheets, items of clothing, or other objects. Once dry, stains that were visible at the scene may not be visible.
- If the stains are located on bedding, mark the side that was exposed during the assault and indicate which end was at the head and which was at the foot of the bed. Allow wet stains to air-dry before folding.
- If collecting and submitting the object itself, no control sample is required. Otherwise, obtain a sample from an uncontaminated area on the surface where the stain was found.
- Before folding an item, place a clean piece of paper over stains to prevent cross-transfer of the stain to other portions of the item. Do not fold the item through a stain.

Dry Stains (Figure 27.4)

- Submit item if practical or cut out the section containing the stain.
- Collect as much of the stain as possible.
- If the item cannot be seized or the stain cut out, collect dried stains with clean, moistened sterile swabs.
- Lightly moisten a sterile swab with distilled or sterile water (do not use saline solutions) and swab the stain.
- Saturate the sterile swab with as much of the sample as possible. It is important not to dilute the stain too much.
- Continue to saturate swabs with the stain until the swab comes away clean or until six to eight swabs have been collected.
- Air-dry the swabs.
- Take a control sample with an additional swab, identically moistened, swabbed on an adjacent unstained area of the substrate, and also air-dried. Package separately as "Control Sample."

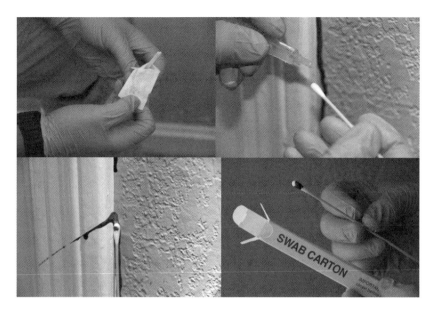

Figure 27.4 Collecting a dry sample of blood after moistening the swab with distilled water.

Wet Stains (Figure 27.5)

- Submit item if practical or cut out the section containing the stain.
- Collect as much of the stain as possible.
- Allow stain to thoroughly air-dry prior to packaging.
- If the item cannot be seized, or the stain cut out, collect wet stains with clean dry cotton swabs.
- Saturate the cotton swab with as much of the sample as possible.
- Continue to saturate swabs with the stain until the swab comes away clean or until six to eight swabs have been collected.

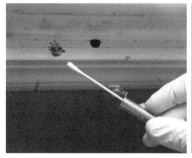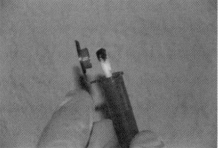

Figure 27.5 Collection of a wet sample of blood using a swab fitted with integrated swab cover to allow for drying and prevent contamination.

- Air-dry the swabs.
- Take a control sample, as described above, using an additional swab and collect separately as "Control Sample."

Liquid Stains (Figure 27.6)

- Withdraw a sample from the depth of the stain (not at the surface or at the bottom) using a pipette or syringe.
- Place sample in an ethylenediaminetetraacetic acid (EDTA) test tube (purple top) for DNA testing. Gently mix by rocking the test tube back and forth several times.
- Place sample in an acid citrate dextrose (ACD) test tube (yellow top) for serology and alcohol testing. Gently mix by rocking test tube back and forth several times.
- Refrigerate sample and send to the lab as soon as practical.
- An alternate, but less preferred, method is to collect liquid stains with a clean, cotton swab.
- Saturate the sterile swab with as much of the sample as possible.
- Saturate and collect six to eight swabs. Let dry before packaging.

Packaging

- Swabs suspected to be from different stains or contributors must never be packaged together!
- All swabs should be thoroughly air-dried and placed in labeled swab boxes. The swab boxes are then packaged in a porous container (bag or box).

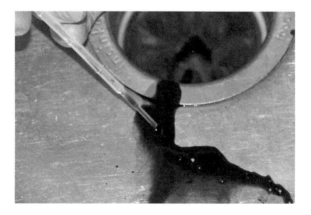

Figure 27.6 Collecting a liquid sample of blood with a disposable pipette. The sample is then placed in the appropriate collection tube.

- Swabs from the same collection sample must be packaged in separate swab boxes, but once containerized, they may be placed in the same secondary package.
- Individual swabs can be marked by the use of tape wrapped around the shaft onto itself, well away from the substance being sampled, where the collector's initials, date, time, and possibly the location from where the sample was taken can be recorded.
- Items of clothing or bedding that contain biological stains must be thoroughly allowed to air-dry before being packaged in a porous container.
- Biological stains should never be permanently packaged in nonporous containers (e.g., plastic bags). The only exception would be using plastic as a temporary container for the purpose of transporting the item to a drying area.
- The time biological materials are allowed to stay in nonporous packaging should not exceed 2 hours.
- All items of evidence should be noted on the proper evidence custody document and entered into the evidence custody system.

Trace Evidence at the Scene

28

Trace evidence is evidence that exists in small quantities or size and may be very difficult to see at the scene. This includes hair, fibers, paint chips, glass, building materials, and soil. A trace evidence notes worksheet is provided in Appendix I that will assist in keeping trace evidence recovery efforts organized and better documented. Trace evidence is unlikely to be detected without a concerted effort and search. This often entails the investigator using a deliberate, time-consuming, hands and knees approach to searching as well as technology aids such as alternate light sources (ALSs).

General Processing Guidelines

- Trace evidence is usually searched for and collected prior to processing a scene for fingerprints.
- Trace evidence is easily overlooked. Its discovery requires a meticulous search.
- Avoid cross-contamination of trace material by thoroughly cleaning collection gear between samples and changing gloves.

Detection

Magnification

- The use of a magnifying glass can greatly assist in the search for trace materials.
- Magnifiers come in various forms, including headband devices that leave the hands free.

Oblique Lighting

- The use of a handheld flashlight or other source of white light, such as that from an ALS, can also assist the investigator in seeing possible trace evidence.
- The light should be held very low (obliquely) to the surface being examined, under darkened or dimly lit conditions.
- Moving the light from various directions will often assist in visualizing trace evidence better.

Ultraviolet Lighting

- Some trace materials will fluoresce under UV light (100–400 nm).
- Using the UV light after the white light may allow the investigator to see material that was not observable under white light alone.
- The UV light should be held at various angles to the surface, but not as low (obliquely) as the white light was.

Alternate Light Source

- Some trace materials will fluoresce when excited by various wavelengths (400–800 nm) of light higher than those produced by UV light.
- The ALS offers a larger range of wavelength options, and it should be used similar to the way the UV light was used, after attempts have been made with white or UV light.
- There are no specific guidelines regarding what wavelengths to utilize, and a broad range of wavelengths should be considered.

General Collection

- Photograph the trace evidence with an evidence-establishing photograph to place it in context within the scene (Figure 28.1).
- Photograph the trace evidence so that it fills the frame of the camera. This might require close-up rings, or a macro-photography lens and settings.
- Trace evidence at the scene can be seized with the item on which it was deposited as long it will not be dislodged or lost in packaging or transit.
- If there is any possibility that the trace material may be dislodged, collect it immediately.
- When collecting trace materials, always follow the rule: bring the container to the evidence, not the evidence to the container. This will prevent inadvertent loss during collection.
- Post-it notes: May be quickly used to collect perishable trace hairs and fibers. Mark the Post-it note with the collection information and then use the adhesive strip to collect the evidence. The note may then be folded over onto itself to protect the trace evidence, and then placed in an envelope or other suitable container (Figure 28.2).
- Trace evidence such as hairs and fibers is often collected with a gloved hand (Figure 28.3).
- Trace evidence may also be collected with rubber-tipped or disposable plastic forceps (Figure 28.3).
- Trace evidence may be tape-lifted from a surface. Once collected, the tape is placed against a clear plastic surface such as a clean document protector (Figure 28.4).

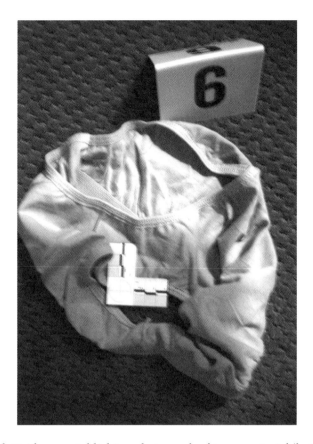

Figure 28.1 Evidence establishing photograph of trace material (hairs) on panties in scene.

- An evidence vacuum is used only as a last resort, and only after other techniques have resulted in the collection of the obvious trace evidence.

Packaging

Trace evidence must always be double packaged. The primary (inner) packaging should coincide with the most effective packaging for the particular lifting method used.

- Double-package trace evidence.
  - A druggist fold (Appendix N) or glassine envelope is the best primary packaging for trace material.
  - A standard envelope will work effectively for the outer packaging.
- **Avoid** plastic bags, as static electricity often builds on their surfaces. This makes them inadvisable for primary packaging.

Figure 28.2 Expedient collection of perishable trace evidence using a yellow sticky note.

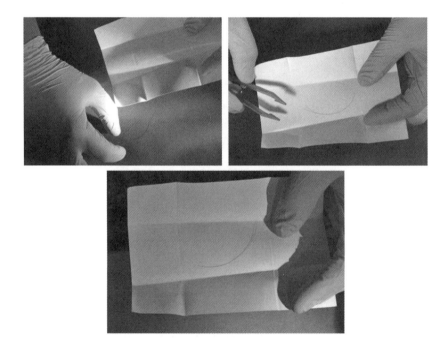

Figure 28.3 Collection of trace evidence with gloved hand and forceps using a druggist fold for primary packaging.

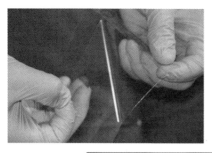

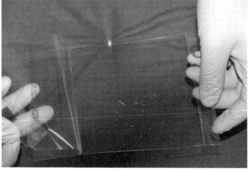

Figure 28.4 Tape lift of trace evidence using a clear adhesive sheet.

- Paint chips should be packaged so as to protect their edges for possible fracture matching. Do not package in cotton.
- Whenever trace evidence is seized from an item, control samples of that material should be taken from potential donor sources.

Hairs

Hairs may be evaluated to determine animal or human origin, region of body from which it came (head, pubic), how the hair was removed (cut, pulled, shed), dyes, and treatments.

- DNA (both DNA and mDNA) testing may be possible to determine the source of the hair.
- Unique dyes or treatments may be present that are consistent with a possible donor source.
- Hairs may often be tested for drug toxicology or longer-term heavy metal poisoning.
- Control samples from possible contributors should include about 20 pulled hairs from the head and pubic region. This may be best accomplished by using the appropriate sections of a sexual assault

evidence recovery kit. Under almost all circumstances the collection should be done by medical personnel as a part of a sexual assault response team (SART) examination.

Fibers

Fibers can be evaluated for determination of the general category of fiber: animal (e.g., wool, mink, fox), vegetable (e.g., cotton, linen), mineral/metallic (e.g., fiberglass insulation), or synthetic and blends.

- The treatments and unique origin of the fibers may allow for determining the source or potential sources of the fiber.
- Control samples from carpeting, ropes, etc., which may have come in contact with the victim or suspect, should be taken.

Paint

Chips and transfers frequently occur when two objects come in contact with each other and where one, or both, have painted surfaces.

- Fracture matches of dried paint may allow a paint fragment to be matched to its origin. The layers, which build up with repeated paintings, may also be sufficiently unique to determine an origin.
- Paint evidence may be present in breaking and entering cases where a tool is used to pry open doors or windows.
- Remember, paint from the scene may also be found on tools recovered from suspects.

Collection

- Collect paint chips.
- Collect small objects containing paint transfers.
- Cut out a section of larger objects containing transfers.

Control Sample

- Take control samples from an unmarked surface near the damaged area.
- Take the control sample all the way down to the unpainted surface.

Known Sample

- Collect any item or paint from the suspected source of the transfer.
- On vehicles, take paint samples from several places around the damaged area.
- It is important to take the full thickness of the paint, all the way down to the metal or body of the car.

Packaging

- Double-pack chips in a pillbox or druggist fold, and then place them in a plastic bag or sealable box.
- Do not allow objects containing paint smears to contact other evidence.
- Seal known paint samples in separate containers.

Glass

Glass is frequently broken or shattered during the commission of crimes. Glass can be evaluated for the general characteristics of the sample and compared with known sources of glass from the scene. Close examination of the edges of broken windowpane glass may indicate whether the glass was broken from inside or outside of the building. Staged breaking and entering scenes can sometimes be identified through a direction of force evaluation.

- Glass evidence at a scene may provide information such as fracture matching, latent prints, direction of force, sequence of impacts, velocity of impacts, and angle of impact.
- When glass is broken, microscopic fragments travel backwards toward the direction of force. The fragments may be found in the hair or on the clothing of the suspect.
- If glass fragments are potentially present on clothing, seize the clothing of the suspect and package it securely
- Have the suspect comb his or her hair over a clean sheet of paper.

On-Scene Examination

The primary radial (long, not circular) fractures on windowpane glass may be used to determine which side of the glass received the force that broke it. This may be important when it is believed a scene is staged.

- Glass both within the frame (not displaced) and loose in the scene (displaced) may be examined. The edge of the primary radial fracture

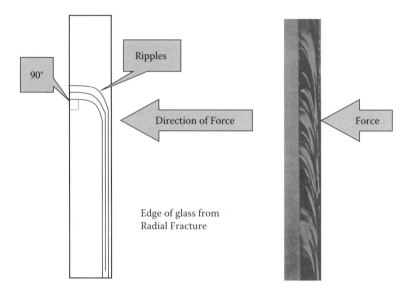

Figure 28.5 Determining directionality in glass fractures: the four "R" rule. Ripples on radial cracks are at right angles to the rear.

is examined for the presence of a wavelike pattern created by small concordial fractures. These waves will run parallel to the surfaces of the glass, and then at one point turn toward the front or back surface at about 90 degrees.

- This evaluation is only valid on primary radial fractures, fractures that originated at the point of impact. Fragments may be present with secondary fractures, but these are not functional for direction of force determinations.
- The rule to follow is the 4Rs: **r**ipples on **r**adial fractures are at **r**ight angles to the **r**ear (direction away from force) (Figure 28.5).
- Compare residues on in-place fragments (fragments still in the frame) to displaced fragments to determine which side of the displaced fragment was inside or outside. Look for oily deposits on interior aspects or dirt on exterior aspects.

Collection

- Photograph and document the location of glass and glass fragments on the crime scene sketch.
- Collect the clothing of suspects and all glass present at the scene, including any glass in the window or doorframe.
- Mark pieces removed from the frame to indicate which side faced inside.

Known Sample

- Collect a known sample of glass when needed for comparison with glass fragments recovered from a suspect.

Packaging

- Wrap large pieces separately in cotton, clean paper bag, or butcher type paper.
- Pack small fragments together in a small container, such as a druggist fold. Prevent shifting during transit.
- Mark "FRAGILE" and "SHARP HAZARD."
- Control samples from broken glass should include glass from the windowpane. The glass should be marked as to its orientation in the window (inside, outside, up, down, etc.).

Building Materials

Collection

- Collect suspect's clothing.
- Collect hair combings from suspect.
- Collect samples from suspected tools used (wood chips, saw dust, metal filings).

Known Sample

- Collect a control sample from each layer the suspect would have had to pass through to gain entry to the area.

Soil Evidence

Soil samples may be critical in linking a suspect to the victim, scene, or conveyance (such as automobile). In some cases, it is helpful to determine if the soil on clothes, tools, or automobiles could have come from a particular location. Soil examinations by a qualified person may be helpful in such cases. Send a sketch to the lab with your evidence, showing where each sample was collected.

Collection

- Collect any small items on which soil is found (shoes, tools, tires, floor mats, clothing, etc.).

- Scrape soil from larger items into a container using a clean instrument, such as a razor blade. On large objects, if only trace amounts are available, collect sample with adhesive tape.
- Samples should be taken from the area of interest as well as 3 and 15 ft from the area of interest and repeated along north, south, east, and west coordinates.
- Collect only from the depth that the activity occurred, such as surface collection (down to about 1 in.), or at the various depths if evidence is buried.
- Samples should be placed individually in canisters, jars, or plastic urine cups.

Known Sample

- Take at least eight soil samples from each area you want compared with the questioned soil. These should be taken from 3 and 15 ft from the area of interest and repeated along north, south, east, and west coordinates.
- Collect only from the depth that the suspected sample was found.
- Samples should be placed individually in canisters, jars, or plastic urine cups.

Alibi Sample

- If a suspect offers an alibi location, where he or she "really" was when the crime was committed, sample the soil from the area identified.
- These samples may then be compared to any soil samples taken from the suspect's footwear, tire tread, wheel wells, etc., and may indicate they were not at the alibi location.

Packaging

- Dry all soil samples before final packaging.
- Wrap small items separately to prevent losing any soil.
- Pack scraped samples from larger items into film canisters, clean baby food jars, or plastic urine cups.
- Pack known and questioned samples in separate shipping containers.

Trace Metals Evidence

Trace metal examinations of suspected bullet ricochets, suspected bullet holes or defects, toolmarks, etc., often yield valuable information. Field chemical testing of possible bullet defects may be warranted in order to appropriately process the scene.

Field Testing for Lead and Copper for Bullet Defects

Testing for Copper

- Dithiooxamide (DTO) and 2-nitro-1-naphthol (2-NN) testing for copper must be done before rhodizonate testing for lead.
- DTO is a colorimetric reagent that will produce a gray-green color in the presence of copper.
- A solution of ammonium hydroxide is sprayed onto the absorbent side of plastic-backed filter paper.
- The wetted filter paper is then pressed against the suspect bullet defect. The hydroxide will solubilize the copper, which will then be absorbed onto the filter paper.
- The orange DTO solution is then sprayed on to the filter paper. If copper is present, a ring of gray-green color will develop around the lifted defect pattern.
- The results should be photographed and the lift retained as evidence.
- If the ammonium hydroxide lift has a substrate color that would obscure DTO results (e.g., something that will not provide sufficient contrast to the green-gray positive color response of DTO), 2-NN may be used instead of DTO.
- Using 2-NN on a lift containing copper will produce a pink color. DTO is then sprayed over the pink and will produce the positive gray-green color if copper is present. Each of the color changes should be photographed and the lift retained as evidence.

Testing for Lead

- Sodium rhodizonate is a chemical reagent that is used to test for the presence of lead.
- When the surface has dried after testing for copper, rhodizonate testing can be done on the same area for lead.
- This is a nondestructive test, meaning other tests can be done to the same evidence.
- A colorless tartrate buffer solution is sprayed onto the surface. The buffer will solubilize lead.
- Then the orange-brown sodium rhodizonate solution is sprayed over the same area. If lead is present, an immediate color change to pink will occur.
- The results of this test should be photographed.
- To confirm that a pink color change was caused by the presence of lead, 5% hydrochloric acid can be sprayed over the pink color (or a

portion of the pink color). If the pink was produced by the presence of lead, the pink color will change to a purple-blue color.

- The results should be photographed and the lift should be retained as evidence.

Collection

- Take items on which the trace metal is believed to be present.

Control Sample

- Collect samples of the material on which the trace metal is present from a location away from the area containing the evidence.

Known Sample

- Take any tools, bullets, or materials that may have made the mark.

Packaging

- Pack to protect against accidental transfers or contact with the area in question.

Trace Explosives Evidence

The collection of trace explosives evidence is a rather unique situation involving attempts to identify the materials used to produce the bomb itself. It comes in the form of explosives residues as well as very small pieces of component materials (wiring, container, trigger mechanisms, wrappers, fragmentation pieces, batteries, etc.) made of plastic, paper, metal, or other materials. The search for trace materials stemming from blasts should be conducted in conjunction with the processing guidelines found in Chapter 14. It is highly recommended that the general crime scene investigator, unless trained specifically in this type of search and collection effort, enlist the assistance of someone specially trained in this field.

Collection of Explosives Residue Materials

This involves the deliberate search and collection of possible trace amounts of explosives materials used in making the bomb. These can be residues from primary or secondary explosives.

- These residues may be located in the crater/seat of the blast, on other recovered bomb component parts, or on nearby surfaces, including preexisting vertical or horizontal surfaces.
- Preexisting surfaces include street signs, vehicles, sides of buildings left standing, and other nonporous and porous objects.
- Priority should be given to charred or deformed surfaces, and porous substrates such as wood and textiles/clothing. These surfaces retain the smaller particles of explosives residues better.
- When surfaces possibly containing explosives residues can be reasonably collected and preserved, they should be recovered and placed in clean, sealed metal cans or containers used for fire/arson materials.
- When these surfaces do not lend themselves to being seized, they should be swabbed for residues. Control samples of the substrate from areas that do not appear to hold explosives residues should also be taken, by either seizing the object or swabbing a clean area.

Collection of Trace Components Parts

This involves the hands and knees approach to searching what may later be identified as smaller pieces of the component materials of the explosive device.

Note: Tools used to excavate and search for or screens used to sieve postblast material should be made of brass, which will not spark when in contact with other metals. This is preferable when practical.

- The use of ½ and ¼ in. sieves will assist in this search.
- The search should begin in the crater/seat of the explosion, and it should involve the removal of soil well below what is simply observed on top.
- The search and collection of these trace materials should continue through the entire area covered by the crime scene search aided by the use of magnification.
- The search must be slow and methodical. All potential trace material must be identifiable to the sector of the scene from which it was recovered.
- All trace materials collected must be packaged in a manner that ensures their integrity and prevents cross-contamination.
- In some cases, explosives residues can be attached to these smaller items, and it is imperative that they be preserved in a manner that allows subsequent laboratory analyses.

Hazardous Materials Evidence

- Before collecting hazardous evidence, obtain advice from the local HAZMAT team. In many cases, they will collect, package, and store the evidence.
- Work closely with HAZMAT to ensure proper chain of custody is maintained throughout the process.
- In cases where hazardous materials are seized, follow the guidance of the local environmental specialists for collection, storage, and shipping/transport.

Entomological Evidence at the Scene

29

The use of insect life cycles and insect succession (the order in which various species colonize necrotic tissue and fecal waste) can provide helpful investigative indicators. Though more traditionally used in death scenes, entomological evidence may be very valuable in both abuse and neglect cases. In cases of severe neglect, diapers, creases surrounding the buttocks and anal cleft, and any area with open sores may be infested with insect eggs or larvae. These may aid in documenting the extent and duration of the neglect. Additionally, foodstuffs left in the room of the victim and other garbage may show signs of infestation that may be used to determine the time they have been present at the scene.

Terminology

Larvae: The immature form of an insect. With flies the larval form is commonly referred to as maggots.

Maggot: The larval form of flies.

Necrotic tissue: Tissue most commonly at a wound site, injury site, or area where blood flow is cut off for a sustained period and where the tissue has died. It is no longer viable and is decomposing or rotting.

Pupa: An insect in an inactive immature stage between larvae and adult.

Pupal casing: The case that encloses the pupa. These are abandoned by the emerging adult insect. They may contain traces of drugs or substances from the original food source (i.e., the victim).

Insect succession: Insects colonize an infestation site in a relatively ordered progression. First are those drawn by the scent of decomposing flesh. They are followed by those that feed on the larval forms of the first invading species, and lastly those that make use of the dried or desiccated remains.

General Guidelines

A forensic entomologist should be able to provide a good estimate of the amount of time that the infestation site has been active. It is incumbent upon the investigator to understand the following:

- Certain species of insects (often flies) will begin to colonize necrotic tissue or fecal waste within minutes of the site being exposed if the right temperature and other conditions (such as daylight) are present. Additionally, early infestation may be limited by movement of the victim, brushing away flies and other insects as they land on the necrotic tissue.
- Flies usually choose areas of the body that provide protection, moisture, and food for their eggs. In neglect cases this often includes open-wound sites, fecal material adhering to the skin, or in advanced stages, the nares (nose), mouth, eyes, and exposed genital area of a victim.
- Most insects that choose to colonize human tissue go through a complete life cycle consisting of egg, larva (maggot), pupa, and finally, adult. The larvae themselves usually go through two or three stages called instars before becoming pupae.
- Using the known times it takes for specific insects to develop from one stage to another under nominal conditions, entomologists can tell how long the insects have been feeding on the tissue. Environmental factors affecting this estimation include temperature, humidity/moisture, amount of sun or shade, and related conditions.
- Some of the resulting adult insects are seen as flies; even after they have gone through a complete life cycle to adulthood, entomologists can continue to make good estimate of the time since infestation using the succession of arrival of other types of insects that come to the body at various intervals.
- It is therefore important to collect a sample of as many different species of adult flies as observed on and around the victim, as well as beetles on or around the victim and flying insects other than flies.
- With many species, only the adults are used to verify the species. This does not preclude analysis if adults are not present. Immature insect forms may be collected and raised to adulthood by the forensic entomologist.
- Often, the largest larvae at the scene will be the oldest of that particular species present.
- If present, pupae can be found. For example, larvae crawl off the body and bury themselves in the carpet or soil under or near the

body, or they may migrate in mass to a nearby shady/protected area and develop a protective shell around them.

- In outdoor scenes, soil samples need to be taken to see if any pupae exist, and if so, what species they are. With indoor scenes pupae may be found under the body, in bedding, or nearby carpeting.

Collection of Samples

Collection from samples is often a difficult task with a living victim. The victim should be rapidly cared for and transported by emergency medical services (EMS) personnel. Thus, coordination of collection may have to be undertaken at the treating medical facility, and accomplished from the removed clothing, diaper, or medical waste. Scene collection may be accomplished from clothing removed from the victim at the scene, the bedclothes of the victim, or the victim himself or herself. Expedient methods may cause the CSI to greatly abbreviate the steps and process listed below in order to capture this perishable evidence.

Adult and Flying Insects

- Using a figure eight motion, collect flying insects with an insect net from the area immediately around and above the victim.
- Place immediately into a 70% ethanol or isopropyl (rubbing) alcohol solution that has been further diluted 1:1 with water. Small glass vials make the best collection containers for these samples.

Crawling Adult Insects

- Collect any crawling insects from the surface of the wound site or body opening using forceps or gloved fingers. *Note*: Do not probe the wound, infestation site, or body opening.
- Very small insects may be collected with an artist brush moistened with the preservative solution.
- Place the collected specimens immediately into a 70% ethanol or isopropyl alcohol solution that has been further diluted 1:1 with water.

Maggots, Pupae, and Other Immature Insect Forms

- Record the temperature of any maggot mass on the victim.

- Record the air temperature at body level for the victim.
- Record the temperature of the surface near the body (e.g., not at the body's interface with the bed).
- Collect the largest maggots visible from the surface of and from the body using forceps or gloved fingers. Just a few of these largest ones will be needed **from each of the separate infestation sites on the body.** *Note*: Do not probe the wound site or body opening, and be careful not to damage the larvae.
- Place the collected specimens immediately into a 70% ethanol or isopropyl alcohol solution that has been further diluted 1:1 with water.
- **Live specimens:** Place about 15–30 of the specimens collected from the same areas of the body in a breathable container with a lid. The container should hold a piece of raw liver, which is placed on top of a layer of clean sand, vermiculite (or potting soil), or dampened paper towel. Place the specimens directly on the liver.
- Punch very small holes into a plastic lid, or use an oversized piece of material cut from a pair of ladies hosiery and held in place over the container with a rubber band to allow air to exchange within the container.
- Fill the remaining space of the container with a clean, damp paper towel that will serve to keep the container moist and minimize the movement of meat and maggots during transport.
  - These insects will be raised to maturity by the forensic entomologist for species identification.

- Mark each container with the investigator's initials and date/time of collection. Also, mark containers that are associated with each other (e.g., such as live and dead samples from the same areas of the body) in such a manner that the specimens can be associated with each other at the lab.
- Transport all samples (dead and live) to a forensic entomologist as soon as practical. *Note*: Do not mix different live species in the same container. For example, carrion beetles will eat fly maggots.

Insects in Soil

- Handful-sized samples can be collected from under (head, body, and extremities), adjacent to, and up to 3 ft from the victim's location in both directions, noting the position of each sample in relation to where the body had been located.
- Scoop soil samples into a locking plastic bag and chill. Transport to a forensic entomologist as soon as practical.

- Carefully examine surrounding soil and soil beneath the body for insects, pupae, and pupae casings. These should be collected and preserved as stated above.

Documentation of Entomological Evidence

- Include a complete set of scene photographs ensuring that the surrounding area is depicted. This information should be forwarded to the forensic entomologist who will complete the analysis.
- Obtain and record climatic conditions, including minimum and maximum temperatures for the 2-week period preceding the discovery of the body, any precipitation during this period and amount, wind speed and direction, relative humidity, and cloud cover. This information may be obtained from the National Weather Service. Appendix L can be used to record the type of information needed by the servicing entomologist.

Contact with the Servicing Forensic Entomologist

- Before transporting the collected samples, it is advisable to contact the entomologist who will be conducting the analysis.
- Explain your collection and preservation process and ask for any additional guidance he or she can give.
- The entomologist often has a collection questionnaire that explains all observations and recordings required for the analysis. If a singular entomologist is utilized by the CSI, it is beneficial to coordinate with him or her in advance of need.
- Discuss an estimate of cost, method of payment, and related business issues, and arrange for transportation of the collected samples.
- Insect samples should be treated as evidence in that any changes in custody should be noted and recorded in case this becomes an issue in court.

Use of Light and Alternate Light Sources (Oblique, UV, ALS, and RUVIS)

30

The use of light at a crime scene has progressed from the simple but effective use of white light from flashlights and handheld ultraviolet (UV) lamps to portable lasers and the alternate light source (ALS). Clean white light (5700 Kelvin, which mimics natural sunlight) is still the best tool of the crime scene investigator, but the ALS assists in observing substances or items that might not otherwise be seen. Oftentimes, these substances or items are critical evidence, connecting the suspect(s), victim(s), or both to the scene, each other, or the crime being investigated. (Due to their technical nature and their limited scene use, lasers will not be discussed.)

Terminology

Absorption of light: Light that is taken up by an item or substance. Many substances absorb some amount of light.

Alternate light source (ALS): The ALS uses a powerful lamp and specific filters to produce various wavelengths of light at a crime scene that cause certain items or substances to fluoresce or absorb light.

Barrier filter: Filter that blocks shorter wavelengths of light and permits the transmission of longer wavelengths, allowing the observer to witness the fluorescing effects of light emitted by an item or substance.

Electromagnetic spectrum of light (EMS): The range of radiation (for our purposes, light) from very powerful gamma rays to less powerful radio waves.

Emitted light: The light given off by a fluorescing item/substance. After absorbing a small amount of excited light coming from the ALS, this absorbed energy from the excited light is reemitted as light, at a longer, less powerful wavelength, producing luminescence in the form of fluorescence or phosphorescence.

Excited light: The light produced by the ALS or other forensic light source that causes an item or substance to emit fluorescing light.

Fluorescence: Luminescence (emitted light) that ends immediately when the excited light is removed from the item or substance.

Infrared (IR) light: (*Infra* means "below.") In the EMS, it is light immediately below visible light (in power), ranging from 700 to 1100 nm.

Luminescence: The emission of light from an item or substance after absorbing a small amount of light energy from an excited light source.

Nanometer (nm): One billionth of a meter. Wavelengths are described by the length of their waves in nanometers (e.g., UV is 200–400 nm)

Phosphorescence: Luminescence (emitted light) where there is a continued emission of luminescing light after an item or substance stops receiving the excited light.

Ultraviolet (UV) light: (*Ultra* means "beyond.") In the EMS, it is light immediately beyond visible light (in power), ranging from 200 to 400 nm.

Visible light: In the EMS, this is the range of light observable to the human eye, ranging from 400 to 700 nm. It consists of a range of colors, from lowest in power to highest in power: red, orange, yellow, green, blue, indigo (ROYGBIV), violet (ROYGBV).

Wavelength (of light): A measure of the distance between repetitions of a shape feature such as peaks (crests) or troughs (valleys). Wavelengths of light are usually measured in distances from peak to peak in nanometers.

White light: Light that is a mixture of wavelengths of various colors appearing as colorless (e.g., sunlight).

General Guidelines

- Many substances at a crime scene, to include body fluids and dyed fiber and hairs, will fluoresce at a different wavelengths (emitted light) than the wavelength of the light used to excite the item. Using specific barrier filters (either goggles or shields/plates), the excited light (e.g., blue light) is eliminated and the emitted light (e.g., semen emits a lime green light) from these substances can then be observed and differentiated from the surface they are on (Figure 30.1 and 30.2).
- Just because a substance fluoresces does not automatically mean it has evidentiary value. It must be considered in the context in which it is observed and then carefully collected, preserved, and forwarded to a forensic lab to confirm what it is.
- Light moves in waves, and the wave is measured from crest to crest in billionths of a meter, known as a nanometer (nm) (Figure 30.2).

Wavelength	Barrier Filter	Evidence
400 nm	Yellow/None	Body Fluids
450 nm	Yellow	Bruising & Bitemarks
485	Yellow	Ninhydrin developed prints
525	Orange	Development of prints with fluorescent powders
530 nm	Orange	General Crime Scene Search
570 nm	Red	Inks and un-dyed cyanoacrylate treated prints
700 nm	Red	Questioned Documents and Subcutaneous Bruising

Figure 30.1 Common wavelengths and filters used in forensic scene examination.

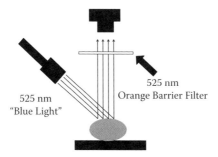

Figure 30.2 Stokes Shift: 525nm excitation wavelength is converted to a longer (lower power) wavelength as it reflects from the surface. The excitation wavelength is filtered out by the barrier filter and the eye, or camera, only sees the longer wavelength light reflected from the item of evidence.

- The shorter the wavelength, (the smaller the number of nanometers), the more powerful and penetrating the electromagnetic radiation. For example, gamma and x-rays have very low wavelengths and penetrate tissue easily. Thus, UV light, which ranges from 200 to 400 nm, is more harmful (e.g., extended exposure can cause burns similar to sunburn) than a red light at 700 nm. There is an inverse relationship between the size of the wavelengths and the amount of power involved in any source of light (Figure 30.4).

Caution: Light at wavelengths in the UV range and shorter is very powerful and can be very dangerous to the eyes and skin. Appropriate protective gear must be used at the scene. Whatever light equipment is used, always be aware of the manufacturer's warnings and follow its safety instructions.

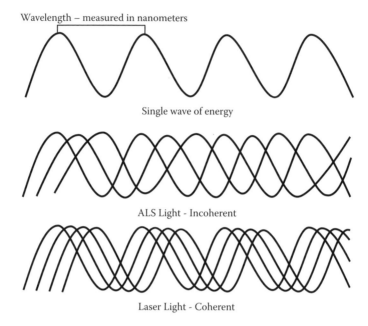

Figure 30.3 Wavelength and wave form in an alternate light source (non-coherent light) and a forensic laser (coherent light).

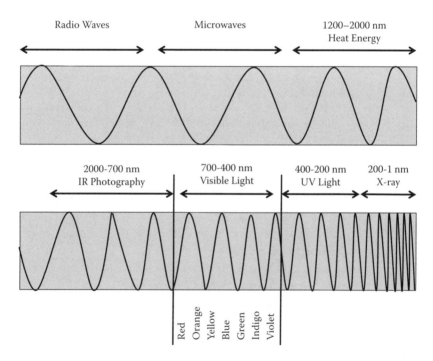

Figure 30.4 Electromagnetic spectrum. forensics most often work within the IR, visible and UV spectra.

- The wavelengths of light used as a forensic tool at the scene range between 200 and 400 nm (UV), 400 and 700 nm (visible), and 700 and 1100 (infrared) (Figure 30.4).
- As with other types of evidence, substances or items that fluoresce and in a given context are believed to be evidence should be documented in place prior to being collected, and then seized and preserved. It is important to note that for proper photographic documentation the camera being used must have the same color of barrier filter over the lens as was used for visualization by the CSI.

Crime Scene Application

White Light/Oblique

- White light comes from many sources, such as the sun, a lamp bulb, or a flashlight. Although it is not usually used to excite fluorescing substances, it is still the most important tool at the scene.
- Note that not all white light sources (e.g., various flashlights and portable lighting) produce clean white light that mimics natural sunlight. Using a source that produces such clean white light (5700 Kelvin) results in more natural colors and more effective searches. Thus, a strong flashlight or the white light offered by the ALS is used at the scene extensively.
- The use of oblique white lighting at the scene is also an important technique. The scene can be darkened, or the light dimmed, and white light applied at various angles and various orientations to the surface, allowing visualization of small items that might not otherwise be observed. Many items of trace evidence, as discussed in Chapter 28, can be seen by using this technique without the need for an ALS or barrier filter to observe fluorescence (Figure 30.4).
- Oblique white light and a magnifying glass cannot be overstated as an effective search tool, leading to the observation and recognition of small items otherwise missed at the scene.
- Applying white light to a dark surface where blood has been shed can sometimes allow the investigator to differentiate the blood from the surface, making both photography and collection of the blood possible. The blood does not fluoresce, but darkens, making contrast with the surface better.
- The use of white light also assists in better observing the roughness or texture of surfaces by showing the depth. This is particularly true when white light is held at an oblique angle when photographing footwear and other three-dimensional impressions.

- Unprocessed latent fingerprints and other important items of evidence can often be observed with nothing more than the use of white light.

UV Light (200–400 nm)

A common UV light can be extremely effective in producing fluorescing effects with certain types of evidence. As observed in Figure 30.4, as the wavelengths get shorter, the power gets higher (and poses a greater risk to our eyes and skin). Shortwave UV light (200–300 nm) is more damaging than longwave UV light (300–400 nm). Older models of UV light may have a shortwave setting; this setting should not be used, as there is seldom a need for the shortwave UV in on-scene processing. It is very important that the investigator use eye protection and long-sleeve clothing when working with UV for extended time frames. As always, follow the manufacturer's safety instructions. Do not risk the danger of eye or skin damage.

- The fluorescence given off by items or substances excited by UV light is seen in the visible range, without the need of a barrier filter. However, since UV light is being used, it is safer to use UV goggles during the process.
- Semen fluoresces well at 365 nm, but will fluoresce in a broad range of UV light.
- Injuries to the skin, such as bruises, may be better observed with UV light. See the appropriate section below for further details.
- Blood can sometimes be observed better with UV light than it can with other ranges of light, depending on the surface it is on. Blood does not reflect the light, but rather absorbs it, making it appear darker or black in color. See the section below on the search for blood.
- Many dyed items (hairs and fibers) can be observed under UV light.

The Alternate Light Source—Variable Wavelengths

When available, an ALS offers the widest selection of wavelengths to use at a scene. Some ALSs offer white light or a UV light as selection options for a complete range of light sources.

Recognizing that not all agencies can afford the more expensive ALS, manufacturers have developed smaller handheld devices that may be limited to one wavelength or a range of wavelengths. They are often called forensic lights or by their manufacturer's name.

Small Handheld Forensic Light Sources
- These are small and portable and may be carried in pocket. They are battery operated.
- They typically provide a single broadband wavelength (generally 450–520 nm), to maximize the crime scene search.
- These lights generally come with a detachable orange barrier filter for viewing.
- They do not produce significant light. They are usually 3 watts or less. As such, they produce a small search radius.

Scene Portable Forensic Light Sources
- These lights are portable and handheld. They may run from household current or optional battery packs.
- They provide multiple wavelengths, often including a broadband crime scene search setting as well as specific wavelengths for more discrete searches. They often have a white light setting as well.
- A variety of eyeglasses (barrier filters) are provided for the specific wavelengths.
- These systems are generally 400 watts or less. They provide a mid-sized search radius and are designed for scene search and processing.

Laboratory Forensic Light Sources
- These systems are high end and expensive. They are not particularly portable, and require 110 volt current.
- They do provide multiple wavelengths, including a broadband crime scene search setting with specific wavelengths for more discrete evidence searches, as well as clean white light.
- A variety of eyeglasses (barrier filters) are provided for the specific wavelengths.
- They are generally bright, at least 400 watts, producing a large search radius. They were designed for laboratory examination of evidence.

Using the ALS/FLS to Search for Trace and Biological Substances
- It is often better to start with the floor or other surface that the investigator might use to walk on to lessen the chance of damaging or removing potentially fluorescing items.
- After searching a specific area with white and UV light, the ALS can be used at various ranges of wavelengths, depending on what type of substance is expected to be found on that particular surface.
- Using the chart in Figure 30.1, appropriate goggles should be worn in order to observe any fluorescence. The color of goggles will change as the selection of an ALS wavelength changes.

- As each target area is examined with an ALS, if the system has the capability, the lamp intensity can be varied; some items will fluoresce better at different intensities.
- The investigator must stay organized in the search techniques overlapping areas in an effort not to miss any item(s) that might fluoresce.
- Depending on the substance involved, a marker can be used for its subsequent location and the investigator can move on to search another area.
- An alternative to marking the fluorescing item or substance is to collect or sample it as the investigator moves from one area to another.
- The investigator should be aware that some items fluoresce well, especially dyed hairs, fibers, and body fluids such as saliva and semen.
- It is best to photograph and sketch fluorescing items or substances in place at the time they are observed fluorescing, prior to their removal or collection.
- Fluorescing trace items should be collected and handled as described in Chapter 28, like any other trace materials.
- Wet or dried biological substances, such as body fluids, should be sampled or cut out and removed as other biological fluids are collected, as described in Chapter 27.

The Use of the ALS with Fluorescent Fingerprint Powders

- Fluorescent powders are very effective on non-porous surfaces that have contrast issues with normal fingerprint powders, such as multicolored or patterned surfaces. Fluorescent powders come in standard and magnetic applications and should be used as nonfluorescing powders are normally used.
- A feather type brush is best for standard fluorescent powder applications, as it applies a smaller amount of powder to the surface, preventing the overloading of powder on the latent print.
- The appropriate barrier filter (goggles) should be worn, depending on the fluorescing properties of the specific powders used. See the manufacturer's recommendations.
- Once observed, fluorescing fingerprints should be documented immediately with photography. Keep in mind that the camera requires the same color of barrier filter over the lens as the eye needs to view the fluorescence. This can be in the form of a screw-on lens filter or an acrylic shield placed in front of the lens of the camera.
- Fluorescing prints can be lifted with clear tape and placed on a black fingerprint card to allow for the best contrast. The card should be marked on the back as a fluorescent fingerprint lift and further marked as any other fingerprint card.

The Use of the ALS to Document Body Injuries

The ALS is a powerful tool to use when searching for potential body injuries such as bruising, or for enhancing those bruises already observed. This can include injuries from blunt force objects or bite marks.

- Both UV and IR ranges of light can cause bruises to stand out more prominently on the skin.
- These types of injuries should be documented with close-up photography using a scale. Remember that the camera lens needs the same filter color as that used to observe the fluorescent effect.
- It may be advisable to repeat this technique over several days to document the changes in the bruising over time.
- Keep in mind that shortwave UV light in particular can be harmful to human skin and degrade DNA evidence; longwave UV (300–400 nm) is preferred, and even then at short intervals. If it is available on the ALS being used, IR would be the safest to use, if it is effective on the particular bruised area.

The Use of the ALS to Search for Blood

Some substances do not emit fluorescing light, and blood is one of those substances. Blood absorbs much of the EMS spectrum, making it appear dark or black against the surface. This produces better contrast with the surface it is on, allowing visualization or better photographic documentation.

- Even under strong white light, blood turns darker, making it easier to distinguish on relatively dark surfaces.
- The ALS, particularly in the UV range, may cause the surface itself to fluoresce, which will increase the contrast with the blood as well.

Chemical Enhancement/Luminescence of Blood

In addition to the use of white light to create a better contrast between dried blood and a dark surface it is on, the ALS can further be used to create a fluorescent effect with the use of a chemical substance like fluorescein when faint amounts of blood may be present at the scene. This substance is a medical dye, and is considered safer to use than luminol. However, it is mixed with hydrogen peroxide, zinc, and other chemicals to make a working solution.

- Unlike luminol (application covered in Chapter 31), which produces a chemiluminescent glow in the dark when applied to bloodstains, fluorescein requires light from an ALS to cause a fluorescing effect.
- The substrate should always be checked for any naturally occurring fluorescence (lime green colored) before application of the fluorescein.

- A positive control test should be conducted first with a known blood source; this shows that the fluorescein mixture is working properly before it is used on scene surfaces.
- The investigator should follow the mixing directions and safety instructions of the manufacturer of the fluorescein kit to ensure the correct mixture is obtained and the procedure is conducted in a safe manner.
- Fluorescein is best viewed under light at the 445–485 nm range to produce the fluorescence as it reacts to blood.
- The test can be accomplished in a dimly lit or darkened space.
- The fluorescein is sprayed directly on the area suspected of containing the bloodstain, and the ALS is shined on the area.
- Yellow or orange goggles (depending upon the nanometers used) are needed to observe the fluorescent effect.
- Any visible reaction should be photographed. Set the camera, with appropriate colored lens/shield, on a tripod and have it ready for use prior to the application of the fluorescein. Be aware that photographic techniques of any type of fluorescence, including fluorescein, require a skill set that demands practice before attempting at the crime scene. The skills are not difficult to master, but do require a mastery of camera controls.
- A positive result with fluorescein does not confirm the presence of blood. False positives are possible with other substances, such as bleach, cleaning materials, some metals, etc.
- The area displaying fluorescence can be cut out or sampled for possible DNA results and laboratory confirmation of the presences of blood (see Chapter 27).
- If negative results are obtained, other presumptive tests or enhancement techniques for blood can be used after the application of the fluorescein mixture.
- The investigator needs to consider the cleanup necessary after applying fluorescein and the chemicals mixed with it, and the possibility of using a professional cleaning service if one is available.

Reflected Ultraviolet Imaging System (RUVIS) (Figure 30.5)

RUVIS is a handheld device that enhances the ability to see and collect evidence by allowing the investigator to actually observe evidence such as latent friction ridges on nonporous surfaces prior to the use of fingerprint powders and other potentially destructive methods. Many surfaces either absorb or reflect UV light. To some degree, this will depend on the angle that the light is applied to the surface. The lens in the RUVIS device allows

Use RUVIS in bright sunlight or total darkness

Figure 30.5 RUVIS system for latent print visualization. (Photograph courtesy of Sirchie®.)

only shortwave UV light to be emitted from it. This allows it to be used in well-lit or dark scenes. As the investigator looks through the RUVIS device, this weak reflected UV light is intensified and transformed into visible light, allowing the investigator to see the print being viewed. RUVIS works on the surface of an item, not the background materials embedded in it. Therefore, it works better on smooth, nonporous surfaces—not rougher ones. Because the device allows the investigator to see the actual print, he or she can rule out smudged or otherwise poor quality prints and move directly to touch DNA processing. RUVIS is very effective for eliminating contrast and background issues (e.g., patterned or multicolored surfaces) and will also visualize latent foot and shoe marks.

RUVIS for Latent Print Searching

- Either the background or the moisture in the print will be seen, depending on the properties and color of the item the print is on and the position and distance the RUVIS is used from the surface.
- If the underlying surface reflects light as well, the latent prints will absorb the light, and the background will appear as a lighter color on the screen of the device and the ridges of the print will be distinguished as a darker color.
- Changes in the angle of application of light can also make the latent prints seem lighter and the surface appear darker.
- Some manufacturers allow for the option of linking a camera directly to the device, thus allowing for simpler photography of the print.

- RUVIS works on the surface of an item, not the background materials embedded in it. It works better then on smooth, nonporous surfaces, not rougher ones.
- The nonporous surfaces that RUVIS can be used on to search for prints include glass, tile, plastic items, glossy papers, and photographs.
- Since the prints have not been processed with powders or chemicals, the collection of print matter for possible touch DNA is further enhanced with the use of RUVIS.
- Always follow the manufacturer's warnings and instructions when using RUVIS, since it uses shortwave UV rays that are harmful to the human eye and skin. This should include eye protection and long-sleeved skin protection.

Other Uses of RUVIS

Besides the search for latent friction ridge detail, RUVIS can be used to search for bruises, bite marks, shoe impressions, and even bloodstains.

Documenting and Processing Bloodstain Patterns at the Scene

31

Bloodstains in the form of characteristic patterns such as spatter, flows, transfers, and drips are associated with crimes of violence and injury and may be interpreted to help in the reconstruction of bloodshed events. These patterns should only be interpreted by a properly trained bloodstain pattern analyst. Bloodstain pattern analysis is best accomplished at the scene by the expert; however, a properly documented and processed complete bloodstain pattern analysis can be accomplished at a later date. The basic procedures for the CSI to follow when documenting a bloodstained scene are:

- Assess the scene and detect all bloodstain patterns on the victim, his or her clothing, and at the scene.
- Isolate individual patterns, particularly where they overlap.
- Identify the patterns as far as your training allows.
- Document the patterns through a mapping technique.
- Identify the discrete portion of the pattern that will be sampled for DNA analysis.
- Document and collect that sample.

Detection

- Bloodstain patterns will often be visible on the walls, ceilings, and floors, as well as intermediary objects associated with a violent incident.
- Identification and documentation of these patterns is essential for proper analysis.
- Though many bloodstain patterns are obvious at the scene, subtle transfer patterns or very fine misting patterns are easily overlooked.
- The scene must be thoroughly searched for any and all bloodstain patterns.

Visual

- Strong white light directed at 90 degrees to the surface is the best method that will allow the viewer to recognize the presence of blood, even on a dark surface.

- A strong white light at an oblique angle to the surface is also effective.
- Use of magnification (20×) when examining the surface to prevent missing small sub-millimeter-sized stains that may be present. This is particularly important when examining clothing items.

Alternate Light Source (ALS)

- Blood does not fluoresce when exposed to any wavelength of light; rather, it absorbs the light darkening its color.
- Using ultraviolet (UV) lighting (350 nm) will not fluoresce blood; however, the blood will darken, creating increased contrast with its background. No goggles are required to view the stains.
- When using wavelengths of 400–520 nm of light, the stains will darken as well. Viewed through yellow or orange goggles, the blood-stain will appear like a dark spot in the background material.

Infrared (IR)

- Blood also darkens when exposed to infrared light, while many dark surfaces tend to be IR reflective, including dark clothing. This combination will make the surface appear lighter, creating significant contrast between the two.
- There are, however, no rules as to what items will be IR reflective or not, so use of IR requires a trial-and-error approach. Sometimes it works in excellent fashion, and other times it does not.
- Due to this behavior, infrared video or photography of darker-colored items is an excellent way to visualize bloodstain patterns.
- Specialized IR cameras are available for forensic work; these are the easiest to use and generally give excellent results.
- Unlike other wavelengths, the use of a normal digital camera with IR light will have no effect. Standard digital cameras are equipped with an internal IR filter that removes all IR light.
- Older digital cameras no longer in use for normal photography can be inexpensively altered to remove the internal IR filter present, making them IR capable.
- IR-capable cameras require care in focusing. The IR focal point is different than for visible light.

Chemical Enhancement

- In some instances (e.g., a death scene reconstruction or when significant cleanup is suspected), once all other scene processing efforts are completed, the use of a chemical blood enhancement technique to better visualize the latent blood may prove beneficial.

- There are a variety of chemical blood enhancement products available. These include various forms of luminol (e.g., Bluestar®, Lumiscene) as well as Luecocrystal Violet.

Luminol

- Luminol causes minute amounts of (latent) blood to fluoresce from a chemical reaction (chemiluminescence). No ALS or UV light is needed.
- Luminol generally does not adversely affect DNA analysis, depending upon the specific formula.
- Luminol will work on surfaces where the blood has been cleaned or in some cases even painted over.
- Luminol is not effective on visible bloodstains; however, it may be used to extend the margins of visible bloodstains if cleanup is suspected.
- It must be used and photographed in near total darkness. Ambient light will greatly reduce the ability to visualize and photograph the chemifluorescence. Bluestar has a reported advantage of being better photographed in low-light conditions.
- It is important to use a small amount of luminol to see if any reaction is present. If a bluish glow is observed, a camera (still or video) can be set up with the use of lighting, using a tripod. More luminol can then be used and captured in total darkness with a second application.
- Photograph with time exposure, and set the background with a fill flash near the end of the exposure to capture the scene itself.

Caution: Luminol is a suspected carcinogen. As such, proper skin, breath, and eye protection should be used. Review the material safety data sheet (MSDS) and apply accordingly.

- Luminol is most effective if applied with a commercially available atomizer or compressed paint gun (the system must not contain metal parts that would be exposed to the spray).

Modified Luminol Formulas (such as Bluestar)

- Luminol-based products.
- Do not adversely affect DNA analysis (caution should still be used to avoid excessive application).
- More sensitive to extreme dilutions of blood.
- Do not require total darkness to be visualized and photographed (ambient lighting should be reduced as much as possible to near darkness).
- More effective after bleach has been used to clean up the blood.

- Apply according to manufacturer's instructions. Be sure to follow safety instructions.
- More effective if applied with a commercially available atomizer or compressed paint gun (must not contain metal parts that would be exposed to the spray).

Fluorescein

- Available as separate ingredients or in kits.
- Two-part application.
- Longer-lasting reaction than with luminol.
- Repeat application is more effective than luminol.
- The reaction is visualized and photographed with an ALS set to 455–485 nm and viewed through either yellow or orange goggles, depending upon the wavelength used.
- Results can be photographed with a camera using the same type of filter needed by the investigator to visualize the results.
- Does not require total darkness as with luminol.

Isolate and Identify Discrete Patterns

The bloodstain pattern taxonomy approach to classifying bloodstain patterns was introduced by Bevel and Gardner in their text *Bloodstain Pattern Analysis* (see Appendix K for Bevel and Gardner's bloodstain pattern taxonomy). This allows for a decision-based approach to identifying discrete bloodstain patterns. The classification of patterns should only be done by those with appropriate training. Although it is not imperative, bloodstain documentation is far better when the CSI has been trained, as a minimum, in basic pattern recognition. Otherwise, it is sufficient to isolate the patterns based on their general appearance and document them using a mapping technique.

Spatter

Linear Spatter (Figure 31.1)

- Spurt (arterial)
- Cast-off
- Drip trail

Nonlinear Spatter (Figure 31.2)

- Impact spatter
- Misting spatter
- Expectorate
- Drip

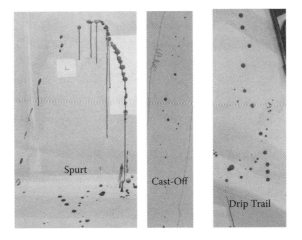

Figure 31.1 Linear spatter patterns.

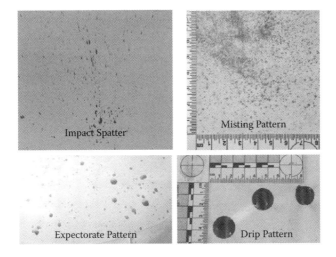

Figure 31.2 Nonlinear spatter patterns.

Nonspatter Stains

Irregular Margin (Figure 31.3)
- Blood into blood
- Gush
- Smear

Regular Margin (Figure 31.4)
- Pattern transfer
- Flow
- Pool
- Saturation

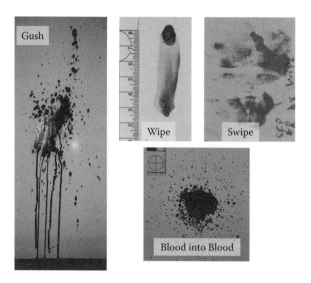

Figure 31.3 Nonlinear spatter patterns, irregular margins.

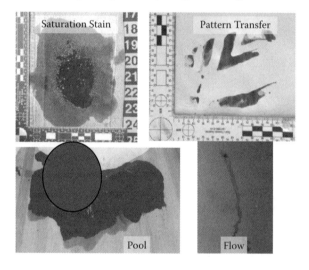

Figure 31.4 Nonlinear spatter patterns, regular margins.

Documentation through Mapping

Bloodstain patterns are significant in the size and shape of the individual spatter/stain, the appearance of the overall pattern, the location of the pattern, and the location of the pattern in association with the body and other patterns. Toby L. Wolson of the Miami-Dade Police Department's Crime Laboratory introduced a concept that is now called road mapping, which effectively places the pattern in context. The technique introduced in this guide for bloodstains, bullet defects, and injuries to the body is based on this technique and is referred to as mapping.

Mapping (Figure 31.5)

This technique works well on all surfaces within the scene, clothing, and bloodstains on the body.

- Take an establishing photograph of the item of evidence or surface that the bloodstain is on.
- Take an additional photograph with a scale.
- Identify the discrete pattern(s) on the surface with letter markers.
- Bracket the discrete pattern horizontally and vertically with large-scaled rulers or ruled tape.
- Take an establishing photograph containing the overall scale and discrete pattern identifiers and scales.
- Take a photograph of each discrete pattern with scale.
- Identify the spatter pattern that will be used for area of origin determination and mark with designators (e.g., pattern A, stains A-1, A2, and A3).
- Bracket the discrete spatter pattern with a horizontal and vertical scale. Ensure the vertical arm of the scale is plumb.
- Take a photograph of the bloodstain pattern with the individual stains identified and marked.
- Take examination quality photographs of a representative sample of the individual stains that make up the pattern.

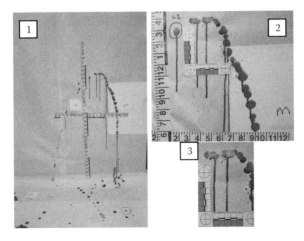

Figure 31.5 Blood spatter mapping: 1) overall with vertical and horizontal scale; 2) pattern "M" framed in vertical and horizontal scale; 3) close up of pattern "M."

- Divide the pattern into thirds either along the pattern's long axis (if linear or curvilinear) or by rings (think of a bull's-eye target).
- Photograph at least three individual stains from each third.
- Sample for DNA a stain adjacent to (and appearing in) the examination quality photograph.
- This will result in at least nine individual stains being photographed and sampled for each pattern type.
- This is a minimum number for documentation; additional stains for a radiating impact pattern will further assist in area of origin determination.
- Take a final establishing photograph of the item of evidence or surface that the bloodstain is on with all identifiers and scales.

Mapping Large Area Patterns

- When presented with a large area or surface containing multiple bloodstain patterns, it may be beneficial to divide the surface into grid squares.
- Mapping may then be accomplished with the staining identified by the appropriate grid squares.

Clothing

Mapping of bloodstains is also effective on clothing items. The procedure is no different than that described for scene surfaces above. The following is an example of sequential mapping photographs used on an item of clothing.

Photography

- Use a high-resolution setting on the camera. Maximize the capture of detail (pixels); this will allow enlarging sections of the photograph for examination.
- Mount the camera on a tripod and use a remote shutter release. Ensure that the film plane (or body of the camera) is parallel to the surface being photographed.
- Use a normal or macro-lens for the camera. Do not use wide-angle lenses. Overlap the photographs, if necessary, for full coverage.
- Establishing photographs of the surface should demonstrate the relation of the surface to the floor, corner of the room, or other recognizable feature.
- Establishing photographs of the patterns should demonstrate the relationship to the surface and a recognizable feature or scale.

- All close-up photographs should be examination quality and include a metric scale (preferably L shaped to show height and width of the stain).
- The L-shaped metric scale should be oriented with the vertical leg plumb; if not, there must be a plumb line indicator on all examination quality photographs taken on horizontal surfaces.

Sketching

- A rough sketch of the location of all bloodstain patterns should be made using an exploded view.
- The rough sketch should be transposed into a finished drawing, including measurements and placements of bloodstain patterns within the scene.

Sampling and Collection

- Using the guidelines contained in "Collection of Biological Evidence" in Chapter 27.
- Sample a minimum of nine stains or spatter within a discrete pattern.
- If practical, remove the wall, carpet, or ceiling sections containing the blood stain pattern.
- Smaller patterns may be lifted using large tape or clear contact paper and placed on panels the same size as the object they were removed from, much like the lifting and preserving of developed fingerprints.

Documenting and Processing the Shooting Scene

32

The shooting scene offers unique challenges for the crime scene investigator. Establishing the shooter and victim's locations in a scene and body positions at the time of the shooting may be critical in resolving the investigation. In order to effectively document the scene, it is necessary to be able to identify all bullet defects, to include ricochets and grazes; determine the direction (trajectory) the bullet traveled; and determine logical shooter positions along the trajectory and the victim's position along the trajectory. This may only be accomplished if thorough documentation of the angle of the shot causing the defect, as well as the precise location of that defect, can be determined.

This documentation and the evidence at the scene should only be interpreted by someone properly trained in shooting incident reconstruction. A properly documented and processed shooting scene may be reconstructed at a later date. The basic procedures for the CSI to follow when documenting a shooting scene are:

- Assess the scene and identify all firearms-related evidence (spent bullet cases, bullets, guns, gunpowder marks, etc.).
- Identify all potential bullet defects, to include ricochet marks and grazes. It may be necessary to chemically test ambiguous marks to increase confidence that they are firearms related.
- Document the patterns through a mapping technique.
- Identify any defects or patterns that will be sampled for gunpowder residue or DNA analysis, or from which a bullet will be recovered.
- Document and collect samples and collect bullets.

Recovery of Firearms Evidence from the Scene

The Weapon

Weapons Safety Is of Paramount Concern
- If the weapon is within an area secured by law enforcement, it should be properly documented and thoroughly photographed in place prior to any manipulation.

- If the crime scene is still dynamic (marginal law enforcement control), the weapon should be expediently documented and made safe, if positive law enforcement control of the area cannot be immediately established.

Documenting the Firearm

- Photograph and place the weapon onto the death scene sketch.
- While completing and documenting initial examination using the firearms documentation worksheet (Appendix J), place the weapon in an unloaded and safe condition.
- Thoroughly photograph the weapon in place. This includes any close-up photography of the serial numbers, unique identifiers, and bloodstains.
- Prior to handling the weapon, if it is safe to do so, process for touch DNA (Chapter 27). Swab the handgrips or other areas you will have to handle in order to render safe and collect the weapon.
- The weapon should be handled with a gloved hand on its knurled surface or other area least likely to contain latent prints. *Note*: It is not advisable to place any item into the weapon's barrel to facilitate collection.
- Photograph the surfaces of the weapon that were not visible in its original orientation.

Making the Weapon Safe

- Render the weapon safe. It is best not to be tentative in an attempt to minimize handling. Firmly grasp the weapon as you would your own, remove the ammunition source, and remove any round remaining in the chamber.
- In the rare instance when a weapon cannot be unloaded at the scene, it must be carefully packaged in as safe a condition as possible, in such a way as to preclude accidental discharge, and the container marked with "Warning, Loaded Firearm." All subsequent personnel and facilities that will handle the evidence must be made aware of the loaded condition of the weapon.

Processing the Weapon on Scene

- Do not unload the magazine. Note the approximate number of rounds and superglue the magazine with the bullets in place and the round ejected from the chamber.
- Discreetly sample any bloodstains adhering to the weapon after they have been thoroughly documented (Chapter 27).
- If possible, superglue the weapon and any bullets removed from the weapon to preserve latent prints or touch DNA.

Collection and Packaging the Firearm

- The weapon must be packaged so as to prevent any movement that might obliterate latent print, trace, or biological evidence.
- The weapon may be secured to a piece of cardboard with plastic tie-downs or similarly immobilized in special boxes made for this purpose.
- **Do not** package the weapon with the ammunition.
- If blood, tissue, or other biological evidence is present on the weapon, it must be thoroughly air-dried before final packaging.

Recovery of a Firearm from Water

- The weapon should be left in the water until all packaging materials are ready.
- Without removing the weapon from the water, it should be made safe in the same manner as described above.
- The weapon should be packaged in a container filled with the same water from which it was seized. Minimum exposure to the air should be allowed. This will retard rusting or further deterioration of the weapon.
- The weapon must be transported to the forensic laboratory as soon as possible.

Recovery of Cartridges, Spent Bullet Cases, and Bullets

- The locations of cartridges, spent bullet cases, and bullets should be carefully documented.
- Bullets should not be dug from objects, but rather, the object or portion of the object containing the bullet should be collected.
- Spent bullets should be placed on the sketch individually and not documented or sketched as a group.
- Bullet cases and bullets should not be marked in any way.
- Cartridges, spent bullet cases, and bullets should be Superglue fumed, individually packaged in individual rigid containers, and the packaging marked.
- Weapons, loaded ammunition, and additional loose or boxed ammunition of the same type and lot fired should be collected to assist in the range of fire determinations.

Additional Analysis Considerations

- Bloodstain pattern analysis
- Shooting incident reconstruction—trajectory analysis

Documenting Bullet Defects

The bullet may strike, ricochet from, deflect from, travel through, or penetrate a variety of surfaces during its travel. Each of these defects must be thoroughly documented.

- Each defect should be placed on the sketch and photographically documented through a mapping technique (Figure 32.1).
- When possible, sequential defects should be designated as such (A1, A2, A3) to designate the bullet defects' sequential relationship as it passes through multiple surfaces (Figures 32.2 and 32.3).
- The bullet's terminal location should be thoroughly documented.
- Lead splash patterns are particularly useful when a bullet is deflected from the surface, or ricochets. Latent lead splash can be made visible by reagent testing of the surface. Lead splash may not be visible in ambient light due to low volume or being deposited on a dark surface.
- Positive tests for copper and lead not only indicate that the defect was caused by a bullet, but also give an indication of the direction of travel. Bullet wipe and lead splash occur on the entry side of a bullet hole.

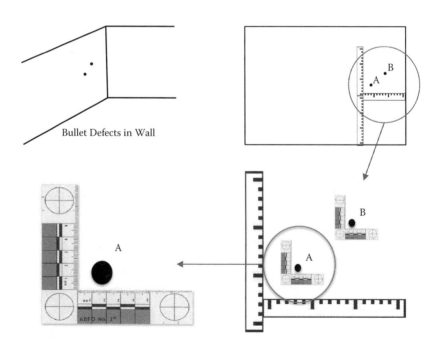

Figure 32.1 Bullet defect mapping.

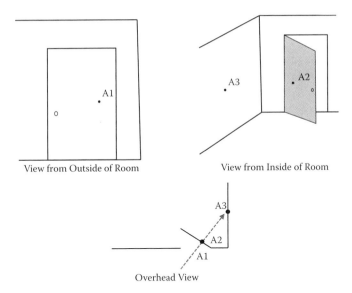

View from Outside of Room   View from Inside of Room

Overhead View

Figure 32.2 Labeling sequential defects from a single shot.

- Ricochets or low-angle defects may demonstrate directionality through the orientation of the lead in mark, pinch point, or bow wave (Figures 32.4 and 32.5).
- A ricochet from a hard, smooth surface may demonstrate an elongated tail in the direction of travel. The orientation of the tail (left or right side of the ricochet) is indicative of the twist of the bullet (Figure 32.6).
- Once documented, a rod and level should be used to demonstrate the elevation angle of the trajectory (Figure 32.7).
- Once documented, a rod and protractor should be used to demonstrate the azimuth angle of the trajectory (Figure 32.8).
- A bullet defect through tempered glass may be marked at the scene with string. This technique preserves the defect location should the glass fall out of the frame (Figure 32.9).

Chemical Testing to Determine if It Is a Bullet Defect

When a bullet comes in contact with a surface, minute amounts of metal may transfer from the bullet to the impacted surface. If it is uncertain whether a defect was caused by a bullet's passage, chemical testing may be accomplished to detect the copper or lead that may have transferred.

Testing for Copper (Figure 32.10)

- Dithiooxamide (DTO) and 2-nitro-1-naphthol (2-NN) testing for copper must be done before rhodizonate testing for lead.

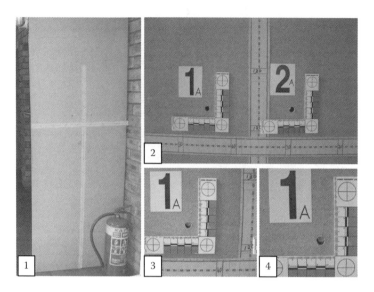

Figure 32.3 Mapping technique: 1) overall of wall with vertical and horizontal scales, 2) defects 1 and 2 with reference to scales, 3) defect 1 with reference to scale, 4) defect 1 examination quality.

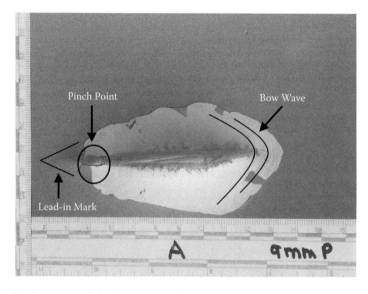

Figure 32.4 Low angle bullet impact demonstrating pinch point and bow wave.

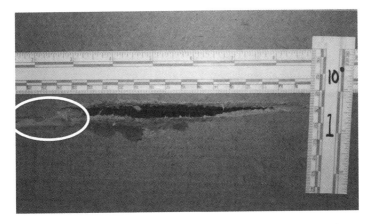

Figure 32.5 Lead-in mark on a 10° bullet defect to wall board.

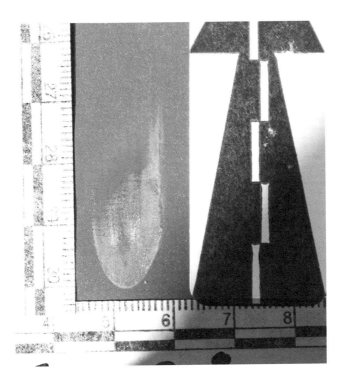

Figure 32.6 Bullet ricochet from a metal surface. The elongated pattern on the right side of the mark indicates the bullet had a right-hand twist.

Figure 32.7 Demonstrating trajectory (elevation) with rods.

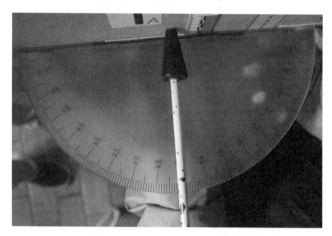

Figure 32.8 Demonstrating trajectory (azimuth) with rods.

- DTO is a colorimetric reagent that will produce a gray-green color in the presence of copper.
- A solution of ammonium hydroxide is sprayed onto the absorbent side of plastic-backed filter paper.
- The wetted filter paper is then pressed against the suspect bullet defect. The hydroxide will solubilize the copper, which will then be absorbed onto the filter paper.
- The orange DTO solution is then sprayed onto the filter paper. If copper is present, a ring of gray-green color will develop around the lifted defect pattern.
- The results should be photographed and the lift retained as evidence.
- If the ammonium hydroxide lift has a substrate color that would obscure DTO results, 2-NN may be used instead of DTO.

Figure 32.9 Strings are used to "bull's-eye" a bullet defect in tempered glass. Should the glass fall from the frame due to heat expansion or movement of the vehicle, analysis may still be accomplished.

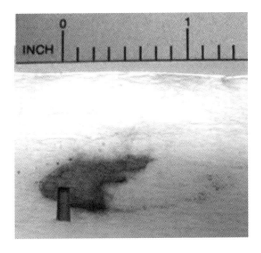

Figure 32.10 Dithiooxamide (DTO) will produce a gray-green color in the presence of copper.

270   Crime Scene Investigation Procedural Guide

- Using 2-NN on a lift containing copper will produce a pink color. DTO is sprayed over the pink and will produce the positive gray-green color if copper is present. Each of the color changes should be photographed and the lift retained as evidence.

Testing for Lead (Figure 32.11)

- Sodium rhodizonate is a chemical reagent that is used to test for the presence of lead.
- When the surface has dried after testing for copper, rhodizonate testing can be done on the same area for lead.
- This is a nondestructive test, meaning other tests can be done to the same evidence.
- A colorless tartrate buffer solution is sprayed on to the surface. The buffer will solubilize lead.
- Then the orange-brown sodium rhodizonate solution is sprayed over the same area. If lead is present, an immediate color change to pink will occur.
- The results of this test should be photographed.
- To confirm that a pink color change was caused by the presence of lead, 5% hydrochloric acid can be sprayed over the pink color (or a portion of the pink color). If the pink was produced by the presence of lead, the pink color will change to a purple-blue color.
- The results should be photographed and the lift should be retained as evidence.

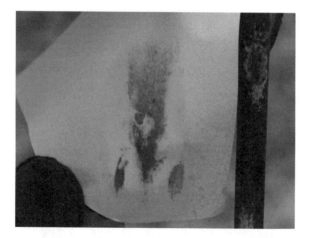

Figure 32.11 Sodium rhodizonate will produce an immediate pink color (not shown) in the presence of lead.

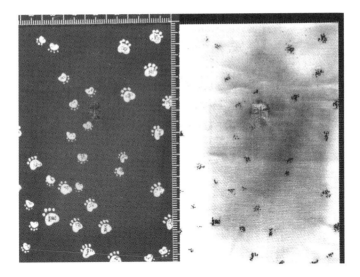

Figure 32.12 Dark print fabric with gunpowder pattern photographed with regular lighting and IR. (Photograph courtesy of Jeff Borngasser, Oregon State Central Point Crime Laboratory, Portland, OR.)

Recovery of Firearms Evidence from the Victim

Detection of Gunpowder Patterns

Visual

- Gunpowder patterns may be visible surrounding a bullet defect or on the hands or surface directly adjacent to a weapon when it is fired.
- If visible, these patterns should be photographed.

Infrared (IR) (Figure 32.12)

- Infrared video and photography of darker-colored items are excellent ways to visualize gunpowder patterns on darker surfaces.
- Specialized IR cameras are available for forensic work; these are the easiest to use and give excellent results.
- IR filters may be used on digital cameras; less expensive cameras have a built-in IR filter that prevents it from being captured.
- IR filters on digital cameras also require care in focusing. The IR focal point is different than the visible light. This may cause difficulty with autofocus.

Collection and Packaging of Clothing

- Clothing may only be removed at the scene with the permission of the medical examiner. This permission may exist as a preagreed

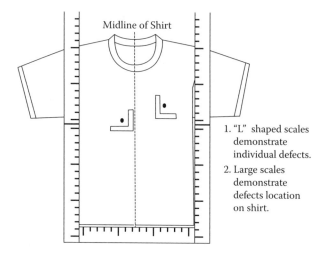

Figure 32.13 Mapping bullet defects in clothing.

protocol when the bloodstain patterns or gunshot residue would be obscured or degraded by the clothing remaining on the body.

- Always seize the victim's clothing as evidence. While powder may not be readily visible over the outer surface of clothing, microscopic examination may reveal fragments of powder caught in the weave of the material.
- The suspect's clothing (outer clothing worn at the time of the shooting) should also be seized. This should include any gloves he or she may have been wearing.
- Clothing with visible defects, gunshot residue, or bloodstain patterns should be photographically documented through a mapping technique (Figure 32.13).
- All clothing collected should be thoroughly air-dried. If bloodstain is present, a piece of heavy paper between layers of fabric can prevent blood pattern transfer.
- Clothing items should be packaged separately in paper containers.
- Weather and environmental conditions such as air movement, precipitation, etc., should be documented to assist in range-of-fire determination.

Documentation and Collection of Gunshot Residue

- Gunshot residue testing should be conducted on the hands of anyone believed to have handled the firearm.
- The victim of a possibly self-inflicted wound should have his or her hands sampled for gunshot residue. This may be done at the scene

with the medical examiner's approval, or the hands may be bagged at the scene and the samples taken at autopsy.

- Use gunshot residue (GSR) analysis to help evaluate whether a person handled or fired a weapon.
- Questions for subjects of GSR examination and collection:
  - When was the last time you handled a firearm?
  - When was the last time you fired a weapon?
  - When was the last time you were present when a weapon was fired, and what was your proximity to the weapon?
  - When was the last time you washed your hands?
  - Are you right- or left-handed?

Appendix A: Universal Precautions

Potentially Infectious Materials

A variety of harmful microorganisms can be transmitted through body fluids, including the hepatitis B virus (HBV) and the human immunodeficiency virus (HIV). Both HBV and HIV are transmitted through broken skin or mucous membrane contact, not through casual contact. Be alert for infectious materials at all death scenes.

Universal precaution: All biological material must be assumed to be contaminated.

Occupational Safety and Health Administration (OSHA) Requirements

Your organizational protocols should comply with 29 CFR 1910.1030, "Bloodborne Pathogens," for death scene investigators having an occupational exposure risk. Contact your public health office for guidance.

Personal Protective Equipment (PPE)

- Determine the appropriate combination of protective equipment. Consult medical specialists if unsure about appropriate PPE.
- Wear double gloves when handling any infectious material or infectious material container.
- Wear full-body overgarments when the splashing or spread of contaminated materials or body fluids is possible (scenes with large amounts of blood, body fluids, or tissue). Full-body coverage includes hood, surgical mask, and eye protection while in the contaminated area.
- Use disposable booties if boots are not attached to the body overgarment. Use disposable shoe coverings to prevent contaminated fluids from being transported to automobiles, offices, and homes.
- Wear double latex gloves when processing the scene.

- Wrap duct tape or other suitable tape around wrists and ankles to secure sleeves to glove tops and overgarments to booties.
- Remove PPE before leaving the immediate scene for any reason. Wash hands thoroughly with water and germicidal soap when leaving scenes. Put on fresh or decontaminated PPE before reentering the scene.

Evidence Collection Safety

- Presume all blood, body fluids, body tissue, sexual assault kits, used medical supplies, biological waste, and drug paraphernalia to be infectious. This includes evidence at sexual assault, drug, assault, bodily injury, arson, and death scenes. Attach biohazard labels to all containers of potentially infectious materials.
- Control access to death scenes containing potentially infectious materials. Limit access to only those people who have a clear need to enter.
- Pregnant investigators should not process scenes where potentially infectious materials are present.
- Put liquid blood, body fluids, and body tissue samples in leakproof containers. Place these containers in sealable plastic bags for secondary containment. Some body fluids, especially blood and saliva, may need to be collected differently and air-dried. See Chapter 27.
- Be alert for sharp objects. Exercise extreme caution when handling needles, syringes, knives, razors, broken glass, nails, or other sharp objects. Mark containers for these items with "SHARP HAZARD" and attach biohazard labels if called for.
- If you are cut or your skin is punctured by a contaminated item, immediately cleanse the wound with an appropriate antiseptic and seek medical assistance.
- After processing a potentially infectious death scene, release the scene to the appropriate authorities responsible for decontamination of potentially infectious scenes.

Removal and Decontamination of PPE

- Prior to leaving the scene, place a large piece of paper or plastic or a bed sheet on the floor of an unaffected area of the scene near the perimeter.

- Stand in the center of the paper, plastic, or sheet. Remove each piece of PPE in the following order and ensure it remains on the paper, plastic, or sheet:
  - Duct tape, if worn
  - Outer gloves, if double gloved
  - Booties if separate from overgarment
  - Surgical mask
  - Eye protection
  - Inner gloves
- Remove the inner pair of gloves by grasping the wrist edge of one glove, and pulling it off inside out.
- Remove the second glove by sliding two fingers beneath the wrist of the second glove and pulling the glove off inside out. These two fingers should only touch the inside of this glove.
- Decontaminate reusable PPE and equipment by hand washing the surfaces of each item with a solution of water and chlorine bleach (1 cup bleach to 1 gallon water). Let air-dry. Place disposable PPE in a biohazard bag for disposal (these bags are usually red or orange and designated with a biohazard symbol on the front). Wear protective gloves and eye protection when decontaminating.
- Dispose of reusable PPE as infectious waste if it becomes damaged, saturated with infectious material, or is otherwise unusable.
- Ask medical specialists to dispose of infectious waste, such as pens, pencils, gowns, gloves, masks, and shoe covers by incineration.

Appendix B: Crime Scene Entry Log[*]

Crime Scene Entry Log

Title: _____ Date: _____

Case number: _____ Investigator: _____

Location: _____

Time log opened: _____ Opened by: _____

Already on scene: _____

_____

_____

Name	Organization	Time In	Time Out

Appendix C: Crime
Scene Notes*

* Available for download from www.crcpress.com/product/isbn/9781466557543.

Crime Scene Notes

Title: _____ Date: _____

Case number: _____ Investigator: _____

Time of notification: _____ Time of arrival: _____ Time of departure: _____

1. Crime scene survey notes:

_____

_____

_____

_____

_____

_____

_____

_____

_____

_____

_____

2. Supplemental reports:

[ ] Crime scene entry log   [ ] Biological evidence
[ ] Photography log   [ ] Friction ridge evidence
[ ] Crime scene sketch   [ ] Trace evidence
[ ] Impression evidence   [ ] Toolmark evidence
[ ] Firearms evidence   [ ] Bite mark evidence
[ ] Immersion burn worksheet   [ ] Bloodstain documentation
[ ] Postblast worksheet   [ ] Shooting documentation

3. Miscellaneous comments:

_____

_____

_____

_____

_____

_____

_____

_____

_____

_____

<u>Crime Scene Notes</u>

Title: _____ Date: _____

Case number: _____ Investigator: _____

Supplemental notes:

_____

_____

_____

_____

_____

_____

_____

_____

_____

_____

_____

_____

_____

_____

_____

_____

_____

_____

_____

_____

_____

_____

_____

_____

_____

_____

_____

_____

_____

_____

_____

Appendix D: Photograph Identifier Slate[*]

[*] Available for download from www.crcpress.com/product/isbn/9781466557543.

Photographic Head Slate

| 0% |
| 10% |
| 20% |
| 30% |
| 40% |
| 50% |
| 60% |
| 70% |
| 80% |
| 90% |
| 100% |

Department/agency: _____

Case/incident no.: _____

Photographer: _____

Location: _____

Date: _____

Appendix E:
Photography Log*

Photography Log

Title: _____   Date: _____

Case number: _____   Investigator: _____

Camera: _____   Lens: _____

Filters: _____   Macro Lens: _____

[ ] Digital SLR   [ ] Digital point and shoot   [ ] Film SLR   [ ] Point and shoot

Film type: [ ] Color print   [ ] Color slide   [ ] Black and white ISO no.

1. _____

2. _____

3. _____

4. _____

5. _____

6. _____

7. _____

8. _____

9. _____

10. _____

11. _____

12. _____

13. _____

14. _____

15. _____

16. _____

17. _____

18. _____

19. _____

20. _____

Appendix F: Friction Ridge Evidence Worksheet[*]

* Available for download from www.crcpress.com/product/isbn/9781466557543.

Friction Ridge Evidence

Title: _____ Date: _____

Case number: _____ Investigator: _____

[ ] PRINT
   [ ] Finger   **[ ] Palm**   **[ ] Lip**   **[ ] Foot**
   [ ] Partial   **[ ] Unknown**

LOCATION:

DETECTION METHOD:
   [ ] Visible   [ ] Oblique   [ ] UV   [ ] FLS

PROCESSING METHOD:
   [ ] Standard powder   [ ] Magnetic powder   [ ] Fluorescent
   [ ] Black   [ ] White/gray   [ ] Bichromatic
   [ ] Cyanoacrylate fuming

COLLECTION METHOD:
   [ ] Photograph   [ ] 35 mm   [ ] 1:1   [ ] Polaroid
   [ ] Tape   [ ] Gel lift   [ ] Mikrosil   [ ] Seize item

[ ] PRINT
   [ ] Finger   **[ ] Palm**   **[ ] Lip**   **[ ] Foot**
   [ ] Partial   **[ ] Unknown**

LOCATION:

DETECTION METHOD:
   [ ] Visible   [ ] Oblique   [ ] UV   [ ] FLS

PROCESSING METHOD:
   [ ] Standard powder   [ ] Magnetic powder   [ ] Fluorescent
   [ ] Black   [ ] White/gray   [ ] Bichromatic
   [ ] Cyanoacrylate fuming

COLLECTION METHOD:
   [ ] Photograph   [ ] 35 mm   [ ] 1:1   [ ] Polaroid
   [ ] Tape   [ ] Gel lift   [ ] Mikrosil   [ ] Seize item

[ ] PRINT
   [ ] Finger   **[ ] Palm**   **[ ] Lip**   **[ ] Foot**
   [ ] Partial   **[ ] Unknown**

LOCATION:

DETECTION METHOD:
   [ ] Visible   [ ] Oblique   [ ] UV   [ ] FLS

PROCESSING METHOD:
   [ ] Standard powder   [ ] Magnetic powder   [ ] Fluorescent
   [ ] Black   [ ] White/gray   [ ] Bichromatic
   [ ] Cyanoacrylate fuming

COLLECTION METHOD:
   [ ] Photograph   [ ] 35 mm   [ ] 1:1   [ ] Polaroid
   [ ] Tape   [ ] Gel lift   [ ] Mikrosil   [ ] Seize item

Appendix G: Impression Evidence Worksheet[*]

Impression Evidence Notes

Title: _____ Date: _____

Case number: _____ Investigator: _____

[ ] **IMPRESSION**

    [ ] **Footprint**   [ ] **Footwear**   [ ] **Tire print**   [ ] **Toolmark**   [ ] **Bite mark**

    [ ] **Soil**   [ ] **Sand**   [ ] **Mud**   [ ] **Underwater**   [ ] **Snow**

PHOTOGRAPHY: [ ] Without scale   [ ] With scale

CASTING METHOD:

    [ ] Dental stone   [ ] Algenate   [ ] Tape   [ ] Stati-Lift

    [ ] Mikrosil   [ ] Silicon rubber   [ ] Snow print wax   [ ] Electrostatic print lifter

[ ] **IMPRESSION**

    [ ] **Footprint**   [ ] **Footwear**   [ ] **Tire print**   [ ] **Toolmark**   [ ] **Bite mark**

    [ ] **Soil**   [ ] **Sand**   [ ] **Mud**   [ ] **Underwater**   [ ] **Snow**

PHOTOGRAPHY: [ ] Without scale   [ ] With scale

CASTING METHOD:

    [ ] Dental stone   [ ] Algenate   [ ] Tape   [ ] Stati-Lift

    [ ] Mikrosil   [ ] Silicon rubber   [ ] Snow print wax   [ ] Electrostatic print lifter

Appendix H: Biological Evidence Worksheet[*]

[*] Available for download from www.crcpress.com/product/isbn/9781466557543.

Biological Evidence Notes

Title: _____   Date: _____

Case number: _____   Investigator: _____

[ ] **SAMPLE**   LOCATION:
   [ ] **Dry**   [ ] **Wet**   [ ] **Liquid**   [ ] **Tissue**

DETECTION METHOD:
   [ ] Visible   [ ] Oblique   [ ] UV   [ ] FLS

COLLECTION METHOD:
   [ ] Swab   [ ] Pipette   [ ] Swatch
   [ ] Scraping   [ ] Forceps   [ ] Seize item

PACKAGING METHOD:
   Test tube: [ ] Purple top   [ ] Druggist fold
              [ ] Yellow top   [ ] Envelope
              [ ] Gray top   [ ] Other _____

PRESUMPTIVE TEST:
   [ ] Positive   [ ] Negative   [ ] Type: _____

[ ] **SAMPLE**   LOCATION:
   [ ] **Dry**   [ ] **Wet**   [ ] **Liquid**   [ ] **Tissue**

DETECTION METHOD:
   [ ] Visible   [ ] Oblique   [ ] UV   [ ] FLS

COLLECTION METHOD:
   [ ] Swab   [ ] Pipette   [ ] Swatch
   [ ] Scraping   [ ] Forceps   [ ] Seize item

PACKAGING METHOD:
   Test tube: [ ] Purple top   [ ] Druggist fold
              [ ] Yellow top   [ ] Envelope
              [ ] Gray top   [ ] Other _____

PRESUMPTIVE TEST:
   [ ] Positive   [ ] Negative   [ ] Type: _____

[ ] **SAMPLE**   LOCATION:
   [ ] **Dry**   [ ] **Wet**   [ ] **Liquid**   [ ] **Tissue**

DETECTION METHOD:
   [ ] Visible   [ ] Oblique   [ ] UV   [ ] FLS

COLLECTION METHOD:
   [ ] Swab   [ ] Pipette   [ ] Swatch
   [ ] Scraping   [ ] Forceps   [ ] Seize item

PACKAGING METHOD:
   Test tube: [ ] Purple top   [ ] Druggist fold
              [ ] Yellow top   [ ] Envelope
              [ ] Gray top   [ ] Other _____

PRESUMPTIVE TEST:
   [ ] Positive   [ ] Negative   [ ] Type: _____

Appendix I: Trace Evidence Worksheet*

* Available for download from www.crcpress.com/product/isbn/9781466557543.

Trace Evidence Notes

Title: _____ Date: _____

Case number: _____ Investigator: _____

[ ] **SAMPLE**   **LOCATION:**
   [ ] Hair   [ ] Fiber   [ ] Soil   [ ] Building material
   [ ] Explosive residue   [ ] Fire residue

DETECTION METHOD:
   [ ] Visible   [ ] Oblique   [ ] UV   [ ] FLS
   [ ] Hydrocarbon detector   [ ] Aromatic   [ ] Canine

COLLECTION METHOD:
   [ ] Swab   [ ] Pipette   [ ] Swatch
   [ ] Scraping   [ ] Forceps   [ ] Seize item

PACKAGING METHOD:
   [ ] Test tube   [ ] Druggist fold   [ ] Paint can
   [ ] Envelope   [ ] Tape lift   [ ] Other _____

[ ] **SAMPLE**   **LOCATION:**
   [ ] Hair   [ ] Fiber   [ ] Soil   [ ] Building material
   [ ] Explosive residue   [ ] Fire residue

DETECTION METHOD:
   [ ] Visible   [ ] Oblique   [ ] UV   [ ] FLS
   [ ] Hydrocarbon detector   [ ] Aromatic   [ ] Canine

COLLECTION METHOD:
   [ ] Swab   [ ] Pipette   [ ] Swatch
   [ ] Scraping   [ ] Forceps   [ ] Seize item

PACKAGING METHOD:
   [ ] Test tube   [ ] Druggist fold   [ ] Paint can
   [ ] Envelope   [ ] Tape lift   [ ] Other _____

[ ] **SAMPLE**   **LOCATION:**
   [ ] Hair   [ ] Fiber   [ ] Soil   [ ] Building material
   [ ] Explosive residue   [ ] Fire residue

DETECTION METHOD:
   [ ] Visible   [ ] Oblique   [ ] UV   [ ] FLS
   [ ] Hydrocarbon detector   [ ] Aromatic   [ ] Canine

COLLECTION METHOD:
   [ ] Swab   [ ] Pipette   [ ] Swatch
   [ ] Scraping   [ ] Forceps   [ ] Seize item

PACKAGING METHOD:
   [ ] Test tube   [ ] Druggist fold   [ ] Paint can
   [ ] Envelope   [ ] Tape lift   [ ] Other _____

Page ____ of ____   Initials _____

Appendix J: Firearms Documentation Worksheet*

* Available for download from www.crcpress.com/product/isbn/9781466557543.

Firearms Documentation Worksheet

Title: _____ Date: _____

Case number: _____ Investigator: _____

Circumstances of recovery: _____

_____

WEAPON:

Handgun: [ ] Automatic [ ] Semiautomatic [ ] Revolver [ ] Bolt action [ ] Break
      action: [ ] Single shot [ ] Double shot

Rifle: [ ] Automatic [ ] Semiautomatic [ ] Magazine fed [ ] Tube fed [ ] Lever action [ ] Break action [ ] Pump
      shotgun: [ ] Automatic [ ] Semiautomatic [ ] Pump [ ] Break action: [ ] Single barrel [ ] Double barrel
      [ ] Bolt action [ ] Double action [ ] Single action

Manufacturer: _____ Model: _____ Serial number: _____

Other: _____

Safety: [ ] Left handed [ ] Right handed [ ] On [ ] Off

Decock lever: [ ] Left handed [ ] Right handed

Magazine release: [ ] Left handed [ ] Right handed

Magazine: [ ] Fully seated [ ] Partially seated [ ] Removed Manufacturer:

Slide: [ ] Forward [ ] Locked to the rear

Hammer: [ ] Fully cocked [ ] 3/4 cocked [ ] 1/2 cocked [ ] 1/4 cocked [ ] Not cocked

AMMUNITION TYPE:

Note: If ammunition differs, designate by cylinder number, magazine number, or evidence item number.

[ ] Ball	[ ] Hollow point	[ ] Wad cutter	[ ] Specialty: _____
[ ] Not jacketed	[ ] Jacket	[ ] Semijacketed	[ ] Other: _____

Caliber: 0.22 0.25   0.32 0.38/357   0.380 0.41 0.44 0.45
Millimeter: 9 mm 10 mm
Gauge: 012   016   020   028   0.410 Shot size:

Manufacturer: _____ Make: _____ Lot number: _____

Begin number 1 with cylinder chamber that is in line with the barrel. Continue
numbering clockwise or counterclockwise based upon the direction the cylinder turns.
Package each round separately.

1. [ ] Fired__[ ] Misfire [ ] Not fired [ ] Empty head stamp:
2. [ ] Fired__[ ] Misfire [ ] Not fired [ ] Empty head stamp:
3. [ ] Fired__[ ] Misfire [ ] Not fired [ ] Empty head stamp:
4. [ ] Fired__[ ] Misfire [ ] Not fired [ ] Empty head stamp:
5. [ ] Fired__[ ] Misfire [ ] Not fired [ ] Empty head stamp:
6. [ ] Fired__[ ] Misfire [ ] Not fired [ ] Empty head stamp:
7. [ ] Fired__[ ] Misfire [ ] Not fired [ ] Empty head stamp:
8. [ ] Fired__[ ] Misfire [ ] Not fired [ ] Empty head stamp:
9. [ ] Fired__[ ] Misfire [ ] Not fired [ ] Empty head stamp:

Appendix K: Bloodstain Pattern Taxonomy*

Used with permission of Ross Gardner from *Bloodstain Pattern Analysis with an Introduction to Crime Scene Reconstruction, 3rd Ed.*

---

* Available for download from www.crcpress.com/product/isbn/9781466557543.

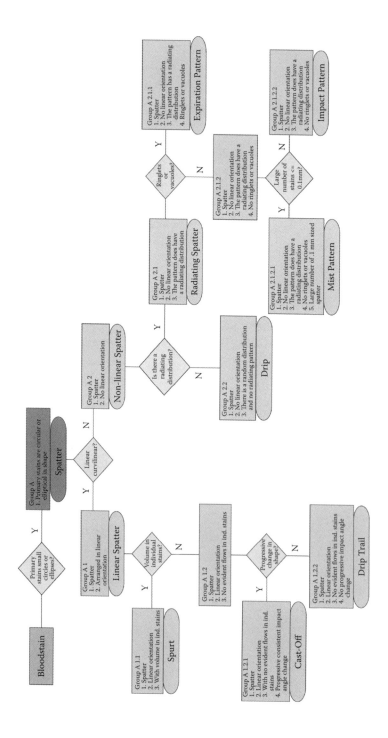

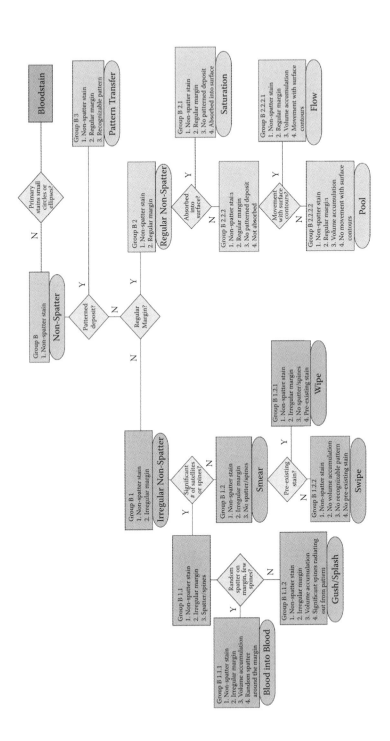

Appendix L:
Entomology Worksheet
(Neglect)[*]

[*] Available for download from www.crcpress.com/product/isbn/9781466557543.

Entomology Worksheet (Neglect)

Victim/case title: _____

Date/time neglect reported: _____/_____ Reported by: _____

Location of neglect: _____

Description of building/residence: _____

Condition/injuries to victim's body: _____

Temperatures of victim's living area taken at various times around the clock (e.g., 3 hours)

Time: _____ Temp.: _____   Time: _____ Temp.: _____   Time: _____ Temp.: _____

Time: _____ Temp.: _____   Time: _____ Temp.: _____   Time: _____ Temp.: _____

Time: _____ Temp.: _____   Time: _____ Temp.: _____   Time: _____ Temp.: _____

Description of insect infestation on victim: _____

_____

Description of adult insects observed in living area: _____

_____

Insect Collection:

Largest larvae observed (live sample + kill sample)

Adult flies and other insects (sample of each placed in kill jar)

Pupae located in carpet, bedding, or other nearby area (live sample + kill sample)

Additional Information Needed:

Complete photographic coverage and sketch of living space

Status of doors and windows: open/closed, broken screens, etc.

Observations about insects in other parts of the residence and their food sources

Area daily weather as reported by National Weather Service for time interval involved

Presence/absence of dirty diapers/underwear or other soiled clothing

Recovery of bedding, clothing, or other items used to cover victim before discovery

Presence/absence of open food in living space and other areas of residence

Humidity level of the main living area

Appendix M: Postblast Scene Management Worksheet[*]

* Available for download from www.crcpress.com/product/isbn/9781466557543.

Post-Blast Scene Management

Team Assignments

SoB	Baker	Thomas	
Zone 1	Smith	Jones	
Zone 2	Fife	Griffin	
Zone 3			
Zone 4			

Case Information

Location	ABC Industrial Warehouse
Date	12 October 2013
Agency	Audubon Police Department
Case Title	121013-077-6ACN

Item	Azimuth	Distance

Perimeter is established at a radius of 1.5 X's the distance from SoB to farthest blast debris located.

Use Polar Coordinate Method from SoB to document location of all suspected

• device components
• biological evidence
• farthest piece of debris

Use sequential numbering for all items of evidence within a sector. They will later be designated 1-1, 2-1, 3-1, 4-1, SoB-1 based upon the sector in which they were found.

Item	Azimuth	Distance

Item	Azimuth	Distance

North

0°

270°

SoB

90°

180°

4

1

3

2

Key

○ Device
△ Biological
□ Structural

Appendix N: Druggist Fold Instructions[*]

[*] Available for download from www.crcpress.com/product/isbn/9781466557543.

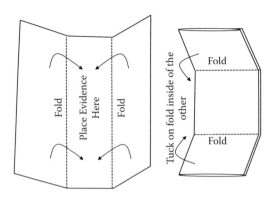

Appendix O: Immersion Burn Worksheet[*]

Immersion Burn Worksheet

Case Number: _____ Date: _____

Title: _____ Time: _____

Victim: _____

Location: _____

Type of basin: [ ] Bathtub [ ] Bathroom sink [ ] Kitchen sink [ ] Other _____

Measurements: Width Length Depth Other _____

Material: [ ] Porcelain [ ] Fiberglass [ ] Steel [ ] Iron [ ] Plastic [ ] Other _____

Manufacturer: _____   Model: _____

Type of fixtures: [ ] Single-temperature control [ ] Dual-temperature control
                    [ ] Spray attachment [ ] Shower head [ ] Bathtub spout [ ] Single spout [ ] Separate
                    hot/cold spouts
Manufacturer: _____   Model: _____

Hot water heater:
Manufacturer: _____ Make: _____ Model: _____
Serial number: _____ Capacity: _____
Thermostat setting: Upper _____ Lower _____

RUNNING WATER TEMPERATURES			
HOT WATER		COLD WATER	
Seconds	Temp.	Seconds	Temp.
0		0	
5		5	
10		10	
20		20	
30		30	
40		40	
50		50	
60		60	
70		70	
80		80	
90		90	
100		100	
110		110	

STANDING WATER—FULLT HOT Temperature Recorded from Mid-Basin at Mid-Depth			
FILL TIME		TEMPERATURE	
		Measured from Time Water is Turned Off	
Depth	Time	Min.	Temp.
1		0	
2		1	
3		5	
4		10	
5		15	
6		20	
7		25	
8		30	
9		35	
10		40	

_____ ran a separate basin of water at my request. The temperature was _____ degrees at a depth of _____ inches 1 minute after the water was turned off. Measurements were made at mid-basin, mid-depth.

Thermometer: Make: _____ Model: _____ Size: _____ Range: _____

Index